# ERRATA

Please read Dr. *W. Donald* Harris on page vii / line 7, on page 10 / line 3 of the picture section following text page 116, and also in the index page 204. Read Rev. *W. Donald* Harris on page xiii / line 11. On page vii / line 10 read Mrs. *Amanda* García. On page xvi read *1940* instead of 1937 as the year in which Dr. Harris received his honorary LL.D. On page 29 / line 12 read *1940* instead of 1938. Page 40 / line 16 read *Sabana* without accent, and on pages 209 / line 8 and line 25 read *(S.G.)* instead of (S.J.). On page 211 / line 1 read *University* instead of Universitiy.

On page 10 / line 5 of the picture section that follows text page 68 read *$5,000* instead of $4,500. On the same page the caption to the bottom picture on the facing page should have listed *Mr. George Steadman* following the name of Mrs. Mary V. de Harris, and *Mr. Fred Whaley* following the name of Dr. Boyd B. Palmer. On page 6 of the picture section that follows text page 84 the last name in the caption should read *Enrique Garcés.*

# Riding & Roping

## THE MEMOIRS OF J. WILL HARRIS

# Riding & Roping

## THE MEMOIRS OF
## J. WILL HARRIS

*Edited by C. Virginia Matters*

## Inter American University
## of Puerto Rico

FRONTISPIECE:
Dr. J. Will Harris, riding and roping
on the Polytechnic campus

For information write:
Inter American University Press
G.P.O. Box 3255, San Juan, Puerto Rico 00936

Designed by Klaus Gemming, New Haven, Ct.
Illustrations printed by The Meriden Gravure Co., Meriden, Ct.
Composed, printed, and bound by Port City Press, Inc., Baltimore, Md.
Manufactured in the United States of America

LIBRARY OF CONGRESS CATALOGING IN PUBLICATION DATA

Harris, John Will, 1876-1956.
    Riding & roping.

    Includes bibliographical references and indexes.
    1. Harris, John Will, 1876-1956. 2. Educators—
Puerto Rico—Biography. 3. Puerto Rico—Biography.
4. San Germán, Puerto Rico. Inter American University of
Puerto Rico—History. I. Title.
LA2317.H425A37    370'.92'4    [B]    74-78373
ISBN 0-913480-23-1
ISBN 0-913480-34-7 pbk.

# TABLE OF CONTENTS

## PART III / THE DREAM FULFILLED

*Illustration sections follow text pages 68, 84, 116*

# ACKNOWLEDGEMENTS

MY SINCERE THANKS go to all those who helped to locate pictures or information and to identify persons and places, among whom I wish to mention the following: Miss Frances Fishburn, Historian of Park College; Dr. and Mrs. José M. Rodríguez Quiñones (Nito and doña Ana); Mr. Ricardo Ramírez Acosta; Dr. Boyd B. Palmer; Miss Zelima Arce; Mr. and Mrs. Raúl Irizarry; Mrs. Lydia Q. de Gregory; Mrs. Teresa Fábregas; Mr. Aurelio Tió; Mrs. Helen Harris Artau; Dr. Donald W. Harris; Dr. José M. Gallardo; Mrs. Laura Irizarry de Bover; Mrs. Georgina Villanueva de Vivoni; Mrs. María Eugenia Aviles; Mr. Israel Planell; Miss Carmen Tuya; Mrs. Joyce Matthews; Mr. Rafael Bonilla; Mrs. Amada García vda de Irizarry; Mrs. Ramonita Martínez (Mona Marti); the staff of the Salón Puertorriqueño, University of Puerto Rico, Río Piedras campus; Mr. Fernando Avila, librarian of *El Mundo;* personnel of the Historical Archives of Princeton Seminary, United Brethren and Congregational Churches; and staff of the Public Library and city government of San Antonio, Texas.

I wish to express my deep appreciation for the cooperation and encouragement given me by Professor John Zebrowski, director of Inter American University Press, while I worked on this manuscript. My thanks go also to Mr. Richard Hall, acting director for the time Professor Zebrowski was on sabbatical leave, and to Mrs. Josefina L. Durán and Mrs. Margaret Flenniken of the University Press staff.

Grateful recognition is here paid to Mr. Sol Luis Descartes, president of Inter American University, for the interest he has shown in preserving this unique history of the Polytechnic Institute and for advancing the publication of the manuscript.

In editing as personal a manuscript as Dr. Harris's memoirs, there is always a question whether to correct or eliminate idiosyncracies of the text or retain them so as to preserve better the characteristic tone of the original and the personality of the writer. I chose to make changes only where they seemed indicated for reasons of clarity and accuracy, often leaving unchanged "telescopic" grammar, arbitrary abbreviations, capitals and punctuation and other divergencies from the standard. For this, I beg the reader's indulgence.

*C. Virginia Matters*

# FOREWORD

GOING OVER THE MATERIAL used in the preparation of this book was a treat for me. I was able to identify everyone in all the pictures which we examined. Not only that, I was overwhelmed by the emotions brought on by the multitude of memories.

J. Will Harris was a man from Texas: his father "early American," his mother full German. I think of him as a pioneer of Puerto Rican education and a messenger of the Gospel.

While a student at Park College in Missouri he had a dream he was never to forget which influenced his life immensely. In this dream he saw a poor young man drowning in ignorance, begging for help. Many years later he recognized the youth in Popo, the first student ever to come to Poly.

After Park College he attended Princeton Seminary and right after graduation married Eunice White, his college sweetheart. The young couple was getting ready to go to Africa when an offer came to move to Puerto Rico instead.

In 1908 the Rev. Harris started a church in La Plata, Lajas. The meeting place was my parents' home where two years later, in 1910, I was baptized a Presbyterian.

While officiating at my father's funeral on April 30, 1919, he called José Rodríguez, Sr., the best friend he had ever had. From then on, I have tried to occupy my father's place in Dr. Harris's affections.

In 1937 the Harris family retired to Dilley, Texas, to tend a cattle ranch. I feel compelled to tell this story as told by Mrs. Harris: Dr. Harris was riding Ranger, his indomitable colt, at a fast clip. The horse heard a rattlesnake and came to a sudden stop. Dr. Harris was thrown so high up in the air he had time to think that if he survived the fall he would dispose of the horse, sell the ranch, and go back to Puerto Rico. Though they returned only to visit, both Dr. and Mrs. Harris told me that had they known how much Puerto Ricans loved them they would never have gone back to Texas.

On their deaths their bodies were cremated and their ashes placed in a bronze urn and brought back by their children to the San Germán Campus to be deposited inside *The Steps*—all that is now left of the old farmhouse where Inter American University began.

Many, many Puerto Ricans join me in putting up a pedestal for the Harris family who live on in the lives of Helen, Donald, Margaret and Cleland, their children. But to a greater extent they continue to live in the life and work of many of us who came under their influence and guidance and were blessed with their friendship.

Personally, I consider it a great honor to have been able to participate in a small way in the development of the superb work done by the Harris family and I hope this work, in J. Will Harris's own words, may convey to everyone reading them some of the spirit which guided him and is his legacy to all of us at Inter American University.

*José M. Rodríguez Quiñones*, M.D.

# A REMINISCENCE

## *A Few of the Many Things That I Remember About My Father*

ONE HUNDRED YEARS after the American Revolution, on January 2, 1876, a baby boy was born in a small town west of Austin, Texas. That area was too settled for the pioneering spirit of the family, so they moved to Frio County, southwest of San Antonio, to the open ranch country. That little boy grew up to be what every young man was in that area—a cowboy. That was my father—strong, an excellent rider and roper, and afraid of nothing.

On March 2, 1912, in the town of San Germán, that same young man, after several failures, announced that he would try again to start a school for poor boys and girls. On that day two young men showed up. One of them went back home discouraged. The other one stayed. The school began and my father called it a success!

*I REMEMBER MY FATHER'S GREAT OPTIMISM*—Nothing could discourage him. I cannot recall ever seeing him depressed a single time. He was driven by a tremendous faith in God and a deep desire to help the poor people of Puerto Rico. Obstacles and difficulties were just things to overcome on the road to fulfilling his purpose.

*I REMEMBER HIM SINGING HYMNS WHILE TAKING AN EARLY MORNING SHOWER* prior to walking to Morning Prayers at the Polytechnic dining room at 6:00 A.M. Three chapters of the Bible per day were assigned. No student could enter for breakfast unless he had his Bible and hymnbook. He believed in starting the day with God.

*I REMEMBER THE STUDENTS GATHERING IN FRONT OF OUR HOME* on the night my father would be catching the 11:30 train to San Juan to take a boat to New York to try to find money to keep the school operating. It was a serious moment. The school needed funds, the journey was long and many times it was very stormy. During World War I many ships were sunk between Puerto Rico and the States. So the trip was not exactly a picnic. The students gathered to sing hymns and to pray for a successful voyage. They would then bid farewell and return to their dormitories.

*I REMEMBER MY FATHER'S STRONG WILL POWER AND COURAGE* in attempting to build a school in the face of insurmountable obstacles, as he was told by even his fellow-missionaries. He was warned that to go against the custom and tradition of the prevailing culture would lead only to failure. Some of the obstacles were:

a  Starting a Protestant school in the midst of a strong Roman Catholic population would never succeed. The oldest Catholic church in the Western Hemisphere is in San Germán.
b  The idea of a coeducational boarding school in the face of the tradition of constant protection of the female sex would lead to failure.
c  The idea of every student working at manual labor in a culture that frowned on work as something done by servants only would also fail.

But all of this only served to increase his desire to try to find a better course for the young people of Puerto Rico.

*I REMEMBER THE LOYALTY OF THE STUDENTS AND FACULTY.* There was an intangible spirit that pulled the group together. They were willing to make sacrifices for the success of the school. Teachers would continue to teach when they not only had not been paid, but even when there was no prospect of payment in the immediate future. Students would continue to work and study in the midst of difficult conditions, and even make jokes about their plight.

*I REMEMBER HIS TEXAS SPIRIT OF THE FRONTIER LIFE.* When we were small, he would tell us bedtime stories of his boyhood life that thrilled us. How far he and his brothers ran when they had ventured fairly close to see the first railroad engine in that area—only to have it shoot off steam! They thought that it would explode, so they took to the woods.

He brought to Puerto Rico wild jabalinas that roam the vaquero country. He kept raccoons in pens. He brought home a coyote whose howl at night brought memories of his early ranch days. He even brought unbroken horses from his sister's ranch to see if he could still break and tame and train a horse as he had done in the past. Ranger, his favorite horse, was a common sight in the area. I was scared to death when I saw my father work hard to get a saddle on him for the first time, and then watch the fierce battle Ranger put up to try to throw his first rider, a former cowboy, now a college president! His big ten gallon hat, Texas saddle, and boots were natural to him.

*I REMEMBER THAT HE WAS SO MUCH LIKE THE PROPHET JOEL—* "And behold your young men shall dream dreams, and your old men shall see visions." I can recall how students would almost laugh out loud when he would begin to describe the many students and buildings the campus one day would have! They were living in shacks and that day looked too remote. But he kept on dreaming and making those dreams come true. If my father returned again to this earth, he would not be surprised to find that his first two students had increased to over 25,000.

*I REMEMBER ABOVE ALL ELSE HIS DEEP SENSE OF MISSION AND PURPOSE.* He believed that somehow God called him to do this specific job—to help bring to the poor boy and girl of Puerto Rico a new life, a life that would be more meaningful, and helpful, and rewarding. He never wavered from this purpose—to be of service to the people of Puerto Rico, and hopefully to all Latin America.

Many fine students have come and gone. Many have climbed to positions of success in their respective fields of endeavor. Knowing my father I would say that his penetrating question to the student and graduate of today would be not what are you doing for yourself? But rather, "What are you doing for the people of Puerto Rico, the Caribbean, and Latin America?"

Our world today needs more dreamers and people of vision. How about going out into your daily life now and making a dream come true for someone else?

*Rev. Donald W. Harris*

# J. WILL HARRIS

## *A Chronology*

1876 Born in Dripping Springs, Texas, January 12.

1893 Working as a cowboy, dreams of God in a rift of clouds.

1894 Admitted to the Presbyterian Church in Cibolo, Texas. Decides to study for the ministry.

1895 Surrenders unconditionally to God, accepting a lifelong commitment. Leaves for Park College in Parkville, Missouri.

1899 Has another dream, this time of children of all colors bathing in the Missouri River. Feels it is prophetic of his future work.

1900 Summer work on an Indian reservation in Kansas. Meets Eunice White there and becomes engaged to her.

1902 Graduates from Park College. Enters Princeton Seminary in Princeton, N.J.

1905 Ordained in Brooklyn, N.Y., April 14. Marries Eunice White on May 17 and accepts a call to a church in Pond Creek, Oklahoma.

1906 After being turned down for foreign assignment by the Presbyterian Foreign Mission Board, he is assigned to Puerto Rico by the Home Mission Board. He and Eunice sail on July 5. Receives first inspiration to serve as a teacher on the island.

1907 Starts teaching in a rented room in a poor family home in San Germán. Buys first lot for a school site. Later exchanges it for another.

1908 Travels to Kansas seeking financial support for his new school.

1910 After negotiating for acreage and buildings in several locations, takes an option on 100 acres on Las Lomas de Santa Marta for $8,000.

1911 Option on acreage extended. Incorporates school as Polytechnic Institute of Porto Rico. In December raises last of money needed for purchase of land.

1912 First school year ends with 12 students.

1916 First high school class graduates with 6 students.

1917 Master plan for Polytechnic campus finished.

1919 Legislature authorizes granting of university-level degrees.

1920 Polytechnic Institute of Porto Rico incorporated in Washington, D. C.

1920 Dr. Harris receives honorary LL.D. from Park College, Missouri.

1921 First college class enrolled. This class did not complete work for a degree, as the demand for teachers in the public schools was such they were all enticed into accepting teaching positions at the end of their second year.

1923    Carnegie Corporation agrees to give $250,000 if the school can raise a matching amount. Second college class enrolled as candidates for bachelor's degree.

1925    Successful finish to fund-raising drive to match Carnegie funds.

1927    First college class graduates with 23 students.

1930    Casa María built as a retirement home for the Harrises.

1937    Dr. and Mrs. Harris say goodbye to the Polytechnic. Dr. Jarvis S. Morris installed as president. Dr. Harris awarded honorary LL.D. from University of Puerto Rico.

1940    Dr. and Mrs. Harris return for Founder's Day.

1946    Return for Founder's Day.

1948    Dr. Harris receives D.D. honorary degree from Polytechnic.

1949    Return for Founder's Day.

1953    Mrs. Harris dies January 18 in Texas.

1956    Name of school changed to Inter American University. Dr. Harris returns for last visit. Dies in Texas from injuries in an auto accident June 14.

Young Will Harris ready to bring dreams into reality.

Dr. Harris in his Texas hat, the way thousands of
Polytechnic students always remember him.

## I DEDICATE THIS BOOK TO

*Alumni, ex-Students, Faculties, Presidents, Trustees, Friends and People of Puerto Rico, for whose advancement Mrs. Harris and I founded our college, now your college.*

*We commit to you, one and all, the ideals in the Articles of Incorporation—the united, normal developments of the* head, *of the* heart, *of the* hand.

*Thus Students can achieve well-rounded characters and attractive personalities, which are resourceful, independent and of a sturdy Christian faith, expressed in service and love to God and man.*

### IN MEMORY OF POLYTECHNIC INSTITUTE
### SAN GERMAN, PUERTO RICO

# INTRODUCTION*

SOME THIRTY-FIVE YEARS AGO Will Harris was a "poor lonesome cowboy," working in the Cotulla country. Now Will Harris, a minister of the Gospel stationed in Puerto Rico, is back on his old "stamping grounds."

But life "ain't what it used to was," in the brush country. When Will Harris was working in the La Salle region in Headquarters House, thirty miles from town, he never went in oftener than once a moon. Now the saddle-weary vaquero comes in at night, has a bath in a regular tub, shaves and cold creams, gets into a party dress including shiny dancing pumps, gets into a car, then rolls into Cotulla for an evening fandango; else he stays at headquarters of the evening, calls up some friends on the phone, listens in on the radio, or reads the daily paper.

In his days Will Harris stayed at the ranch, played solitaire, or maybe monte with the Mexicans, heard the wolves howling in the brush, the owls hooting in the oaks, or maybe went out and took a look at the stars and wondered if he "would ever amount to anything."

If Will Harris will go over to the Cotulla Courthouse the night of the annual old folks ball, he will find the vaqueros from all over the country there, from Fowlerton to Big Wells, from Encinal to Pearsall. Chub Poole, high sheriff, will be teaching some fair lady how the waltz is done, Howard Quinn will be stepping keen, Dick and Dutch Knaggs will be putting on a show, C. F. Binkley will be looking on and evidently liking it, for he has money to go and look in on any place he wants to, L. A. Kerr will be on hand, likewise Burney Wildenthal and Jack Baily and Onie Sherran.

But thirty-five years ago if that sort of thing was staged the gang would leave their ranches on horseback early in the morning, and at the close of the next day be riding back to the home corral. Now they are back at daylight.

Will Harris has two brothers still left in La Salle, Charlie and Ed, and two sisters, Mrs. W. H. Jacobs and Mrs. H. A. Sackville.

* From "Texas Trails," in the *San Antonio Light,* 1928, reprinted by permission. Dr. Harris chose this for his Introduction.

# PART I

# Early Days

# Chapter 1

## *Two Decades in Southwest Texas Brush*

THE CURTAIN was falling on the past in 1876. The Indians were giving way to the inevitable. General Nelson A. Miles captured the Apache Indians and their chief Boyathlay (The Yawner), better known by his Spanish nickname, Gerónimo, with his whole tribe Chiricahua, and brought them to Fort Sam Houston in San Antonio in 1886.[1] We children, however, covered up and kept quiet in bed when the owls began hooting on two sides of our lonely ranch home during full moon season. This was the time and the way Indians came to set fire to the settler's home. The buffalo days were also ending.

Not many years later, some eight or ten, the settler's custom of putting his brand on all maverick calves (the unbranded calves) and of his killing for meat only mavericks, became unethical. But the word *ethical* was not in the Texas cowboy's vocabulary; in fact, he did not know there was such a thing as a vocabulary. Schools lasted only three months and the racehorse course of instruction was in reading, 'riting, and 'rithmetic.

Then came a law ending maverick days in Texas. Some vaqueros, however, learned to respect law only through the hard way—a court reprimand, or a penitentiary sentence. Fred was a Canadian boy sent to a Texas ranch with a label around his neck to make sure the trainmen would put him off at the right siding in the Southwest. He grew up here without father or mother. The last time I saw Fred was in 1893 when he reached his hand through the bars of the Cotulla jail to shake goodbye to me. They sent him to the pen.

To protect and calm his five sons, my father sold our home in Dilley and moved down on the Mexican National Railroad, traded his cattle to don Antonio Bruni for sheep—a hard pill for his boys to swallow. I was now sixteen years old, with two brothers and a sister older, and two brothers and a sister younger. I had seen a woman die a natural death. It never occurred to me that men could die a natural death. Even old gray-bearded Mr. Stein was killed by his horse. Most men died in the smoke of a Colt revolver. One man was condemned to death by a court—the first time a court ever did such a thing—and was hanged in the open jail yard of Cotulla where everybody could see it well done.

We loved the semi-savage life of this still wild, unpeopled cactus country known now as the Southwest, with its superabundance of game everywhere, its open spaces covered with sedge grass (we called it sage grass) waist high, its brush thickets filled with "Mexican lions," jabalinas (peccary), coyotes, and with our back gate opened after dark by a hungry desperado to get filled up and to take a day or two of food as he dodged the sheriffs and rangers in his escape across the Rio Grande. A stray preacher would occasionally come into our home about the middle of the week and father would invite the neighbors fifteen miles away for Sunday preaching. He would preach under a brush arbor. Al Franklin and my older brother Charlie were the first young people to join a church in 1888. Mother kept us near the house, especially during moonlight nights when Indians were supposed to be prowling around. Si Parks's mother had lost her first husband in an Indian raid, in what is now my ranch at Rock Crossing. Father plowed a circle around our home to prevent the prairie fires from destroying our log house. John William Harris (that's me) was born January 12, 1876, in a log house, Dripping Springs, Texas.

BADGER CLARK
CUSTER, SOUTH DAKOTA

16 March, 1949

Dear Dr. Harris:

"The Old Cowman" was written in southern Arizona forty-odd years ago, at the time the first nesters were stretching their one- and two-wire fences in the Sulphur Springs Valley. The line about letting the fences down is literally true. An old-timer rode into the ranch one morning growling about the fences. It had never occurred to him to follow the new section lines. He had stuck to the old familiar trail, leaving a new trail of sagging wire for the nesters to replace.

Certainly you may use the verses. I had not suspected they had crossed the narrow seas to Puerto Rico, though they have covered a good deal of territory in the West. They formed part of my book *Sun and Saddle Leather,* which sold well for thirty years. It is out of print now, but I have hopes that the Yankee publishers in Boston will put out another edition, the fourteenth, within a year or so.

Apparently you have no intention of resting on your laurels. But what a life! I speak often at high schools and colleges, and am acutely aware that today's young people need to have their hearts educated as well as their heads. If I had a billion I would endow every Christian college in the country. I believe it was Gilbert Chesterton who said that being born was like going down a dark street, climbing into the window of a house at random and getting along with the people inside the best you can for the next twenty years.

As I grow older I never cease to thank the Lord that I "selected" a Methodist parsonage—though a Presbyterian manse would have done as well had the same parents come with it.

> Very truly yours,
> /s/ *Badger Clark*

## The Old Cowman

I rode across a valley range
I hadn't seen for years.
The trail was all so spoilt and strange
It nearly fetched the tears.
I had to let ten fences down—
(The fussy lanes ran wrong)
And each new line would make me frown
And hum a mournin' song.

Oh, it's squeak! squeak! squeak!
Hear 'em stretchin' of the wire!
The nester brand is on the land;
I reckon I'll retire.
While progress toots her brassy horn
And makes her motor buzz,
I thank the Lord I wasn't born
No later than I wuz!

'Twas good to live when all the sod,
Without no fence nor fuss,
Belonged in partnership to God,
The Government and us.
With skyline bounds from east to west
And room to go and come,
I loved my fellowman the best
When he was scattered some.

Oh, it's squeak! squeak! squeak!
Close and closer cramps the wire!
There's hardly play to back away
And call a man a liar.
Their house has locks on every door;
Their land is in a crate.
There ain't the plains of God no more,
They're only real estate.

There's land where yet no ditchers dig
Nor cranks experiment;
It's only lovely, free and big
And isn't worth a cent.

I pray that them who come to spoil
May wait till I am dead
Before they foul that blessed soil
With fence and cabbage head.

Yet it's squeak! squeak! squeak!
Far and farther crawls the wire!
To crowd and pinch another inch
Is all their heart's desire.
The world is over-stocked with men,
And some will see the day
When each must keep his little pen,
But I'll be far away.

When my old soul hunts range and rest
Beyond the last divide,
Just plant me in some stretch of West
That's sunny, lone and wide.
Let cattle rub my tombstone down
And coyotes mourn their kin,
Let hawses paw and tramp the moun', —
But don't you fence it in!

Oh, it's squeak! squeak! squeak!
And they pen the land with wire.
They figure fence and copper cents
Where we laughed round the fire.
Job cussed his birthday, night and morn
In his old land of Uz,
But I'm just glad I wasn't born
No later than I wuz!

*Charles Badger Clark, Jr.*

# God Appears in the Rift of Clouds

One January night in 1893, with my clothes drying out before a fire in the tent after a three days' cold winter rain, I was sleeping in a camp with brother Charlie, surrounded by 3,000 sleeping sheep. I dreamed I saw God in the rifts of the clouds. I heard Him say, "Thou shalt be punished for the iniquity thou hast done." I awoke somewhat frightened and shocked into serious thought. The three years of sleeping on the ground at night and looking at the stars had given me time to study and wonder how the stars kept going without collisions.

The next time I went to the ranchhouse, I brought back an arithmetic and a Bible, expecting to find out about celestial bodies and their movement. So I started reading Genesis and, before finishing Exodus, I was convinced that I was far from sainthood. For two weeks and more, I prayed simply but sincerely for a new heart which in time began slowly to clean out in long streaks till one day it was clean, but still somewhat stained. I applied to Cibolo Presbyterian Church for admission to the only organized church south of the Frio River. My family's old friend, Thomas J. Cavender, a Bapist deacon, was present and objected on the grounds that Will Harris was "wild and would dance." I had carried a Colt, loved always, and still do, to shoot and never could see the sin in dancing, nor in circuses, nor in decent theaters later in life. But soon I found that pious people had held all such as taboo and held firmly to Adam and Eve's escapade in the definite year of 4004 B.C. So, I was not admitted. I kept coming, and so did the deacon. Finally, he took a Sunday off to round up his cattle and the pastor had the session admit me in 1894. He baptized me. My mother also joined at the same time on restatement of her faith. She had been a Lutheran in Germany. I exceedingly re-joiced. Mother's father, John Wm. von Buckow, a captain in the German Army, graduated from the University of Bonn with the grandfather of the late Kaiser.

## Decided for the Ministry As Life Work

I told the pastor, W. H. Wright (the Presbyterian missionary sent down from Pennsylvania to convert the Texas cowboys), I would like to become a minister. He explained that I would have to study many, many years in school, and also three years more in a theological seminary. That pleased me. But where? Father wanted me to go to Texas A&M, then a teachers' college of some 100 students. My mother thought it was best for me to get out of Texas. God led me to take my mother's advice and, like Jacob of old, I left my native state—Texas.

Pastor Wright recommended Park College, Missouri. He had graduated at Amherst. I was afraid to remain in the state of Texas, for I might return to ranch-ing and bronco busting in which I was dyed in the wool. I applied to Park College, Missouri, and was turned down.

I wanted to make some money and go off to some school somewhere. God had definitely called me and was leading me on. The more I heard of Park College, the more I determined to go there. My father gave me ten acres of his fifty acre field in which to plant cotton. Cotton was only three cents per pound. I made ten bales, but I was sure my father had slipped in three or four bales when I was in Pearsall High School for two months trying to learn enough to be admitted to Park Col-lege. The ten bales brought me a total of $150.

My best preparation was the night before I left home down on the Arroyo Martín. There I knelt down on the curly mesquite grass till near midnight, talking things over with the Lord. I was preparing to cut loose from my ranch home the next day, January 5, 1895. Gradually, I came to see that I had to renounce my desire and hope of someday being governor of Texas, and also the hope of owning a big cattle ranch, and surrender unconditionally to God, then and there, once and forever. This I did. I only asked to have the conscious presence of God with me, and strength to do His will as He would reveal that will to me, day by day. I promised Him I would never stop and would try to do the impossible without doubting, if He would only go with me. His promise was, "I am with you always."

Col. J. P. McAfee had come recently from Missouri and built the first general merchandise store in Dilley. He was a roommate and classmate of his cousin, John A. McAfee, the founder of Park College.[2] Col. J. P. went back home to Columbia, Missouri, for a visit and called at Park College to plead for my admission. Again I applied and, with Col. J. P.'s recommendation, I was admitted, to enter January 5, 1895.

Sister Alice had, in 1887, married a Mississippian, Will Jacobs, called "Civil Will" to distinguish him from his cousin "Wild Will" Jacobs. Seven years later I was paying him $5.00 for his wedding suit, a black woolen, semi-cutaway—a split-tailed evening thing. He had worn his pants till one knee was almost in threads. The coat was used very litttle, if any, after the wedding. I bought it for my very best, if and when I was admitted to Park College. As it turned out, I had only that suit. Mother took a piece of coarse white linen, covered it with black silk, and patched it underneath the thinly worn trouser knee. Long before I reached Park, the white linen was peeking through.

Will Harris throws his lasso into the unknown future and prays.

## The Cowboy's Prayer

O, Lord, I've never lived where churches grow,
I've loved creation better as it stood
The day you finished it, so long ago.
And looked upon your work and called it good.

Make me as big and open as the plains;
As honest as the horse between my knees;
Clean as the wind that blows behind the rains;
Free as the hawk that circles down the breeze.

Just keep an eye on all that's done and said;
Just right me sometime when I turn aside;
And guide me on the long, dim trail ahead—
That stretches upward towards the Great Divide.

*(Author unknown)*

# Chapter 2

## *A Decade in Yankeedom*

I BOUGHT A CARDBOARD VALISE, one of those that open into two halves. Sister Alice made me a jelly layer cake, about six inches high. Mother baked me a big loaf of lightbread, which with the cake and a leg of lamb father roasted for me, just filled one side of the valise.

The few clothes I possessed filled the other half of the valise.

On January 5, 1895, I caught a cattle train to San Antonio, where I waited a night and a day for another cattle train I hoped would go to Kansas City. With the permission of George W. Saunders, the founder of the Union Stockyards of San Antonio, I slept on the porch of the stockyard's office building, with not even as much as a rock for a pillow. So far, Jacob was one ahead of me.

Next day, about sundown, I caught a cattle train for East St. Louis. There were sixty cars of cattle. Some of the boys were so drunk that I found myself punching cattle for them in nearly half the train. The cowhands fell onto my valise and broke one side open, ate most of my cake and lamb. One of the fellows (a telegraph operator from El Paso) called me "preacher." He was so grateful for my services in punching his cattle for him that he went to a friend in St. Louis Union Station (which had recently been built as the first Union Station in America) and got me a half-fare ticket to Kansas City.

Five days after leaving Dilley, on January 10, 1895, I arrived in Parkville—dirty, tired, and smelling like a cattle train—not having bathed or shaved en route, but was glad to see the college and Mackay Building. A nicely dressed student, Henry Hepburn, the college baker,[1] showed me to the office building, but did not go in with me, such a questionable Texan as I appeared to be. With my saddle blanket, which I had bought from Buck Rowland, strapt to my valise covering up the broken-in side, I walked in and up to the office on the second floor. Three students, Dora Withrow, Adelina Peters and Nora Shipley, were sitting on a bench as I passed in and laughed their heads off at me. This was our introduction to a later friendship that has lasted through the years.

The President[2] sat at his desk looking non-plussed at me and said, "Come in." He asked who I was and soon found out what I did not know in books. He called in three women teachers, Isabel McCrea, Clara Bell Hastings and Agnes Dilley,[3] who went with him into a huddle in the corner of his office—glancing sidewise between whispers amusingly at me, a five foot, nine inch, hundred and sixty pound cowboy from Texas—as they tried to arrive at a decision on just what to do with me. He dismissed the teachers. I had been standing all the time, with my Texas slouch hat in hand, by the side of my valise. Again he took his seat and said for me to go over to Bergen Hall, Room No. 4, on the outskirts of the campus, go down to the old well in the corner of a yard near Barrett Hall two blocks away, draw all the water I needed for a bath, and "after you get washed up and shaved, come back tomorrow!"

The Missouri River was frozen over with 18 inches of ice. The well rope was a cable of ice. The board sidewalk was covered with slick ice. I fell down and spilled my bucket of water on the first trip. I was at last where I wanted to be, in college, in my dancing pumps! Field Edmonstone in Col. McAfee's store had told me to throw away my boots and wear these pumps.

Next day I returned all dolled up with my only clean shirt on, but no tie (never owned a tie), and was shown down to a room of faculty children taught by Margaret Demuth,[4] a consecrated recent graduate of college under appointment as a missionary to Persia. She told me I had to make up the first half-year of the classroom work which I had missed; that I had four and a half years more in preparatory school and four years in college to graduate. I left Texas to find my sentence of nine years' work in Park College, which I did in seven and a half years, worked four and one-half hours daily, awoke at 3 A.M. to study.

I was given a front seat on her left. My school desk was made for a child. I had to sit like the girls rode their side saddles in Texas. Next day there squeezed into the seat behind me Fred Huckvale[5]—a slender, six-foot, half bald-headed cowboy from Idaho with a long brown mustache. His presence made me feel much relieved, and less humiliated.

Miss Demuth announced that next Friday we would begin our Rhetoricals. I looked back at Huck and he shook his head. Neither did he know what that was. Friday was the day for the teacher to whip all the big boys in Texas. "I know," said Huck, "but I'll not take that now." It seemed to me that a pretty girl—even whipping me—would not hurt, much. No one on a ranch ever asked questions. We did not know of such a book as a dictionary, and had never heard of the library. So we lay low till Friday's Rhetoricals arrived.

Miss Demuth looked pleasantly at us next Friday as she asked, "Will Mr. Harris and Mr. Huckville remove the table from the platform?" as she walked off with her chair. Huck remarked to me as we sat down, "This is it." The teacher asked Alice Wilson, a nine-year-old, to recite. Alice walked up on the platform, wearing a rather long dress with panties tied with ribbons around her ankles, caught her skirt and panties between thumbs and fingers, and bowed, announcing the title and author of her poem. I looked back at Huck, who was shaking his head and blushing. After it was over, we told the teacher we could not do that. We had mental arithmetic—six months of it—to make up. She countered by telling us to recite anything we had ever learned.

On the way to Huck's room, we discussed our problem. He had learned *The Charge of the Light Brigade*. I remembered a poem I had learned in camp in Texas, written by E. U. Cook, a man from Iowa, who was manager of the Keystone Cattle Ranch across the Frio River, near Pearsall. It was printed in the *San Antonio Express* about 1893. In fact, I had been one of a crowd to see the author off on the train as he returned to Iowa for the last time in 1894.

Our rhetorical day arrived on a Friday "afternoon" (we said "evening" in Texas). I was first on the program. Huck was to follow me. I walked up on the platform like I was going to mount a bronco, with one eye on the teacher. Had a window been open, I would have jumped out of the corral. I made my bow and blurted out *Hell in Texas* by E. U. Cook of the Keystone Cattle Ranch, pulled up my reins and stuck in the spurs.

## Hell in Texas

The Devil in Hell, we're told, was chained,
And a thousand years he there remained.
He neither complained nor did he groan,
But determined to start a hell of his own,
Where he could torment the souls of men,
Without being chained in a prison pen.
So he asked the Lord if He had on hand
Anything left when he made the land.

The Lord said, "Yes, I had plenty on hand,
But I left it down on the Rio Grande.
The fact is, old boy, the stuff is poor,
I don't think you can use it in hell any more."
But the Devil went down to look at the truck,
And said if he took it as a gift he was stuck,
But after examining it carefully and well,
He decided the place was too dry for a hell.

So, in order to get it off his hand,
The Lord promised the Devil to water the land,
For He had some water or rather some dregs,
A regular cathartic and smelled like bad eggs.
Hence the trade was closed and the deed was given,
And the Lord went back to His home in Heaven.
The Devil then said, "I have all that is needed,
To make a good hell," and hence he proceeded.

He began by putting thorns all over the trees,
And mixed up the sand with millions of fleas.

He scattered tarantulas along all the roads,
Put thorns on the cactus and horns on the toads,
He lengthened the horns of the Texas steers,
And put an addition on rabbits' ears.
He put a little devil in the bronco steed,
And poisoned the feet of the centipede.

The rattlesnakes bite you, the scorpion stings,
The mosquitoes delight you with their buzzing wings.
The sandburrs prevail and so do the ants,
And those who sit down need half soles on their pants.
The red pepper grows on the banks of the brook,
The Mexicans use it in all that they cook.
Just dine with a Mexican and you will shout,
"I have hell on the inside as well as on the out."

The devil then said that throughout the land,
He'd arrange to keep up the devil's own brand.
And all would be mavericks unless they bore,
Marks and scratches and bites and thorns by the score.
The heat in the summer is one hundred and ten,
Too hot for the devil and too hot for men.
The wild boar roams through the black chaparral,
'Tis a hell of a place he has for a hell.

Huck was to have followed me, but the pale perturbed teacher arose stiffly and announced, "The class is excused," and pulled out upstairs to the President's office, two steps at a time. Huck assured me as we walked to our room, "You'll be rounded up tomorrow as sure as thunder." We never heard another word about it.

Twenty-five years later, I stopped by Park College and found her son and daughter in the graduating class. My old teacher was back on furlough from Persia. I hurried over to their mother's home in town, knocked on the door. A pretty girl came to admit me. In walked my old teacher. She gazed at me for a moment (she did not know I was in the land) and exclaimed as she threw her arms around me, "Will Harris! Do you remember that poem?" I did. And I appreciated her warm embrace. If only Huck had been there, too!

Refreshing rains ended the two-year drought and E. U. Cook then wrote

### *Texas as a Paradise*

The Lord said he wished to show
To His erring children here below
That He had plenty in His store
For those who knocked at Heaven's door,
And hence would give to some bright land
Samples of blessings from His right hand;

And if you think there's cause to doubt it,
Just listen to how God reasoned about it.
These gifts I can't give to the States in the East,
The weather's too damp for both man and beast,
And the Northern States I consider together,
I made a mistake when I put up their weather,
For in blizzards and cyclones, tornadoes and cold,
No one can enjoy good gifts, I am told.
This is too cold hence westward I shall go
To the land where the fig and the orange trees grow,
For here it is true is a beautiful land,
But then here's the fogs, the dust and sand;
And those who enjoy these gifts as they must
Can't do it in the sand and the fogs and the dust.
At last reaching Texas, a State of some size,
He decided to give her His capital prize:
He opened wide His bountiful hand,
He dispersed His blessing all over the land,
And hence we enjoy as these blessings of ours
Ten months in the year the most beautiful flowers;
And nights most delightful, fanned by the breeze,
That comes sweeping across her from over the seas;
And Italy's skies with our own won't compare;
Nor is her land more fertile nor ladies more fair
And the grasses that grow on the range of ours
Are kept beautifully green by these sweet summer showers,
And as we know, to enjoy our wealth,
We must first secure the blessing of health.
Hence we declare to the sick in each clime
That health you can have, if you come here in time.
And now to our friends in the East, North and West
We want you to come here and with us be blest.
For God never intended that we all alone
Should enjoy all these blessings that He has bestown.

*By permission of the old Buckhorn Saloon,*
*now a museum.*

## A New Life-Objective Is Awakened

In Park College, under C. B. McAfee's[6] leadership of morning prayers, I learned "The eternal God is your refuge and underneath are the everlasting arms." Deut. 33:27. "I will make you a blessing." "Only goodness and mercy will follow you." Psalms 23:6.

If my footprints of yesterday are to be "goodness and mercy" for the encouragement of those who follow me, I must then "Follow in His steps" and live His life. An unconditional surrender to God early in life is the open door to all that is good in abundant living for God and man in the Kingdom of God on earth. Psalms 84:11—

> For Jehovah is a sun and shield:
> Jehovah will give grace and glory;
> No good thing will He withhold from them
>     that walk uprightly.

At first, I could not see the love of God—only a drawn sword for me if I turned back. Through the years of experiences, I can now see the hand of a loving Father's care and His thought of me in everything—"All things work together for good to those who love God, who are called according to His purpose." Romans 8:28. Every experience is intended for a step upward into fellowship and understanding of Divine Love and Guidance. Everything is food for the soul to the one who follows "in His steps." Dr. Sheldon's book *In His Steps* helped me.[7]

During my many but fleeting years at Park College, I had no financial help other than what I could earn by odd jobs, such as sawing oak wood into stove length at fifty cents. For cutting it into three pieces, Mr. Koehler[8] gave me seventy-five cents a cord, etc. Once my brother Charles sent me $15.00. Twice Col. J. P. McAfee, of Dilley, sent me $25.00. A total of $65.00. I wanted to work my way and had to send my parents' remittances back to them before they ceased. When I offered payment of Col. McAfee's $50.00, he refused and *asked me to pass it on to some good, needy boy after I had finished my college studies. This planted an idea in me to found another Park College,*† in Texas or somewhere, where students could work their way to an education under wholesome Christian direction.

## A Threefold Vision of My Life-Work

There are dreams and dreams. I had a second dream that left me a changed candidate for the ministry—changed as a result of this dream, from wanting to be a T. DeWitt Talmage,[9] into an inner urge, *a consuming desire to help other young people to get what I was receiving at Park College.*†

I was rooming in Hill House with a Kentucky debater, whose themes were usually on predestination, foreordination, the Will of God, etc. Every evening after supper, Tom Robinson would begin, before a group of boys in front of Copley Hall, a half-hour soapbox discussion to help digest his food. He was a breezy, longwinded Southerner, and thoroughly enjoyed talking.

---

† This printer's sign will be used throughout the book to indicate phrases that Dr. Harris himself emphasized by underlining or by other means in his manuscript.

The Missouri River washed along one side of the college campus. It was at this time a surging stream, deep and boisterous, up and down which steamboats plied, on which I enjoyed riding down to Kansas City. The Burlington Railroad edged its way between the college campus and the river; and, being buttressed with rock, held the river back from devouring our campus.

In my dream I was walking down the track of the Burlington Railroad, when a young man touched me and said, "Come with me." I followed him as he called my attention to the turbulent river that now splashed at our feet. It was filled a half-mile wide with white, black, brown, red children, chattering, laughing in the water up to their armpits. They kept on passing down the stream as the waters circled in whirlpools and gurgled around the projecting rock-built bends. He said to me, "This is a vision of the people among whom you are to live and work. Among these people you must serve and help to save."

He then said, "Come with me up above." He showed me on the railroad siding a long flatcar on which there was a very big draft horse pulling blocks of gold, two feet square and five feet long, toward the upper end of the flatcar toward a storage house. The harness was cutting sores into the shoulders and sides of the horse, so heavy was his load. The wheels under the flatcar were rolling downhill but the horse, pulling his blocks of gold, thought he was making the uphill grade toward the storage house.

My attendant said, "Do you understand what this represents? The horse represents the wealthy people of the earth, thinking mostly in piling up more and more gold, and not seeing what you have just seen in the river, the children who need their help. Your work will be to get this gold turned to producing, in these children, well-rounded lives, resourceful, independent and of a sturdy Christian faith."

He took me again by the arm saying, "Come along with me to the railway station." There he picked up from the ground, by the east side of the depot, a steel frame of an umbrella and gave it to me, saying, "This umbrella represents what you are now. The old torn covering must be replaced. It needs to be filled in with the best material. You are going to pass through many trials in a land of hot sunshine, cold rains, and stormy winds, in accomplishing the work given you to do." With those words he left me, and I awoke.

My bedfellow, Tom, had been awakened by my tossing around and wanted to know what was the matter. I told him my dream. Next evening, as he illustrated the Divine Sovereignty of God with my dream, all the boys laughed and I never told it again till in Princeton Seminary.

Dr. Vos of Princeton,[10] lecturing on dreams, stated that dreams are sent in a time when the spiritual life of a people is low. MacMillin, my classmate, looked laughingly at me, "Bill, your spiritual life is low!"

At any rate, this dream has given me strength and multiplied my zeal to help others to a higher, better life of abundant living. I read all the biographies to be found in the library, to find out how they did it. I never, at the time or since, have had much esteem for mere grades. In my college later in Puerto Rico, I tried to eliminate all emphasis of teachers on grades. I never failed in an examination, but I never worked for any but medium standing in examinations which I did, and do now, detest.[11]

During my senior year at Park College the students elected me to represent them as student elder in the Session of the college Presbyterian church. I also taught a Sunday School class of college girls, and occasionally preached in country churches.

# Chapter 3

## Riding Curriculum of Park and Princeton

### First

IN THIS CORRAL I found an idea which is like a consuming fire. My professor of Latin, Dr. A. L. Wolfe, was also my Sunday School teacher. He asked the class: "Is your life a career or a mission?"

The dictionary in the library—I had by then learned there was a library and also a dictionary—the dictionary said: "A career is a course of professional or business employment which a man chooses because it offers advancement or honor." A man pushes his own cart to his own desired end. Julius Caesar is a good historical example. The dictionary also said: "A mission is that which one *is* or *feels he is*† destined to accomplish." Jesus Christ embodied this idea. He was *sent*† by His Father.

I took my Bible, which I had secured by memorizing and reciting the Shorter Catechism, and in red ink lines I connected the verses of John's Gospel setting forth Christ's assertion that He had been *sent*. The following references set forth what I found in the Gospel according to St. John.[1]

*3:17* For God Sent the Son into the world.

*4:34* My food is to do the Will of Him who Sent me and to accomplish his work.

*5:23* He who does not honor the Son does not honor the Father who Sent Him.

*5:24* He who hears my word and believes Him who Sent Me.

*5:30* I seek not my own will but the will of Him who Sent Me.

*5:36* These very works which I am doing, bear me witness that the Father has Sent Me.

*5:37* And the Father who Sent Me has Himself borne witness to Me.

*5:38* You do not believe Him whom He has Sent.

*6:29* This is the work of God that you believe in Him whom He has Sent.

*6:38* I have come down from heaven not to do my own will but the will of Him who Sent Me.

*6:39* And this is the will of Him who Sent Me that . . .

*6:44* No one can come to me unless the Father who Sent Me draws him.

*6:57* As the living Father Sent Me.

*7:16* My teaching is not mine but Him who Sent Me.

*7:18*  But he who seeks the glory of Him who Sent Him is true.

*7:28*  He who Sent Me is true and Him you do not know.

*7:29*  I know Him, for I come from Him and He Sent Me.

*7:33*  When I go to Him who Sent Me.

*8:16*  It is not I alone who Judge, but I and the Father who Sent Me.

*8:18*  The Father who Sent Me bears witness to Me.

*8:26*  He who Sent Me is true.

*8:29*  He who Sent Me is with Me.

*8:42*  I came not of my own accord but He Sent Me.

*9:4*  We must work the works of Him who Sent Me.

*10:36*  Do you say of Him whom the Father consecrated and Sent into the world, "You are blaspheming"?

*11:42*  That they may believe that Thou didst Send Me.

*12:44*  He who believes in Me, believes not in Me but in Him who Sent Me.

*12:45*  He who sees Me sees Him who Sent Me.

*12:49*  The Father who Sent Me has Himself given me commandment what to say.

*12:50*  What I say therefore I say as the Father has bidden Me.

*13:20*  He who receives Me receives Him who Sent Me.

*14:24*  The word which you hear is not mine but the Father's who Sent Me.

*15:21*  They do not know Him who Sent Me.

*16:5*  I am going to Him who Sent Me.

*17:3*  That they know Thee, the only true God, and Jesus Christ whom Thou has Sent.

*17:18*  As Thou didst Send Me into the world, so I have Sent them into the world.

*17:21*  That they may all be One . . . . so that the world may believe that Thou hast Send Me.

*17:22*  That they may become *perfectly*† one so that the world may know that Thou has Sent Me.

*17:25*  And these know that Thou has Sent Me.

*20:21*  As the Father has Sent Me, even so I send you.

Jesus Christ chose this way. See John 10:17-18, "I lay down my life that I may take it again. No one takes it from me, but I lay it down of my own accord." See also Luke 13:33. His way led to Calvary. "Nevertheless I *must*† go on my way today and tomorrow and the day following."

This is the way I have always felt since January 5, 1895. I could not turn back. A drawn sword followed me daily. I kept on keeping on, till the pull of the Gospel before me took the place of the push of the brandishing sword behind me. The Mission Life is the way the Master traveled. We must follow in His footsteps. "I am with you always." This Way became brighter daily ever since I learned in Park College that St. John had recorded how Jesus lived for "today, tomorrow and the day following."

I have recorded this to encourage all the students of Polytechnic to make their life a *Mission,* a *Sent Life,*† for every vocation is a sacred vocation under God, just as sacred as that of the one who preaches from the pulpit and deals with expounding the truth. Life, all of life, for all Christians is sacred and equally holy, under God.

## Second

How to live with and for as equals all races of peoples.

## Third

How to see GOD in all the universe, including the tiniest and the greatest of His creation, for creation shows only the back of God. Exodus 33:20-23.[2]

## Fourth

The value of adhering to a schedule for work, study and mental training.

## Fifth

True Education is three-fold, represented by the Head, mental; by the Hand, manual labor; by the Heart, religion. These three fields of study and practice lead the individual into possession, under the direction of the Holy Spirit, of right attitudes in relation of the individual to himself, to others and to God. The path to these attitudes are set forth in natural creation and revealed in the Bible as THE CHRIST-WAY.

## Sixth

The Bible is the faithful written word of God's revelation to man as man is progressively able to understand God. It begins as a written revelation with Moses and ends as a written revelation in Christ Jesus. It is better understood as learning, under the Holy Spirit's direction in the fear and love of God, increases from generation to generation.

These ideas started with my Christian professors, especially Dr. Cleland McAfee in morning prayers and privately from Dr. A. L. Wolfe.

## Seventh

Still in the brush. To be roped in later.

I was fully convinced that God had called me to do a special work. For this great task I prayed God to send me a helpmeet—a Park College trained partner.

I needed such a person. Contemplation of that work made me sweat, "perspire" they said in the North.

Mr. Howard B. McAfee[3] asked me to take a walk with him one afternoon and he showed me where he expected to erect future college buildings in Park. The long hill facing the river was for girls' dormitories. The boys' campus extended from Mt. Zion east and north and between was to be for teachers' homes, library about where [it] is and Science Hall nearby. Above the cow barn was to be the lake for supply of water to the college. He never knew what he planted in me for use in Puerto Rico . . . a Master Plan.

Uncle Sam McAfee[4] asked me to go as a missionary for the summer to the Kiowa and Fox Indian Reservation in Kansas. I went to White Cloud, Kansas, where I found a family of Indians who took me to the Reservation Headquarters where I ate and slept. The work of the one in charge was to give out clothing and money to the Indians. I knew nothing about what I was to do except to preach to the Indians. The small chapel was never painted. Headquarters gave me the key to the front door. There was only one door. Inside I found a pulpit, two rows of benches called pews and an old worn out organ in which a mother rat had her nest in the bellows. The keys stuck. I mended the bellows and papered the key-propellers with my knife. All was set for a service.

I borrowed a horse and rode all over the two tribal territories. The Indians spoke English but could not understand why they should go to church. I found some families who were well educated in Carlisle Indian School,[5] had nice homes and children who played the piano.

The last Sunday of the summer found a large crowd of Presbyterians from Horton and Hiawatha churches who had come for the dedication of the church. No preacher came. I did not know how to dedicate. We had a short service. A layman made a talk. The keys of the organ stuck from time to time. I went over and loosened the keys to the amusement of everyone but the organist. We had a closing prayer and it was dedicated.

Everybody went over to some large trees on an Indian's farm. August is always hot in Kansas. Under the shade of the trees the ladies spread tablecloths and placed abundance of food. I noticed a spry but disappointed looking young lady on the other side of the tablecloths. George Girard[6] was with her. He introduced me to her. I was pleased, for she was to enter my junior class in Park because she could not financially continue in Emporia College. Her eyes were like diamonds, whole-souled smile as she talked to her friends, a charming and winsome personality. I did not then think that Miss Eunice White was in answer to my prayer. Occasionally I saw her working in the laundry and packing fruit in the college cannery and in class.

A shower of meteors appearing every 40 years was to be seen soon. Professor Mattoon[7] divided the class; Miss White and I were in the first division of the astronomy class. We saw no meteors, for the night was dark and cloudy. The second division went the following night at 2 A.M. and saw jillions of meteors. I proposed to four boys that we invite a girl companion for each of us and ask Professor Mattoon to be our chaperon. I invited Miss White. The professor did not show up. It was cold and I took a lap-robe along for Miss White and me. We sat with the others, except Arch Law and Ulna Pryor remained in the room of the 12-foot telescope and kept the coffee boiling for the others. We saw many, many showers of meteors falling out of the Sickle.

The rising bell rang at 5:45 for breakfast. The girls had not asked for permission. Edith Wilson hurried to crawl in thru her room window. She stepped upon the wooden door leading to the coal bin below and broke through, falling into the soft coal bin some feet below. The matron ran down with her lantern to see what had happened and all the girls were placed under restriction till January 1, 1901. Emporia College had no such strict rules and Miss White was innocently caught in what she did not approve. I went to President Lowell McAfee and asked him to let me serve the restriction instead of the girls, for I had proposed the observatory watch meeting. Of course, the older girls should have secured permission but they did not, since Professor Mattoon was to have accompanied us. A letter came from Miss White, and, boy, she laid me low where I belonged but did it in such an understanding but firm way. I then and there decided God had answered my prayer. Johnnie Meyer caried notes, two or three a week, for us. I proposed to Eunice and she said she would give me an answer Christmas Day. Her mother invited me to Hiawatha for Christmas. The clock struck twelve and it was Christmas Day. I pressed for an answer. She arose, started to walk upstairs to her room. I knew she would say no. On the third step she stopt, turned around and said, "YES," as we kissed for the first time—which love grew daily for fifty-three years.

## *Eighth*

I was now all set for life and in the Corral with Eunice whom God had sent me from Heaven.

# Graduated from Princeton and Married

My three years in Princeton Theological Seminary[8] were pleasant and profitable, especially in outside contacts with men like Robert E. Speer, Secretary of the Presbyterian Foreign Mission Board, C. A. R. Janvier[9] of India, and Harry Ford, a private secretary in Philadelphia—men who helped me to clear my vision and understand my responsibility to the world.

The *Princeton Weekly* announced: "On Friday evening, April 14, 1905, W. A. McCoy and J. W. Harris, both of Princeton Seminary, were ordained as evangelists in the Lafayette Avenue Church of Brooklyn, N. Y." Dr. Cleland McAfee who had in Park College ordained me as an elder gave the charge to McCoy and me. John Underwood, of the Underwood Typewriter Co., laid his hand with Dr. McAfee on my head in the ordination service.

Upon graduation from Princeton, May 11, 1905 (Eunice's birthday on which we had planned to be married!) I left for the Kickapoo Indian Reservation in Kansas, where my classmate, Eunice E. White, had recently arrived from her three years of missionary work in Indian Territory[10] and Tennessee. Her parents were missionaries to the Indians in Kansas. Our wedding was attended by relatives and Indians of this Kickapoo Reservation, celebrated at high noon, May 17, 1905, in the missionary home. Here we spent two weeks in the home of Eunice's happy family of father, mother and three smaller sisters. I also got acquainted with the Indian Presbyterian Church and with the non-Christian assembly of Indians held at sunrise. On the way for a last visit with my parents we visited a vacant church and accepted a call to preach for them after our visit in Texas.

We supplied the church in Pond Creek, Oklahoma Territory, for ten months. We could not rest because in this town of 567 there were seven preachers striving with each other in frustration, where one church could have done the job.

My seven and one-half years at Park College and three more in Princeton had opened my eyes to the frustration of the overlapping denominational competition of our Christian attempt to bring in the Kingdom of God.

I had spent two summers visiting and speaking in three or more Presbyterian churches weekly in Missouri while a student in Park College. Some churches refused to allow me to speak or to mention missions. I had done missionary work in 1900 among the Kiowa and Fox Indians of Kansas. I had also done missionary work among the Hungarians of Philadelphia, among the various foreign-born of Minneapolis, Minn., and I had preached to Texas Mexicans under mesquite trees —these and their like were neglected by organized denominations. I had seen half-filled churches side by side, or across the street from each other, whose very hymns of praise mutually interrupted their worship hour. A classy church, a color and racial discriminating church, and oftentimes a church divided into selfish cliques (a self-centered setup), coupled with the ever increasing number of reforming divisions, seemed to me to be absurd as well as futile. This Pond Creek Presbyterian Church had the finest building in Pond Creek, had all the wealthy people as members, was a fine cross-section of the newly settled territory of Oklahoma, but its members were divided. The right side of the church looked out the windows when a soloist sang from the left side of the church. A lecturer with his stereopticon came to town to lecture on the Prodigal Son and show slides illustrating his talk. A picture machine was not allowed in the church building. He had to go to Town Hall. Dr. Alexander, Bishop of Derry, enlarged on Job 31:17 "If I have eaten my morsel alone," very much to the point:

"If I have eaten my morsel alone"—
The patriarch spoke in scorn;
What would he think of the Church, were he shown
Heathendom, huge forlorn,
Godless, Christless with soul unfed,
While the Church's ailment is fullness of bread,
Eating her morsel alone?

"I am a debtor alike to the Jew and the Greek,"
The mighty Apostle cried,
Traversing continents, souls to seek,
For the love of the Crucified.
Centuries, centuries since have sped;
Millions are famishing; we have bread;
But we eat our morsel alone.

Ever of them who have largest dower
Shall Heaven require the more;
Ours is affluence, knowledge, power,
Ocean from shore to shore;
And East and West in our ears have said:
"Give us, give us your living bread,"
Yet we eat our morsel alone.

"Freely, as you have received, so give,"
He bade, who hath given us all;
How shall the soul in us longer live,
Deaf to their starving call,
For whom the Blood of the Lord was shed,
And His Body broken to give them Bread,
If we eat our morsel alone?

# PART II

# Puerto Rico—
# The Beginnings

# Chapter 4

## *Roping in Co-partners*

## Application Made for Foreign Work

WE APPLIED to the Presbyterian Foreign Board for work in Mexico or Central America in April, 1906, but were turned down. There was no vacancy. Our papers were given to the Presbyterian Home Missions Board. My professor in Park, Joseph Ernest McAfee, newly elected Associate Secretary of the Home Mission Board, vouched for us, and Dr. C. L. Thompson telegraphed us our appointment to Puerto Rico. Saved again by the labors of a third McAfee!

THE BOARD OF FOREIGN MISSIONS OF THE
PRESBYTERIAN CHURCH IN THE U.S.A.
156 FIFTH AVENUE, NEW YORK

May 26th, 1906

The Rev. J. Will Harris,
Pond Creek, Oklahoma Territory

My dear Mr. Harris:

Dr. Brown is away at the Assembly, and I write in his absence to acknowledge your letter of May 11th. I do not wonder at your unwillingness to stay in a village of 700 people with seven churches, and I hope the way may open for you to some more destitute field. We shall be glad to speak to Dr. Thompson or Dr. Dixon of the Home Board about you. They have not come back from the Assembly yet, but I will send Dr. Thompson a note which will be awaiting him on his return. Porto Rico[1] and Cuba, as you know, are fields under the care of the Home Board.

Mr. Janvier has written in very cordial terms regarding you and I shall quote what he has said in a note to Dr. Thompson.

Very cordially yours,
/s/ *Robert E. Speer*

THE BOARD OF HOME MISSIONS OF THE
PRESBYTERIAN CHURCH IN THE U.S.A.
156 FIFTH AVENUE, NEW YORK

June 8th, 1906

Rev. J. Will Harris,
Pond Creek, Oklahoma

Dear Brother:

Referring to yours of the fourth of June, it gives me pleasure to confirm the telegram I am sending you now to the effect that you have been accepted for Porto Rico and you will be appointed by the Board at its meeting on Thursday of next week.

The terms of your appointment are a salary of twelve hundred dollars and traveling expenses to the field. I have indicated to you that we would like to have you go at the earliest practicable date. The middle of July will be satisfactory to us. The steamer on which you will go sails on Saturday. We would like to leave indeterminate the question of your location until we have had a conference with you here.

Will you kindly notify us when you expect to leave Kansas, and the Treasurer's office will send you transportation or orders for transportation from Kansas to New York; also name the place from which you will start.

We are very glad to have you thus give yourself to the work in Porto Rico. You are by your knowledge of Spanish especially fitted for it, and we believe that a wide and useful field is open for you there. We are sending two other young men down—Mr. Smith from Auburn Seminary, and Mr. Odell from Princeton; it is possible you know Mr. Odell.

Our Porto Rican work is full of interest and we congratulate you on the opportunity there and the work on having one who in language and other ways is so well equipped. You speak of being rusty in your Spanish; you will have several weeks in which to brush it up.

Waiting to hear from you, I am,

Fraternally yours,
/s/ *C. L. Thompson*
Secretary.

We sailed on the S.S. *Philadelphia* of the Red "D" Line for Puerto Rico July 5, 1906. We were assigned to the San Germán district,[2] extending from the peaks of Cerro Gordo on the north to the Caribbean coast on the south and Mona Passage on the west. The district included San Germán (our home), Cabo Rojo, Lajas, Ensenada [Guánica] and Sabana Grande, a wonderful field of fine, energetic local Presbyterian people, ready and raring to go.

At that time there were no native ministers in Puerto Rico. Now, in 1952, there are no continental[3] ministers, and have not been for a long time, in the Presbyterian mission work of Puerto Rico. My assistants in charge of my eight churches and the thirty out-stations were: don José A. Martínez and his wife, doña Josefa Nazario (doña Pepita), our Bible reader; don Emilio Castillo, don Juan Segarra, don Celso Calderón and don Juan B. Soto. This last named was a very studious young man with a B.S. degree. His preaching was philosophical and far above the heads of the people. He came over on his horse from Cabo Rojo and asked my advice about remaining in missionary work or studying law. I advised him to finish his law course, for we needed Christian lawyers. He soon had his LL.B. and had finished his law course, became a State Senator [later], and Chancellor of the University of Puerto Rico. At the University's commencement of 1938, Chancellor Soto, upon recommendation of Honorable José Gallardo,[4] Commissioner of Education, president ex-officio of the Board of Trustees of the University of Puerto Rico, and graduate of the Polytechnic Institute, confered on me an LL.D. degree. The advancement in life of Doctors Soto and Gallardo shows what integrity of Christian character, plus hard work, will do. I am proud of Dr. Soto and Dr. Gallardo.

Here in Puerto Rico, it dawned on me that my dream in Park College of children in the Missouri River was a true vision of my mission in life. The streets, highways, and country paths of Puerto Rico were filled with thousands of smiling, bright, and eager children, of all classes and colors: white, black, brown and yellow,* very few of whom were in school.

Rev. J. L. Underwood was one of three missionaries brought in from Latin American republics to organize the work in Puerto Rico, which had become a part of the U.S.A. He organized a Theological Training School in Mayagüez. He was granted permission to go to the States and take a refresher course in theology. While there studying, Presbytery was influenced to ask the Mission Board not to return Underwood to Puerto Rico. He was sent to the Philippines. I am thoroughly ashamed of my acquiescence to this action, pushed through Presbytery in 1910. I had substituted for Rev. Underwood in the training school, teaching church history and homiletics, and took charge of the English-speaking church service in Mayagüez on Sunday mornings.

We worked out a charter for the training school's development into a Men's College and Theological Seminary combined. Presbytery approved the project and sent it on to the Mission Board in New York, where it was turned down. I suggested that the president of the Training School solicit funds outside of the Board and develop his school independent of the Board. He was too loyal a Presbyterian to think of going against the expressed denial of such by the Mission

---

* A handwritten correction "tan" by an unknown hand appears in the typescript.

Board. The project was then definitely dropped. Like so many missionaries and preachers, he followed the Mission Board and not the Lord's leading to a bigger field of service. Sometimes even a good board is wrongly influenced.

When our household effects came, we carefully kept all the boxes for a possible return to Texas after my first year's contract ended. My father wrote me an encouraging letter stating that I was under the U.S.A. flag which was far better than being under the Mexican flag, to which country I wished to go. Said he: "When Porfirio Díaz[5] ends his peaceful reign there will be years of revolutions in Mexico. Call the Porto Ricans a royal family and you will soon see in them noble traits to be developed."

Two young men, graduates of colleges in the U.S.A., Lcdo.[6] Pedro Amado Rivera and his cousin Cástor Rivera, a licensed doctor in dentistry[7] invited me to ride my horse and to accompany them one afternoon, as they rode up and down the streets of San Germán. This was then a regular event of fiesta[8] life . . . All the people and pretty girls waved at the youthful riders as scores of them rode their fancy-gaited horses down the streets in front of their houses. It seemed to me I had never seen so many handsome young men and beautiful girls and well-dressed happy old folks as I did that day. My impressions of Porto Ricans were most favorable.

I had written J. Ernest McAfee of my intentions of going to Mexico. He sent me the following, one of his chapel talks in Park College.

## *Thanks in Unison*

Thanks for a chance; to see a land to save, and hold it the key to the world's saving. Thanks for a vision of God's purpose in the ministry of his gospel. Thanks for the push of the past into a livelier and more energetic future. Thanks for dirty cities—not for their dirt, but for their promise of glory after the cleansing. Thanks for a country-side all overgrown with sin-weed and ignorance-dock—not for the unsightly over-growth, but for the sure marks of a fertility needing only the zealous attendance of God's husbandmen to bring out God's green and yellow fields. Thanks for a great hurrying, impetuous, unsatisfied, even rebellious people, that hurrying they may make eager progress toward godliness; that impetuous they may grow passionate for righteousness; that unsatisfied with cheap material baubles they may dig for and find the treasure of the soul's peace; that rebellious against degrading impositions they may gladly accept the mastership of Him whose yoke is easy and His burden light. Thanks for things to mend, a disordered society to set to rights, broken lives to reconstruct, sinners to save. Thanks for a chance.

Thanks for faith; for the confidence to believe in God and the power of his salvation in spite of all—because of all. Thanks for the grounds of faith; the immutable promises of God, whose will has gone forth that all men should be saved and come to the knowledge of the truth. Thanks for the reassurance of faith; the demonstration of saved lives, the ever-enlarging company of those who know and love God and set zealously to work out a sealed salvation. Thanks for a gospel of which none need feel ashamed, a salvation which is effectual, however new and fibre-testing be the strain. Thanks for known truth, for tested promises, for a Christ who can save because He has saved. Thanks for faith and a prayer for more.

Thanks for wisdom to plan and zeal in achievement. Thanks for a Church which is winning a conquest. Thanks for keener discernment of what the needy need, of what the lacking lack. Thanks for a ministry of grace which applies, which touches the wound, which does not so far miss the mark. Thanks for old men eager to redeem the time, for young men passionate to set to work. Thanks for sane men whose spirits God has set aflame with holy zeal.

Thank God for Himself, His world and a task.

During his four years as leader of Park's chapel service, this and similar five-minute talks were given five times weekly.

That experience with the two young men and the effect of my former teacher's *Thanks in Unison* prepared me for the acceptance of my Divine commission on the road a few days later.

It was with deep conviction ever afterward that I sang with my students the hymn in Morning Prayers:

### *Just When I Need Him*

Just when I need Him, Jesus is near,
Just when I falter, just when I fear;
Ready to help me, ready to cheer
Just when I need Him most.

Just when I need Him, Jesus is true,
Never forsaking all the way thro';
Giving for burdens pleasures anew,
Just when I need Him most.

Just when I need Him, Jesus is strong,
Bearing my burdens all the day long;
For all my sorrow giving a song,
Just when I need Him most.

Just when I need Him, He is my all,
Answering when upon Him I call;
Tenderly watching lest I should fall,
Just when I need Him most.

# Chapter 5

## *A Voice from Heaven Speaks*

IN NOVEMBER 1906, Pedro, a fisherman of [Bo.] Las Salinas[1] on the Caribbean shore, invited don Emilio Castillo and me over to his house fast by the seashore, where some 150 children and parents were waiting to request me to come and teach them how to read the Bible and to write. The breakers on the reef one-half mile off shore made me uneasy; being a novice I was afraid the sea might roll in upon us. Pedro told me of the fire-flecked waters of the Devil's bay near by, now called "Phosphorescent Bay."[2] I promised to do all I could to get them a school, but I told them I could not be their teacher.

After the meeting in don Pedro's house, don Emilio and I rode our horses while his peoncito, "Juancho," trotted along ahead of us with his lantern in hand and the folded Bilhorn organ on his head. I left don Emilio in Lajas, his home, and rode on alone to San Germán. The hour was about midnight. I was thinking of the children in Salinas and their desire for a school. I could not go over there and teach them. I could get someone else to do it. Like these children, had I not once longed for a school while I was a lad on the Rio Grande in Texas? I could not forget their eager faces as they sat on the ground around the fisherman's shack. They touched my heart deeply.

The Lord had changed my childish ambition to become governor of Texas and called me to the ministry, in which I hoped to become a T. DeWitt Talmage. After my dream of children floating down the Missouri River, my ambition was to return to Texas and build another Park College for Texas youth, who at that time found it hard to go beyond reading, writing and arithmetic. When I sailed for Puerto Rico I seemed to leave such ideas behind and expected to do in Puerto Rico purely church work. My college founding had been left at the dock in Brooklyn. But these Caribbean children had awakened in me the old urge of building a college.

I was riding Old Bay, the laziest horse I had ever ridden, with a rough trot, short and bumpy. Don Emilio had arrived at his home in Lajas and I kept on riding and thinking of those children on the shores of the Caribbean. At a turn in the road around the rock hillside near the farm of Antonio Christian, I was in deep meditation and forgot even the rough gait of Old Bay, when suddenly I heard in my whole being a voice, saying: "You! You are to do it!" The Lord Jesus spoke to me. Like Moses of old I began to make excuses. I really felt I was not capable of doing the work of building a college in Puerto Rico—so far from my own people and in a land of strangers, without money with which to make a beginning. To do this I would have to return often to the U.S.A. for money and leave my wife and her newborn baby, Helen,[3] in La Paloma—the name of the house in which we lived, a big rambling house of large rooms, no water, no electricity, with an outdoor toilet 200 feet in the rear, on the outskirts of San Germán. I could not leave them.

All the time my soul reverberated with that voice, "You are to do it!" My excuses fell flat; I accepted the commission, though I could not see just how and where to begin.

Puerto Rico was not prepared for an institution like Park College. A normal school was started in Fajardo in 1899, was moved to Río Piedras in 1901. The University of Puerto Rico was started March 12, 1903, as a teachers college; in 1910 the University offered the beginning of a liberal arts course.

At the end of the sixth grade licenses were given to those who wished to teach in the rural schools, where 80% of the people lived. Public schools were run in two sections—morning and afternoon divisions under the same teacher. Even so, only a few of the thousands of first graders could be admitted.

I saw distinctly that people both in the church and school would have to be taken where they were and led on to a place very worthwhile their going. Fourteen years later we were enrolling students in the Polytechnic for College.[4]

Early in 1907 I employed Miss Guillermina Nazario (a sister of doña Pepita Nazario), who had a rural license and was living in [Bo.] La Pica, of Sabana Grande . . . a very active girl in church work in La Pica.

Into a narrow front room of a poor family's house,[5] Guillermina gathered some thirty tots—eager to learn and who could not find seats in the public schools of San Germán. She had no school furniture. I devised a 3′ × 4′ blackboard made out of pine boards. They were taught the alphabet and numbers, memorized Bible texts and learned to pray and to sing hymns. This was in San Germán, Barrio Santa Rosa, near the Longfellow School. I bought a lot from don Pancho Rivera by the side of don Juan Ortiz Perichi's house. Ortiz Perichi traded a better location to me for my lot by his house.[6] I advanced the money and built a concrete school and chapel combined on the lot don Juan had traded me, and paid for it principally from rent money allowed by the Women's Mission Board. This was the begininng of what, in 1912, became the Polytechnic Institute.

In the meantime I went to [Bo.] Ensenada and told Mr. A. J. Grief, vice-president and general manager of Guánica Central, of the people's request for a school. He asked me to request the Presbyterian Church to take charge of the district; that he would help put up buildings, and establish the schools needed. I wrote to the Presbyterian Board of Home Missions offering that Board, in Mr.

Grief's name, the exclusive right of the educational work in the Guánica Central's territory. The Board turned it down.

Mr. Grief then made the same offer to the Catholic Church, of which he was a member. It could not undertake the work.

He and I then bombarded the Department of Education, till they responded. Now, that district has many rural schools, an elementary and high school. We were surprised to find that most of the rural people in that section were unmarried. Mr. Grief paid the Catholic priest the cost of his fee for marriage, and thus many families celebrated weddings of fathers and mothers. The Protestant churches performed weddings without fees; and judges of court were required by law to marry couples free of all charge.[7]

## A Site for Enlargement of My School Purchased in 1908[8]

Seeing that the Presbyterian Church schools, i.e., the Theological Training School of Mayagüez, would not be developed into a college and the Colegio Americano of Mayagüez had no plans for development into a coeducational Christian college of liberal arts and sciences, nor did the Presbyterian School at Aguadilla dream of anything but a temporary aid to the public school system, I determined to continue developing my school, in embryo, in San Germán into a Park College.

My purpose was to develop a school like, but better than, Park College, where boys and girls chosen from good homes, with intellectual and physical ability, could find a college course possible, even though they had no money to pay for tuition and board. I knew from college experience that in erecting the college buildings, roads and cultivation of farms or in shops, in offices, in the kitchen, in serving tables, and in caring for the grounds—all this could always be given to students, as Park College did in my day. The value of their work would be accredited on tuition and board. To be really successful, all student work must be supervised by specially qualified and trained directors. This I learned at Park College also to be the most difficult positions to fill—impossible, in fact, to secure at the reasonable teacher's salary. The highest salary in Park College was paid the director of masonry. Years after this, Dr. Marquis found a man to take charge of our Polytechnic carpenter shop, a fine Christian fellow. We wrote him and his reply was that by taking an awful licking, he would be able to do it for only $8,000 a year! . . . nearly four times the salary of the president of Polytechnic at that time.

I could not develop my idea on the little lot where I had operated my school in San Germán since 1907. A friend, don José M. Acosta, had a livery stable near my home and an adjoining acre of land for resting his horses back of the Presbyterian Church in San Germán. He would not sell it. The highway and railway had been completed to Ponce and automobiles began to carry passengers. Don Pepe[9] read the signs of the times and consented to sell me the acre for my school after months of my repeated requests. I paid him $300 for the acre. The Registry of Property in San Germán records January 19, 1910, as the exact date.

I was not satisfied with the size of my college site, but it was as big as I could get at the time. The acre was bigger than the people of San Germán felt I needed.

## Secured Money for Boarding School

I was sent to the Presbyterian General Assembly at Denver, Colorado, as a delegate from the Presbytery of Puerto Rico in May 1909. Mrs. Harris and our baby, Helen, went with me. We had a three months' furlough. On our return through Kansas to visit Eunice's family, we picked up three $300 yearly pledges, amounting to $900 over a term of three years, for my college in San Germán, one from D. H. Hills,[10] of Salinas, Kansas. Two of the pledges, which Eunice secured for us in Hiawatha and Horton, were from Women's Missionary Societies in Kansas. The Women's Mission Board in New York stopped the Kansas Missionary Societies from making more than one payment, which they had already sent in, on grounds that my school was not under their jurisdiction, which was true. I had been operating it from the first as a private project. Their aid was simply a token of good favor and blessing. These were the first donations for the future Polytechnic.

When we returned to Puerto Rico, I began (in my spare time) to draw plans for building a dormitory on the acre of land I had contracted to buy. Don Isidro Palmer[11] hauled gravel and sand for the construction work. There were many odds and ends in my mission field demanding my attention after the three months' vacation in the States.

I tried, but failed, to get the Board of Home Missions to take the deed to the acre of land which I had bought adjoining the Board's property in San Germán [12] and to refund the $300 to me for the foundation of my building. When the city of San Germán offered me $1,000 for a street right-of-way through the acre, the Board then gave me the $300 I had paid for the acre, and it was then (1910)[13] deeded to the Mission Board.

## San Germán Mayor Offered Cuartel* as Site

The Mayor of San Germán, don Enrique Rossy, a graduate of Cornell University, suggested that I accept the old Spanish barracks in San Germán for my college, that in recent years had been vacated by the American Army.[14]

Ulises Gregory, Juan N. Matos, Julio Montalvo and Enrique Rossy[15] took me up to see the barracks and walked with me over some 20 acres of adjoining land, belonging to doña Filomena Quiñones,[16] which they proposed to secure for my school, since I felt I needed more land than the mere acre which the barracks covered.

This met with public favor. The mayor asked the San Germán City Council to draw up the deed for the transfer of the barracks from the city to me for my school, then functioning in Barrio Santa Rosa of San Germán since 1907. The Council concurred and the deed was drawn up.

Several months had passed since the City of San Germán had asked me to accept the barracks for my college. Now we were well into the year 1910. I wanted possession of the old Spanish barracks, now the property of San Germán. I had raised the money, which had lain idle, and the donors were wondering what had become of their donations.

I had spoken to Ursula Nazario, sister of doña Pepita Nazario, and to Esperanza Acosta, sister of Ramonita Acosta (wife of Judge Juan Faría)[17] to come over to San Germán and board in private homes and go to my school until I could get the first building of my college erected. They did so.

The president of the San Germán City Council lived out beyond the Río Grande,[18] on the road to Sabana Grande. Either the river was overflowing its banks or he was sick at every monthly meeting of the Council. All other members and the mayor had signed the deed of transfer, only the signature of the president, don Jesús Nazario, was needed to make it legal. Opposition to this then broke out in May 1910 and grew, as the following *hoja suelta* ** indicates (purportedly written by Ulises Pabón). The translation is by my son, Dr. Charles Cleland Harris:

### TO THE MEMBERS
### OF THE MUNICIPAL COUNCIL OF SAN GERMAN

You are representing the people, who, as a body, are composed of persons belonging to different religious institutions; therefore, you honestly cannot show preferences toward some and prejudices towards others, but ought to inspire your acts and decisions only in the light of true justice.

* Barracks.
** Broadside or flyer.

Rumors are circulating to the effect that, spontaneously and without a written solicitude of any authority whatever, you are endeavoring to vote for an ordinance that would create a possible means of surrendering gratuitously, to a determined religious sect, a building of great value and importance to our future which is owned by the Municipality. It is difficult for us to believe that the honesty and practical wisdom which characterizes those who form the body of the Municipal Council of San Germán, will permit you to proceed in that unjust and illegal manner, but, if the influence and meddling intervention of some people were to place the honorable Municipal Council in an indecisive situation in which to act with justice, we wish to point out that that situation can be altered if you will cast off such influences and remember that your representation is due all people without distinction of religious differences.

Act with prudence and moderation; do not allow yourselves to be flattered by the promises of installing in the building something which might mean progress, because once the property of the Municipality is lost, there remains nothing guaranteed to the people, and the future consequences of such an act can not be underestimated.

Any partial and unjust decision will deserve public censure, and by such a decision you will show that you belong to a privileged institution and are thereby failing in your duties.

If, as we believe, you are wise and learned, you will not adopt any resolution whatever, without having first considered the popular will.

Don Ulises Gregory, the political leader of the Republican Party of San Germán, asked me to wait till after the November election and he would see that I got the barracks for my school. If he, Gregory, allowed the transfer now of the barracks to my school the vicar and seven priests of San Germán had advised him that they would throw their strength into the opposing political party. I lost the barracks, which was a blessing in disguise.

This was a disappointment, but since Dis-appointments are HIS-appointments, I turned again to my acre of land in San Germán, determined to move forward at once.

Since my night of prayer in Texas on the Arroyo Martín in 1895, I had made it my practice after every failure to gather up whatever resources I had in hand and to tackle the task I had undertaken, maybe in a different way but as the most important thing to be done . . . as a new opportunity to follow in my Master's steps. My prayer was then and always is: "Lord, stop me if I am wrong, divert me if I am running down the wrong road, but I will never stop going, looking, and expecting you to lead me where you have planned for me to serve best."

I have never wept over what I never had, nor munched my fingernails in regrets of having worked and failed. "All things work together for good to those who love God, to them who are called according to HIS purpose" has certainly been true in my own life and in my observation in the lives of others. I always tried to do the best I could do with what I had in hand. At first, in 1906,[19] it was a little day school which grew into higher grades with about 100 students and two teachers by 1910. In 1908 [sic] I bought an acre of land which I knew was all too small for my plans, but it was all I could then get. In 1909 I jumped at the offer of the barracks and a possible 20 acres adjoining it. That failed to be given me.

I returned to my acre. I owned it personally. It is good to invest in something you can step on. Don Isidro Palmer had hauled sand and gravel in 1909, while I designed a girls' dormitory. I had dug a water well on that acre in February 1910 and erected a windmill for the water supply. On February 10, 1910, Donald's birth was announced to me from [Bo.] Ensenada[20] and the well was finished. The city had no water system, only private cisterns in wealthy homes. The poor people carried their water from the river[21] in five gallon cans or bought water from peddlers at five cents per five gallon can. The streets and plaza were lighted up by kerosene lamps. The plaza had recently been paved by José Antonio Vivoni during his term as mayor. Streets were unpaved and there were no sidewalks. This was all for the good because horse races could, and did, prosper along Luna Street. Young men rode fine arch-necked horses up and down the dirt streets on feast days and Sundays . . . . of course there were no autos[22] and no airplanes.

I spent my spare time now in preparing plans for enlarging my Colegio[23] on my acre of land by my home in San Germán back of the church.

## Juan Cancio Ortiz Lugo, Mayor of Mayagüez,[24] Offered Me a Site for My School

Mayor Enrique Rossy's offer of the San Germán barracks to me in 1909 was blocked by the opposition in 1910, as stated in an earlier chapter.

I then turned to my acre adjoining the property of the Presbyterian Church in San Germán, perfected the plans for a building, staked out the foundation lines for digging the ditches the next day and was checking on the exact positions of the corners, when don Juan Cancio Ortiz rode up on his horse from Lajas. His peoncito came trotting along behind him to take the horse back to Lajas after don Juan Cancio caught the 5:30 P.M. train at the lower station for Mayagüez, his new home.

Don Juan Cancio sat on his horse, looked at the cords and asked what I was doing. I told him that I had failed to get the barracks for my school. Don Isidro Palmer had hauled the gravel and sand and I was going to start building at once. The *hoja suelta* of the San Germán opposition had reached Lajas. He had read it and that was why he rode by to see me. He said: "San Germán *es cobarde.** I am

---

* San Germán is cowardly.

not afraid of all the priests in the Island—not even of the Pope at Rome." He urged me not to spend my money in building and offered to give me the buildings and site in Lajas[25] for my school: "Take your school away from this unworthy town." I asked him if he had the right and power legally to give me his buildings and also if I could buy more land adjoining his buildings. I knew that the land on which the buildings stood belonged to José ("Cheo") Ramírez and to the Zapata family. Don Cheo had 42 acres on which two of the buildings stood and don Juan Cancio thought that I could buy the 42 acres from don Cheo, whose wife and family were members of the Presbyterian Church there. This was very encouraging to me and it looked like the Lord had opened a real way for me to get a site big enough for the beginning of my college.

I felt quite certain that if don Cheo refused to sell his 42 acres, don Juan Cancio would let me have all I needed out of his extensive holdings in Lajas.

Don Juan Cancio and I went over[26] to see the Attorney General, Hon. Foster V. Brown, concerning don Cancio's power to transfer the property of his defunct IAAO in Lajas to me for my school in San Germán. The Attorney General said there were no conditions attached to the Legislature's act which was voted to encourage don Juan Cancio in his attempt to help the needy fatherless boys of Puerto Rico and don Juan Cancio could do what he pleased with the buildings.

Returning to Lajas, don Juan Cancio tore a leaf out of his ledger and wrote a simple short transfer from himself as once president of IAAO of Lajas to Rev. J. Will Harris, not to the Presbyterian Church or Presbytery of Puerto Rico, but to Rev. J. Will Harris for his school in San Germán. Mr. Grief, the largest contributor to the IAAO of Lajas, approved the transfer.

Professor Fernando J. Rodil was head of the IAAO of Lajas during the two last years, 1908-1910, and was still with the Palmarejo public schools of Lajas. He was an elder whom I ordained in the Palmarejo Presbyterian Church, as was don Juan Cancio. Rodil proposed to me that we try to enlist don Juan Cancio in the revival of his old school, reorganized with a definite religious program. Rodil sent our circulars to families of ability who could pay all their boys' expenses. Eleven boys enrolled when the public school opened in September with Rodil as principal. Doña Guesa[27] continued as matron of the boys. Rodil also solicited funds from individuals for what was proposed as the "Palmarejo Institute" so as to distinguish it from the IAAO. Four of his eleven boys soon left for their home. Don Juan Cancio refused to have anything whatsoever to do with the revival of the IAAO, even under the new name of Palmarejo Institute.

While Rodil was making this effort to enlist don Juan Cancio's interest, I was trying to buy more land than the acre on which the buildings stood. Otherwise, I would not transfer my school to Lajas from San Germán. Don Cheo first agreed to sell the 42 acres, then postponed all decision on the sale of his property. I offered him $50 per acre. He raised it to $100 per acre. I accepted the $100 figure.

When the deed of contract was presented to him he would not sell. I then asked don Juan Cancio for a site. Don Cancio hesitated, but finally took me to see a 60 acre tract nearby. After walking over it with me he decided it was not a proper site for my school. I called on don José Ortiz, don Cancio's brother, but he did not want to sell. I saw several others in Lajas, to no avail. In fact, Lajas, like don Juan Cancio did not want to revive the IAAO or anything else like it.

Fernando J. Rodil decided his endeavor to revive the IAAO of Lajas was impossible and resigned at the end of October 1910 as teacher under the Department of Education, entering private business. I am glad to have had the pleasure of marrying Rodil to an attractive and winsome young lady teaching in Hormigueros.

Both Rodil and I gave up Palmarejo on November 1, 1910, as impossible. I was left with four buildings and no place to put them down. The Lajas Public School Board continued to use two of the buildings for two years while erecting the present rural school building in Palmarejo.[28]

## Again Looking for a Site

Senator José Castillo of Sábana Grande found a nice 60 acre tract on the highway near Sabana Grande. It belonged to two spinsters. I went with don Pepe Castillo to see them. My ears had become irritated with "We do not want to sell our land." I hoped these ladies would be tender-hearted. But they, too, like the others, looked at me—a penniless missionary preacher—and gently said: "We do not care to sell." They were all afraid I would get on their land and never pay for it.

The IAAO of Lajas had been commonly called "El Instituto." Unfortunately, my school only three miles away was also called "El Instituto," following closely on the IAAO's death. Few people outside of San Germán ever knew that I had had a school of 150 students in San Germán since November 1907 with Guillermina Nazario as its director, and Eva Espada as assistant.

The popular mind outside of San Germán confused the names of the Lajas school and mine in San Germán because of the popular allusion to both as "El Instituto." Few of the Lajas people ever heard the name of IAAO de Lajas for it was referred to always as "El Instituto." When the IAAO de Lajas was closed down and the following year my school in San Germán was incorporated as the Polytechnic Institute of Porto Rico, it soon became known as "El Instituto" for short. The people of Lajas thought "El Instituto de Lajas" had been transferred to San Germán and that the Polytechnic Institute of Porto Rico was simply a continuation of the IAAO de Lajas. No one investigated the origin of the two schools. Many of the next generation in Lajas really believed the two schools were one and the same. I and don Juan Cancio knew the difference. All the older generation of San Germán knew the difference, for they had offered me a site in 1909, the barracks, for my then school which had outgrown its clothing.[29]

## Francisco Lagarde, a Merchant of San German, Offered to Sell Me a Site for My School in 1910

I was again up against a wall. I had gone in the wrong direction and had to retrace my steps, but not to my acre. I needed a larger site on which to erect my ideal college which God had showed me in college days at Park.

God moves in a mysterious way. I had looked all around for a possible site for my college during the years since I arrived in 1906. Right under my nose, God had prepared seven hills, known for nearly 400 years as Las Lomas de Santa Marta,[30] adjoining the city of San Germán. These hills had been consecrated by the Pope in Rome as the location for a college for the home-makers of the future. The Pope meant girls. I added boys, for it takes trained girls and boys of Christian character and common sense to become future home-makers. These hills were prepared by the Creator just for a beautiful college campus.

The owner, don Francisco Lagarde, suddenly fell sick and was not expected to live many months. He sent for me and expressed a desire to help me find a site for my college, said he owned the finest place in the Island and wished me to go up with his brother Ramón and see it. I went to just within the borders and decided it was too hilly and the hills were too steep. A couple of days later two nephews of don Paco[31] came back with an extra saddle horse and urged me to look again at the site. We rode all over it, and I then saw the finest layout for a college campus, good soil, very steep hillsides, with ample room for buildings innumerable.

Don Paco said that he expected to die but wished to do something for his town before dying, that he would sell it to me, 100 acres for $8,000 and would contribute $500 of the amount to me, and let me have reasonable time to raise the money. He had taken it over from Manuel Padilla in payment of a $3,500 note for provisions bought of don Paco's store. I gave him $250 for the three months' option, and left for New York.

# Chapter 6

## *Money Problems*

### Solicited Donations to Pay for Site

I, A PRESBYTERIAN MINISTER, took a letter from Mr. A. J. Grief, a Catholic and manager of Guánica Central, to Mr. John E. Berwind, an Episcopalian, of the Berwind White Coal Company, No. 1 Broadway, in New York. In San Juan I had picked up three postal cards. One was a palm bark country house with the grass-covered roof[1] bulging out with children in the door and window and overflowing into the yard. Another colored card of the father of that family, plowing with a yoke of oxen bound by their horns to a stick plow (showing the need of such a school as I proposed). A third card of the usual well-to-do city and suburban dwelling in which about ten percent of the people lived. I told Mr. Berwind that I proposed to take the people where I found them and move them upward in life to a place very worth their while. He looked holes in me and said he would give me a thousand dollars on my return from Philadelphia. He was the only rich man I knew in New York City. I had only a month of vacation for the trip. A week up and a week back on the boat and two weeks in the States.

Having spent two years of week-ends in Philadelphia while in Princeton as assistant to Rev. C. A. R. Janvier of Holland Memorial Presbyterian Church, I knew a few rich people there. Dr. Janvier, the missionary from India, gave me a letter to W. J. McCahan,[2] a sugar man, who gave me his check for a thousand dollars as he sat comfortably in a long back chair for a snooze in his office at noon. After several attempts, I got in to see J. Milton Colton, who gave a check for $500 when I showed him McCahan's $1,000. I knew John Wanamaker and had once asked him to pay the carfare to Park College for Z. Bose, a brilliant Hindu boy, while I was still a student in Princeton. In 1943 Time Magazine reported Bose as traveling to Japan to get Japanese to unite with India in driving the English out of the Orient. I expected, at least hoped, Wanamaker would give me $5,000. He was very gracious and asked about the Hindu. I showed him the three cards and the two checks and my promise of $1,000 from Berwind. He said, "I will send you my check in a couple of weeks." I got it—$10! It came every year for a long time about Christmas season with a personal note from Mr. Wanamaker.

[ *42* ]

I had to hurry back to New York and catch my steamer. I called on Mr. Berwind, who was hard of hearing but able to hear all I told him and could see the checks I showed him. He called in his clerk, who went back and brought a check which Mr. Berwind signed and handed me for *two thousand five hundred dollars*!† Glad? I could have exploded!

Don Paco was recovering when I returned to Puerto Rico and offered me $500 to cancel the trade. I advanced a like sum for the extension of the option from January 6, 1911, to January 7, 1912. He charged me $275[3] for rent on the old farmhouse up to January 7, 1912.

I wrote to my brother Clarence to come over from Texas and help me erect concrete buildings. He had had special training in the erection of buildings in Park College. He turned me down but offered to help me financially when he made his cabbage crop in the Rio Grande Valley. A freezing norther struck his cabbage and he was left bankrupt. Three weeks later he landed in Puerto Rico and began, a year later, the erection of the present buildings of the Polytechnic Institute.[4]

## Advanced Students Moved to Site

Miss Eva Espada remained downtown teaching the lower grades. There were at this time about 150 students enrolled in my San Germán school. (This transfer was made after Three Kings' Day, January 6, 1911.) Seven boys from the public schools in the old Palmarejo Institute in Lajas entered my San Germán school. They would not conform to our rules and were sent back to their homes after a week or so. At the end of the term in June Miss Nazario went back with her children to my school downtown, Mr. Clarence went to teach for a year in Aguada public schools, and Miss Pardo went into the public schools in San Germán, while I sought financial support in the U.S.A. and Puerto Rico.

# A Board of Trustees

As soon as the option on the site was extended for a year from January 6, 1911, to 1912, I began to name and organize the first Board of Trustees and to incorporate my school as the College of Porto Rico. This charter as I drew it up was presented to Porto Rico's Executive Secretary, Drew Carroll, for official approval. He refused to file the charter under that name, College of Porto Rico, on grounds of confusion possibly with the proposed University of Porto Rico, and also because of the unincorporated College of Porto Rico, a girls' school in San Juan.[5] I needed legal advice. Rev. E. A. Odell, pastor of the Hugh O'Neil Presbyterian Church in San Juan, introduced me to Atty. Charles Hartzel;[6] Mr. Hartzel called up Carroll for a hearing on the name. Rev. Odell suggested that I take the next name on my list which Rev. E. A. McDonald had suggested, Polytechnic Institute of Porto Rico, adding, "Since you are not certain what your efforts will bring forth if your baby lives to grow up and Polytechnic covers almost any kind of college, and the name can be changed later."

Next morning, I presented the charter under the other name, Polytechnic Institute of Porto Rico, and it was approved by the Executive Secretary as the name of an "Educational institution designed to develop mentally, morally, and physically, and to train in the knowledge of practical arts and sciences, the youth of both sexes. Said institution shall be non-sectarian, but evangelical in principle, adhering to the Holy Scriptures as the infallible rule of faith and practice and imbued with the spirit of Christian charity and liberty." Dated April 24, 1911.

The trustees were members of various Christian denominations, and were the following: George R. Colton, Mason, Governor of Puerto Rico;[7] Dr. C. L. Thompson, Secretary of the Presbyterian Home Mission Board; George F. Tibbits, General Secretary of the YMCA; The Right Reverend James H. Van Buren, Episcopal Bishop of Puerto Rico; Reverend E. E. Wilson, Methodist; Reverend N. H. Huffman, United Brethren; Reverend C. S. Detweiller, Baptist;[8] A. J. Grief, Manager of Guánica Central, Catholic; Lcdo. A. M. Dávila, Protestant druggist;[9] [and] the following Presbyterian ministers: J. A. McAllister, E. A. Odell, E. A. McDonald, J. Will Harris and Presbyterian elders J. J. Seibert,[10] Carlos V. Urrutia, Dr. Manuel Guzmán Rodríguez, Sr. J. Fernando Rodil and Juan Cancio Ortiz Lugo.

## Policy of the Polytechnic Institute of Porto Rico

My purpose in starting the school, now known as the Polytechnic Institute of Porto Rico, was to develop a first-class college imbued with a spirit of

1. Work
2. Study
3. Religion

To make this development of the skilled hand, trained intellect, and developed heart life available alike to the poor and rich.

To accomplish this end I needed helpers, teachers and willing workers, holding similar views and hopes, inspired by the same ideal. It was from the beginning thought best that the qualifications for teachers should be thus characterized:

a  By a simplicity of Christian faith.
b  By a single moral standard for men and women, for teachers and students.
c  To embody in his life a model of the best things for the student to imitate.

The teacher, like the preacher, must first *be* † what he professes. The student should find in his teacher a life worthy of full emulation. A shining example of true Christian character is worth more than a thousand essays *on* Christian character.

d The teacher's work is to encourage the student to study, to grade his ability, to master an assigned lesson and especially to help the student while passing through the discipline of a college course, to find in Jesus Christ not only the model of a perfect character but the incentive to the fullness of his own physical, intellectual and religious life and aspiration.

e The teacher should attend and encourage the student in his religious and social meetings.

f Since it was thought not expedient for the student to play cards, dance, and other amusements questionable as to their influence for good, as also the use of tobacco, it followed logically that the student's model, the teacher, should refrain from those things also.

g Teachers should copy only the strong, worthy features of other schools, not their accidental faults.

h Wholesome criticism is the life of any institution. Gossiping criticism, or that made to any but the one authorized to hear it, is injurious not only to critic but also the institution or society to which he belongs.

We should always remember:

a It is not what I get out of life but what I put into life that counts.

b The sacrifice of certain personal rights and liberties is the price of peace and prosperity.

c That this is a Christian institution founded upon the open Bible, prayer, faith and hard work.

d If wisdom's ways you'd wisely seek,
Five things observe with care,
Of WHOM you speak, To WHOM you speak,
And HOW, and WHEN, and WHERE.

## Returned to States for More Money

I took December 1911 off to round up more money in the States. About $2,000 was gleaned here and there. Miss Clara Hazen, founder of the Marina Neighborhood House in Mayagüez, gave me the name of a generous man, E. O. Emerson, Sr., in Titusville, Pa. I left New York on the night train to see him. I called at his office early next morning and was told he was in the Waldorf-Astoria, New York City. I took the train back to New York in time to call on him at 8:00 P.M. He was sick with a cold and talked to me a minute. I asked him for $1,500 to complete the amount needed to pay for the site. He promised to send me a check when he arrived home. As the boat left New York, I dropped him a reminder that I had only till January 7 to make the final payment in full, wished him a Merry Christmas and sailed for Puerto Rico.

To play safe, I asked don Cancio to buy two of the four buildings in Palmarejo, since he needed them in which to store the produce from his large farms near Palmarejo. He loaned the money to Cheo Ramírez, since they were on Cheo's land, who bought them for $1,000. But in time don Cancio had to take them for the debt. The $1,000 first contributed by don Cancio came back to him fourfold in these two buildings valued at $4,000. I had used up all our meager savings to cover expenses north.

It was Friday, mail day from the States. Option was up the next Monday morning. Ramón López, my house boy and later one of the original twelve students, brought me our mail with a letter from E. O. Emerson. I thought to myself, "Here is $1,500, $300 to make up the needed balance and $1,200 on which to begin my school." Eunice and Miss Petrie, of the Mission Board, were in hammocks on the balcony upstairs. I hurried up there, in hopes floated like a balloon, opened my letter and found a $300 check! Glad, but somewhat taken down. The Lord has never given me more than I needed, but always supplied my needs fully. The following had given me undesignated money: Dr. E. R. Hildreth [11] and E. A. McDonald, $10 each, Mrs. William Borden (of Borden Milk), $150, and Mrs. Harris found that we could give $30 to make up the needed $200.

On January 7, 1912, I took over the deed to my site at last, after six years of seeking.

PRESBYTERIAN MEDICAL MISSION
*Willis W. Creswell, in Charge*

Mayagüez, P. Rico, 1-5-1912

Poly has bought and paid for her farm
Without a quiver,
Here's thanks to the man, woman and child
Whoever the giver.
Hurrah! for the Institute and the
Man at the head.
But tomorrow is Tres Reyes so,
I'm off to bed.

With all due apologies to Bill Nye,[12] you have our heartiest congratulations on having signed the deed.

As always,
/s/ *Willis W. Creswell,* M.D.

I had to take the deed in my name, in trust, because my newly named (by me) trustees did not wish to shoulder the responsibility of operating the college. I was young and I rejoiced! In 1920 I deeded the property to my new Board of Trustees.

The Mission Board had stopped payments from the Ladies Missionary Societies in Kansas. Mr. Grief had increased Guánica Central's $300 pledge to $1,000 a year for five years in installments of $83.33 monthly, to begin when I opened classes. This he carried out for a couple of years. French T. Maxwell succeeded Grief as general manager of Guánica Central. Maxwell immediately changed all further payments to continue for the remaining three years but only for the ten months of classroom work. We thus lost two monthly payments yearly.[13] Years afterwards Maxwell said to me, "Harris, I used to consider you our worst enemy in Puerto Rico. I have come to see you are our best friend, and your school is the best institution in the Island."

# Chapter 7

## *The First Day of School*

### The Founder's Day

I NOW HAD THE DEED to the 100 acres of land as *The Site*† for my college—Hallelujah!

I had arranged for two young men from the Presbyterian Church of [Bo.] La Pica to come as students and we would begin work on building up a Christian educational institution.

We had planned to open the Polytechnic March first. That being Sunday, I told Popo [1] and Lupe to come from La Pica, their home, Monday morning, March 2, 1912, Texas Independence Day! Popo came from La Pica for church Sunday night and remained in the home of a friend overnight. He and I started up the hill just about daylight the next morning, I on my horse with tools and Popo's bedding, and Popo walking along by my side with his *maleta** of clothing. The sun came up in all its glory as we walked up *The Steps*† that morning. We swung open the double doors and wooden windows to let the glory of God's presence from the canopy of Heaven shine in upon all that was in the beginning of the first day of the life of the Polytechnic.

We waited quite a while for Lupe. We learned later that Lupe came, looked from San Juan St. (now Harris Ave.) at the old house and in disgust turned and hurried back to La Pica. We lost 50% of our enrollment that morning of the first day. Popo remained with me, faithful at all times. He was the son of a carpenter. With an adze, saw and auger, he made our first yoke for oxen and helped in the carpentry work at all buildings till the day I left, March 2, 1937, a faithful and honest workman, and an elder in the Presbyterian Church.

God bless you, Popo.

> EDITOR'S NOTE: *This description of that first day of the Polytechnic, a Monday morning, March 2, 1912, written 30 years later, is placed here because it reveals more clearly Dr. Harris' emotions as he recollects opening the school of which he had dreamed since a student at Park College.*

* Suitcase.

There was no drum to beat the first march to *The Steps*. I was riding Borinquen with Helen riding in the saddle in front of me. Popo walked along beside the horse, recounting to me the difficulty he had in finding the location the day before. We passed the old Cuartel and down the narrow path of Santa Marta and turned into the dingy, forsaken house back a hundred yards from the road. It was not worthwhile for any mortal to attend the opening of the first day's life of the proposed school. Even Popo questioned its permanence as we walked up *The Steps* together, and out on the rickety balcony. It was early Monday morning, March 2, 1912.

The ecstasy that thrilled me, in the face of the hazardous adventure on that morning, seemed to lift me above the foreseen struggles of founding an institution of learning so diametrically opposed to the accepted system of centuries. I rejoiced in the conviction that the invisible audience of future young people and the public in general would some day accept what I was there trying to establish, that heavenly hosts were accompanying us—that an all-possessing conviction gripped me at the birth of our college: "We Two Must Win in the End, Jesus and I." *

\* \* \* \* \* \*

A menu of rice and beans, small piece of bread in the morning and the milk of one cow were the daily rations. This was served on a long bare table three boards wide. Boxes and benches were the chairs. No tuition or board was charged.

Enrollment grew to eight men and four women, average age twenty years old. Doña Ana E. Martinez, (doña Nená) was in charge outside of classes. I taught them for a while, with the help of Mrs. M. E. Martínez for a time. Then Guillermina Nazario took over the classes to the end of the year. All worked 4½ hours daily and [were] paid no money. Matriculation was $5 or a month's work. They all worked during July for matriculation of the previous year and during August for the coming year of 1912-1913. No one could pay the $5 matriculation fee. Only one could pay part of the tuition and board. Twenty-three additional students were admitted the following year, 1912-1913, on the same condition—working one month for matriculation fee.

Let future generations always remember the daring and faithful ones who so heroically helped during March to June 1912. They were: Leopoldo (Popo) Ortiz Vega, La Pica; Juanita and María Ortiz Vega, Popo's sisters; Antonio Lugo, [Bo.] Caín Alto; Antonia Lugo, Caín Alto, who married Popo (the father of the Lugos was a cousin to don Cancio Ortiz Lugo); Tomás Murphy, Caín Alto; Artemio Ortiz [Bo.] Los Llanos, relative of don Cancio Ortiz; Vicenta Toro Quiñones [Bo.] La Plata, a sister of Rev. Felipe Toro and a cousin to Dr. José M. Rodríguez Quiñones (Nito);[2] Ramón Ortiz, La Pica; Rafael Pérez, Aguadilla; Ramón López Vega, San Germán; Julio Rodríguez, Lajas, who graduated from Louisiana Agricultural College after finishing high school in Polytechnic.

---

\* Paraphrase of the last line of a poem that appears on page 89. Evidently, the poem was of some importance to Dr. Harris.

He is the only one of the twelve originals who holds a college degree, and was the only one with a handicap, cross-eyed, which he himself later in life paid the surgeon to correct.

# Year 1912-1913

Brother Clarence returned and took charge, as classroom teacher in the morning, of the work department during the afternoons and study hall at night during 1912-13. During summer vacation, students cut down trees for sills and uprights and erected a two-story shed of galvanized iron roof and palm sides.* This shed provided us with two classrooms and a dining room upstairs. Downstairs gave the men (for some of them had mustaches) a place to hang up their hammocks and cots. They hung their hammocks up high because the goats I had bought for producing meat always rushed under the shed when it rained and oftentimes into the bedroom.

Our water supply was a large cistern. Artemio fell head-first into the cistern and spoiled our drinking water. A well was dug in the draw and boys carried the water up the steep hill in five-gallon Standard Oil cans for cooking and the weekly bath.

Reverend Odell wrote me from San Juan about a very pretty girl named Georgina Villanueva, who wanted to come over and teach. Miss Georgina Villanueva, of San Juan, had recently graduated as valedictorian from the Asheville Normal and Collegiate Institute in North Carolina. I telegraphed for her to come at once. She arrived the day before school opened September 1912 on the afternoon train. She was indeed a most beautiful girl of sixteen summers with a winsome smile and big endearing eyes that would have set the Texas prairies on fire. I led the way up the steps to her room, six feet wide and ten feet long, which Eunice had prepared for her arrival. Across the rear end was a single bed. A small writing table and an oil lamp on one side, a chair in front of a mirror on the other end and, in the corner, a washstand and pitcher of water. She stood gazing out of the ant-eaten[3] window for a moment. A gust of wind blew her wide-brimmed, soft black hat up and I saw the tears running down her cheeks. But she was made of true steel, and we all admired and loved her.

I left again for New York and Philadelphia. Mr. McCahan gave me $3,000 for a girls' dormitory. With hand-made concrete blocks, the boys under Mr. Clarence's direction soon had the three-story building ready for use.[4] It had six balconies and twelve rooms. Before this was finished, I went again to New York and Mrs. Arthur Curtis James, Sr.,[5] gave me $2,500 for a similar section for a boys' dormitory on the other hill. Later her son, Arthur Curtis James, Jr., gave me

---

* Palm frond sides.

$2,500 for section two. (Now remodeled and called "Clarence Harris Memorial Hall.")

## Three Benefactors

There were 100 acres of land in the site purchased from Lagarde. Between the highway and our 100 acres lay some 40 acres, including one single tract of 15 acres owned by Aurelio Córdova. The remaining twenty-five acres were known as Trujillo. This had been allotted to the slaves when they were freed by the Act of Spain in 1876.[6] It was a densely populated section possessed by the ex-slaves without title to the land.

Mr. James N. Jarvie [7] sent me $40,000 with which to buy this necessary additional land. I sallied forth to buy out the squatters.* The parcels on which the huts stood by the score were ill-shaped and every one fenced with a thorny hedge. This hedge was often ten feet wide, especially between disagreeable neighbors, and was the occasion of many disputes and allegations of boundaries. In some cases I had to pay each neighbor clear across the hedge to the opposite side a double amount of money for the hedge, to end their bickering over their boundary lines. A few held private documents which overlapped. I needed legal help to insure clear abstract titles.

A man of pure Spanish descent, whom I had known in his teens, returning from the States with a legal degree to practice law, had hung out his shingle as Licenciado Eusebio López Acosta. Arrangement was made with him to do the legal work for the Polytechnic. Neither of us, at the time, dreamed that the work was so difficult and would last so long a time.

My work was to contract with the owners for the purchase of the land, allowing them to remove their huts at a settled price; take dimensions of the many-sided lots, quite often only a few feet larger than the hut. Licenciado Acosta [8] would then go with me and get the signatures to the deeds. This intermittent buying and signing deeds lasted for years. It was a long-drawn-out and tiresome job. I could buy a ranch of 5,000 acres in Texas easier than separating any of these poor, ignorant people from their wee bit of land. Often I had to buy other land and trade it to them for their place. It was amusing and interestingly different in nearly every family. One day, Lcdo. Acosta asked a father how many children he had. It astounded the man. He could not say and called his wife. She said fifteen, the oldest of whom was twenty-one. He remarked, as he pointed to his wife, "and this one will be sixteen." Lcdo. Acosta looked at me smilingly, remarked "Golly," as he wrote down fifteen children and one to come. The final cost of the

---

* Dr. Harris uses the term squatters loosely. He obviously means titleless residents.

40 acres averaged $1,000 per acre, or twelve and a half times more per acre than the original 100 acres had cost.

The work was not yet done. A civil engineer had to make an exact survey of the land purchased over the years. Lcdo. Acosta grouped all these individual purchases over some dozen years, took them with the survey to the Mayagüez Court, to make sure that every tiny piece had been legally deeded to the Polytechnic. Then he had the whole survey of land with clear abstract titles recorded in the Registry of Property in San Germán; keeping in bound personal files, as Notary, all the original transactions.

However, this was not all. I kept on buying adjoining land in small and larger tracts as long as I was president till 1937, and Lcdo. Acosta kept on making deeds with absolutely legal clear abstract titles.

This continuous legal and friendly service was given without thought of remuneration for services rendered, at a tremendous cost of stenographic work in his office, of his time and thought in travel and investigations of the Registry of Property, binding every year the original for his files, plus willingness to produce information at all times to the Polytechnic. I had held the deed from 1912 [9] in my name, in trust, which he finally drew up in a transfer deed to the present Board of Trustees of the Polytechnic Institute in 1920.

I am certain that Lcdo. Acosta will be surprised when he reads this, for he has forgotten all those years of loyal and friendly service of long ago. He was during all those times a very busy lawyer and has continued to be so. These were incidental breathing spells during the years of arduous strife of life to which the triumph of all good is the reward.

This is the benefactor whom we very belatedly wish to honor. His Spanish ancestors have left their indelible imprint on American life and customs, so has this worthy son of noble sires left an enduring monument in the clear abstract deeds of every foot of land now owned by the Polytechnic Institute, on the sacred Hills of Santa Marta. The presidents and the trustees can always sleep soundly and rest securely because of this efficient work done by Honorable Lcdo. Eusebio López Acosta. His services are mystically mixed up with the rock and soil which support the buildings of our college rounds "in one of the most beautiful hill-surrounded sites which the imagination can conceive . . . a tropical version of Williamstown, Massachusetts, with a climate that, without irreverence, may be described as heavenly."

Another benefactor, Mr. Charles William Stoughton, A. I. A., architect and landscape gardener, made the master plans, locating on the site the buildings, esplanade, drives and walks for the projected "University of the Antilles," every building in the right place and the whole tied together by Greek-Renaissance style of architecture adapted to modern usage.

The third benefactor was the Rev. Edwin A. McDonald, a fellow Presbyterian missionary, having served both in Mexico and Puerto Rico. Mr. McDonald prepared an illustrated lecture of the Polytechnic. This was in 1916, before moving pictures. He had 120 slides of color made at his own expense, bought a projector which required a rheostat because electric current was not uniform in those days. This rheostat weighed about 30 pounds, the box of slides weighed 20 pounds. [He also brought] a telescope valise filled with literature on Polytechnic for free distribution after each lecture and, last, a leather suitcase of clothing. These had to be carried by hand from depots to hotels and to lecture halls. There were no taxis; street cars were rare, dropping you off several blocks from the church. It was a heavy load. I accompanied him for a season each year. He visited and lectured in practically every church in New Jersey, Pennsylvania and New York States in the three years he served Polytechnic, free of charge.

At the last as he left his apartment on Amsterdam Ave., New York City, he slipped and fell on the ice and broke his hip. A cab picked him up and drove him to the Presbyterian Hospital where they laid him down on a blanket near the office for a couple of hours. His patience was ebbing, and also his strength, because of the pain. He asked the office to call Dr. Henry Sloane Coffin,[10] a friend of man in need at all times, whom he knew. Dr. Coffin came down some four hours after the accident and the hospital fell over itself taking care of Mr. McDonald, for Dr. Coffin was a director. They had considered him an old man of the town and forgot he was wrapped up on the floor. After this accident Mr. McDonald, one of our greatest missionaries in Mexico and Puerto Rico, was compelled to give up all active work. He publicized the Polytechnic as no one else ever did, or probably ever will. He and his wife went to Des Moines, Iowa, to find that their 30-acre property had been encircled by the city. They sold lots, gave a block for a high school. She became an invalid. He attended her for years. He dropped dead at the foot of her wheelchair. Three days later neighbors discovered the crushing misfortune of the helpless wife.

These three outstanding benefactors are the greatest in their field, not in money, but in service rendered as an expression of their inward soul and faith in Polytechnic, as Lawyer, as Architect and as Missionary, a service that can never be repeated nor duplicated, enduring to the end of time.

In celebrations of Founder's Day these three men will be extolled as unselfish servants of God, as doers of kindly deeds and as persevering, faithful cooperators with the founders of our college.

What my son, Professor Dr. Cleland Harris, wrote as a tribute to a great man recently passed on to his reward, I wish to apply and to use for these great benefactors, individually:

What is it about Uncle Howard[11] that made him great? I think I know: he didn't know that he was "contributing," "performing," or "serving" such things as "favors" and "services." Those many acts of his were as much a part of his normal life as breathing was. Had he known the implications of his acts, he would have lived to have been only a "fine" man. It is the unawareness of self which endeared him to the hearts of many of us. He didn't know; he wasn't conscious of himself. It is that unawareness of self that has made him, who would have lived and died a fine man, live forever a great man.

I most gratefully apply this quotation, written by my son, to these three benefactors whose services were given at a time when I had no money to reimburse them, nor had they any idea or thought of payment. The first was a Spanish Don, the second a New England Yankee, and the third a Scotch-American, symbolizing the culture of old Spain, the practical scientific achievement of America, and the spiritual fervor of a Scotch missionary, thus bringing together these great cultures in the development of the Polytechnic Institute as a leader along lines that will some day realize that Heavenly bond of Christian brotherhood, uniting all mankind in cooperative service and enduring love.

I bow in deepest appreciation and gratitude to these three noble men, so different and yet so much alike. God raised them up and the work of one was useless without the others. Together they gave a solid earthly foundation: Lcdo. Eusebio López Acosta produced the legal, clear abstract titles of all the deeds to property; Charles William Stoughton produced the master plans and architectural uniformity of all buildings; Rev. Edwin A. McDonald proclaimed the spiritual foundation on which the college is built. These three men brought together in a synthesis the cardinal principles of Christ, the cherishing of which will ultimately unite all that is good in the Latin-American, Anglo-Saxon and Celtic civilizations.

## A Foreword *

The above bird's-eye view of the Polytechnic Institute of Puerto Rico, located on the Santa Marta Hills in San Germán, is the architectural drawing of the vision of the founder, the Dr. J. Will Harris. It is a fully accredited Liberal Arts College. The enrollment for this year (1955-1956) is 783 regularly enrolled full-time students. The thirty-eight faculty members direct classroom affairs and student activities under the new president, Dr. Ronald C. Bauer.

The college campus and college farms contain 250 acres. Seventeen reinforced all-masonry buildings and Heylman Athletic Field grace the Seven Hills erected to the memory of as many different individuals, except one which is Borinquen Hall, the Indian name for the Island. A small endowment fund was also built up over the years.

All this came about under the direction of Dr. Harris, the founder, with the able

* This Foreword by Dr. Leker was included by Dr. Harris with a few pages quoting from a commemorative booklet written about 1955 by Dr. Harris. It is not known whether Dr. Leker's contribution was written for the booklet or for another occasion.

cooperation of his wife, Mrs. Eunice White Harris, and of his brother, Mr. Clarence Harris.

This book discloses the nature of the man and of his work—"an achievement," as Dr. Marquis states, "never before equaled by the founder of any American College."

*Charles A. Leker*
Retired Professor of Psychology

# Recognitions of Special Merit

Enrollment increased rapidly in 1913. Miss Manuela González, a graduate of Northfield[12] with highest honors, came to teach. She was small and timid but with a powerhouse of spiritual fire and vigor. She had no written rules of class discipline, but students broke their backs to excel. She inspired students and teachers to be content only with the best and in the pathway of life when they come where the road forks, to turn always to the right.

One of my boys from the San Germán church, Pedro P. Casablanca, came to teach. He had graduated from the Normal School of the University of Puerto Rico. (There was no higher course then given in Puerto Rico.) He had also received the highest grades. He was serious and a commanding, efficient, Christian teacher, always willing to go the second mile.

To these first four teachers: brother Clarence Harris, Georgina Villanueva (now Mrs. William Vivoni), Manuela González (now Mrs. Antonio Rivera), and Pedro P. Casablanca, I owe a lasting debt of gratitude, and their names should be engraved on The Steps in bronze and in the affections of every student's heart.

Without these faithful, self-sacrificing, patient individuals, working hand-in-hand with me during the first days and nights for decades, there could never have developed the college of today. They were all different as the poles apart, yet united they made a strong team pulling the best things of the past into the reality of the present for future strength of all who follow them. Time and time again and again they had to wait till I could raise the money to pay their small salaries. They lived in shacks, ate very plain food, voluntarily limited their wants, yet faithfully worked on till success was realized. Polytechnic Institute of today is as much their glory as mine. May God bless them richly and reward their services made in His name, down to old age.

Brother Clarence was the first of the four to pass on and to enter the Golden Gates on Sunday, March 6, 1949. He evidently was taken sick while repairing a field fence, for he had driven the staples into the post only half way, walked out into the brush, where he was found dead later. He had spent ten years of delightful service on his own farm. Jesús llegó a él y él con Jesús partió.* His favorite hymn was:

> Lead me gently home, Father
> Lead me gently home,
> Lest I fall upon the wayside,
> Lead me gently home.

Let me mention by name only those who for decades helped as faithful teachers: Charles A. Leker,[13] the man able and willing to do almost everything. Rachel Akers Palmer [14]—the persistent, efficient, and precise teacher of highest Christian character. Boyd B. Palmer,[15] the gentle, pleasant and steady teacher who loved all, students, teachers, and the people of Puerto Rico. Dr. Ismael Vélez,[16] the author-scientist of Poly, an outstanding professor with the most extensive knowledge of tropical botany of his time. Mrs. Lydia Quiñones Gregory, secretary to the president and Alumni Association,[17] is the efficient, lovable, cheerful soul worthy the special citation recently honoring her long service to the college and the alumni. We, Mrs. Harris and I, thank you, and also express our appreciation of all who have helped for a shorter time.

There were during the years many others who helped in every possible way to build up Polytechnic. This book is too little for recounting their noble deeds and words. It took all of them pulling as one, in the realization of our and your school. You are all dear to us. We love you all. Love never dies . . . if it does it was never love.

There is one who was not at the beginning, but one whom God prepared to come at the proper stage of development. *If an institution can make one dollar do the service of two dollars and can, over the years, accurately show how every dollar is spent wisely,†* that institution will never go begging.

To do this I needed a person of integrity, of keen intellectual power, of honest and accurate judgment, for the systematic recording of all essential facts and figures; a person who could reason with teachers, students, and parents. Patria A. Tió[18] (now Mrs. Ramón Ramírez López) was all this, and more.

She composed, in English and Spanish, business letters, social letters, letters to different Presidents in the White House and Congressmen, and letters of condolence to the bereaved or to parents whose child was failing, much better than I could do.

Above all, she showed the world of business how the Polytechnic received the donations and fees and accounted for every penny. No auditor ever found a mistake in her books during the many years Patria was my secretary and treasurer. Some years as much as $150,000 and more passed through her books. The busi-

---

* Jesus came to him and he departed with Jesus.

ness end of the Polytechnic was so administered that it pleased all employees and pleased me exceedingly. It was stimulating, gave confidence to donors to continue giving to, no more *my* school, but *our* College.

In the name of the Polytechnic Institute, and of us all who labored with you for the Polytechnic, trustees, administration, faculty, students, alumni and friends, I thank you with my whole heart, dear Patria!

Word has just come of Patria's home-going—cerebral embolism . . . less than an hour of suffering. "On to the last minute she kept planning, organizing and helping others gather themselves around worthwhile motives." At 6:30 A.M., Sunday, July 31, 1955, she passed into the eternal Sabbath Day when her Master called her to service above. *Adiós, Patria. Adiós, mi querida Patria!*

## Polygraph *of March 15, 1931, Reports:*[19]

For a long period of years Mr. Clarence Harris has had more to do with the actual building of the physical plant of Polytechnic Institute than any one person. But although the buildings, the farm and dairy may be what the casual visitor sees when he comes to our campus, we, faculty and students, know that Mr. Clarence has been building characters and moulding lives that will, in places far distant from our campus be living witnesses to his years of sacrifice, hard labor and devotion to this institution. And side by side with Mr. Clarence stands Mrs. Harris, Doña Mary, as we affectionately call her, whose kindly and efficient management of the student dining room contributes much to the health and happiness of the entire student body.

Mr. Clarence came to Puerto Rico in 1910 to help his brother, Dr. J. W. Harris, found and organize the Polytechnic Institute of Puerto Rico. At first as a teacher, later as a vice-president, he has striven to develop in this school, principles and ideals similar to those of Park College in Missouri, from which he, as well as Dr. and Mrs. Harris, graduated. As long as any of us can remember Mr. Clarence has been working to make this campus a happier, more comfortable college home, as a more efficient means of education. Dormitories and dining room, faculty homes and classrooms and administration building—all have been constructed under his supervision. Whether new equipment is to be installed in a laboratory or improvements or upkeep attended to on the farm or in the dairy, Mr. Clarence is the man who sees the job carried through.

Although he has been more than a director; he has been an an example of that important phase of our college program in which we endeavor to recognize work as a necessary and valuable factor in the development of youth. Mr. Clarence is not only a supervisor of construction; he is a builder of men. Because he touches all of our lives so vitally. There is one of Mr. Clarence's personal ambitions upon which we do not like to think—his desire to live again in his boyhood home in Texas.

# Chapter 8

## *The Polytechnic Idea*

### Q. E. D.*

IN OUR EARLY MATHEMATICS we learned those letters could be used at the end of the solution of a problem. It takes time to establish the truth of a statement or of a project. Mathematical truth was a development over thousands of years. China, India, Arabia, Egypt and Greece all struggled with mathematical problems. It was in recent centuries that Kepler, Newton and Leibnitz made revolutionary records, which moved forward to the present day when Einstein, the Comptons, Oppenheimer and a host of other scientists split the atom and produced atomic energy, thus leading us on to still greater discoveries for the advancement of mankind.

So, education is gradually enriching its system of instruction in the stored-up knowledge of the world with applied practice of the heart and hand along with the head of man. Education should not be for specialists only. In fact, specialists are to be the exceptions in the educational program for the development of abundant living in this life.

In founding my college, and it took six years of trial and failure, my *first objective* was an old one . . . to introduce the students to the stored-up knowledge of the ages found in books. This can best be done by qualified teachers who teach the students, and who have access to libraries, laboratories and other equipment for the development of student thought. This objective found approval from the very first.

My *second objective* was Religion in the true sense of the word, *religare,* to bind back man, the created being, to God his Creator; to get students to see that man in spirit and body has a vital relation with God and dependence upon God. Communion with God and learning to walk with God are as vital to the living soul as food and air are to the living body, without which there can be no healthy spiritual and physical growth. Man must have an intelligent knowledge of the Bible, not as a Protestant, Roman Catholic, or Hebrew book, but as the written and faithful record of God to man as men progressively are able to understand God. The Bible begins as a revelation of God in darkness and ends as a written

* Quod erat demonstrandum.

revelation of God in the light and fullness of Christ Jesus, the Son of God. The complete interpretation and understanding of that revelation never ends. It should be and is better understood as learning in the fear and love of God increases from generation to generation under the leadership of the Holy Spirit.

A definition of a man of faith given by Robert, our seven-year-old, to his mother, is, "A man who believes what God says and does what God tells him to do." The development of such a man of faith was our chief aim from the very first. This was attained through the public and private study of the Bible, public and private prayer by everyone, by singing hymns and daily religious services and by active religious work in the college and in the rural districts near the college and in the city, where students and teachers held Sunday Schools for those without such privileges. Protestant and Roman Catholic students united in these services. The basic things of Christ's teachings are common to all, Roman Catholic and Protestant. We never allowed a separation of students into groups that tended to divide the student body religiously. Such would weaken the Gospel's appeal as a Gospel for *all* human beings. The positive exposition of the Gospel finds a ready reaction in the heart of all believers. It is this ecumenical creed of the Christ that will bind us all together as brethren. For other than that weakens the appeal to all men. It proved a success by bringing all students into one group of followers of Christ. "I pledge allegiance to the Christian flag and to the Saviour for whose kingdom it stands; One brotherhood uniting all mankind in service and love."

> You are writing a gospel,
>      A chapter each day,
> By deeds that you do,
>      By words that you say.
>
> Students read what you write,
>      Whether faithless or true.
> Teacher what is the gospel
>      According to you?
>
> (*Author unknown*)

I cannot recall what my teachers explained to me, but I can never forget what kind of a gospel they lived before me in every class daily and in every walk of life on the campus.

My *third objective* was co-educational training on a home level. Hillside Campus for the boys and Hillcrest Campus for the girls as dormitories. All students worked together in those things necessary, as in the erection of buildings, in the laundry and kitchen; all ate in the same dining room at tables of their choice in permanent seats as far as possible; all attended classes and had a daily social hour together.

This probably at the time created more misgivings, even from our well-wishers, than any other phase of our pioneering work. From the first I held a private conference before admitting any boy finally, impressing upon him that we were trying to live as in a home and were glad to welcome him into our household, and wished to have him treat every girl in the school as he would like to have other fellows treat his own sister and that this was his privilege, dignity and honor to assume at this time. This developed self-respect, love of home, and the power of right attitudes in the student.

Norma Livia Laforet was waiting tables and, as she served a boy, he made a slighting remark to her. She slapped him a terrific blow in the mouth. The boy protested to me. At the next meal hour, after investigation, I commended Norma Livia publicly. Such an act by a boy was never again repeated. Our co-educational system never produced a moral failure, as was feared it would by many good people. The girls lifted the boys to higher standards by showing in and out of classroom and work their equality and capacity for self-government in personal life and action.

My *fourth objective* was Manual Labor for all boarding students. My dear friend, don Juan Cancio Ortiz, was sure it would not work with anyone who had an eighth grade diploma. Though he himself believed in it, he had failed in Lajas to get boys to work with their hands. Presbytery's Committee on Education of Candidates for the Ministry asked me to excuse their candidates from all work. They feared that ministerial candidates would develop an inferiority complex if they had to work; also, that when placed in charge of a church, the people would consider these young men inferior because they had to work. Some continentals asked me to prepare cooks and house servants for them. They could not see the value of labor for the poor boys and girls I had enrolled in my school . . . poor in financial resources but rich in potential possibilities. Work was a real obstacle for a while. Some considered my school a Correctional Institution.

We had to live in old houses and shacks at first, sit on board benches at tables covered with oilcloth in the dining shed. Rice, beans, bread, soup, milk and coffee with occasional meat was our menu, prepared, cooked and served by the students. Students did all the work under supervision. I reminded them often that if they suffered without succeeding to better things, it was that the next generation of students might succeed without suffering. The fighting endurance had to be kept at white heat in the student morale to win a victory not only for themselves but for those who would follow them. *They were setting standards and marking the way for all time.†*

In order to get girls from the town to come to the Polytechnic, I gave a nice young girl, María Quintana, free tuition. If my memory serves me rightly, María graduated with honors, along with José M. Gallardo, who became the Commissioner of Education for Puerto Rico. Many other girls from town soon were attending classes. One thing soon appeared to shatter Old World theories of man's superiority in brain power over woman . . . the girls were making just as high grades as the boys and were running away with highest commencement honors, even in mathematics.

In these last three Objectives, *I had to do pioneering work.*† In Puerto Rico I found a fertile field of energetic and bright youth for my hopes of building a second Park College. My college dream was coming true here in Puerto Rico with thousands of youth not able to get even a primary education. Most of them had to stop at the fourth grade, if they were fortunate enough to be in school.

I could not rest till I started to help them. Nothing but book learning was attempted in public education of that day, as the highest essential preparation for life. I was told I could not hope to go beyond just classroom study as set forth in public education of the Island transplanted to Puerto Rico by continentals. I was more convinced daily that there was something more in man that needed training and developing along with his intellectual mental gymnastics.

I believed that every student should be required to do his best and, God helping me, I would make it possible for him to do his best:

In classroom studies of stored up knowledge,

In daily *Manual Work* building up, developing and maintaining the physical plant of the college with *his* hands,

In learning how to walk in the footprints of the One All-Wise Master, Christ Jesus,

In a college with a natural home atmosphere whose residents are young men and women of culture.

I felt that this was the only kind of an institution which I cared to spend time and energy in developing, where students get a general training for living the right kind of life as a Christian citizen in an everchanging world of possibilities and adventure.

Improvement along all four of these Objectives should be made all the time. Eternal vigilance on the part of trustees, faculty and president is the price to be paid in maintaining a just and impartial emphasis on all four Objectives. Specializing in any one Objective and slacking up on the others will fail our charter requirement "to produce well-rounded character, resourceful, independent and of a sturdy Christian faith." The holding firm to all the Objectives will develop in the student a man of Christian faith who will strive to attain the Brotherhood of Man and the Fatherhood of God in Christ Jesus.

Dr. Frank Crane [1] has long ago said: "Slowly the world is learning that the best element in education is the work the child does to get it."

It is a pretty safe general rule that an education for which one has not struggled is of little value to him. Effort, self-denial and labor are the only roads to anything in

|  | JAN. Genesis | FEB. Leviticus | MARCH Joshua | APRIL 1 Kings |
|---|---|---|---|---|
| 1—— | 1-3 | 13-14 | 1-4 | 1-2 |
| 2—— | 4-6 | 15-17 | 5-8 | 3-6 |
| 3—— | 7-9 | 18-21 | 9-11 | 7-8 |
| 4—— | 10-13 | 22-24 | 12-14 | 9-11 |
| 5—— | 14-17 | 25-27 | 15-18 | 12-14 |
|  |  | Numbers |  |  |
| 6—— | 18-20 | 1-3 | 19-21 | 15-17 |
| 7—— | 21-23 | 4-6 | 22-24 | 18-20 |
|  |  |  | Judges |  |
| 8—— | 24-26 | 7-9 | 1-3 | 21-22 |
|  |  |  |  | 2 King |
| 9—— | 27-29 | 10-13 | 4-6 | 1-3 |
| 10—— | 30-32 | 14-15 | 7-9 | 4-6 |
| 11—— | 33-35 | 16-18 | 10-13 | 7-9 |
| 12—— | 36-38 | 19-21 | 14-16 | 10-13 |
| 13—— | 39-41 | 22-24 | 17-19 | 14-16 |
| 14—— | 42-44 | 25-27 | 20-21 | 17-19 |
| 15—— | 45-47 | 28-30 | Ruth | 20-22 |
|  |  |  | 1 Sam. |  |
| 16—— | 48-50 | 31-33 | 1-3 | 23-25 |
|  | Exodus |  |  | 1 Chron. |
| 17—— | 1-3 | 34-36 | 4-7 | 1-9 |
|  |  | Deut. |  |  |
| 18—— | 4-6 | 1-4 | 8-11 | 10-13 |
| 19—— | 7-9 | 5-7 | 12-14 | 14-17 |
| 20—— | 10-12 | 8-10 | 15-17 | 18-21 |
| 21—— | 13-15 | 11-13 | 18-20 | 22-25 |
| 22—— | 16-19 | 14-17 | 21-24 | 26-29 |
|  |  |  |  | 2 Chron. |
| 23—— | 20-23 | 18-21 | 25-27 | 1-4 |
| 24—— | 24-27 | 22-24 | 28-31 | 5-8 |
|  |  |  | 2 Sam. |  |
| 25—— | 28-30 | 25-27 | 1-3 | 9-13 |
| 26—— | 31-33 | 28-29 | 4-7 | 14-18 |
| 27—— | 34-36 | 30-31 | 8-11 | 19-22 |
| 28—— | 37-40 | 32-34 | 12-14 | 23-25 |
|  | Lev. |  |  |  |
| 29—— | 1-4 | CHAP. 8 | 15-17 | 26-28 |
| 30—— | 5-8 | ........... | 18-20 | 29-31 |
| 31—— | 9-12 | ........... | 21-24 | ........ |

|  | MAY 2 Chron. | JUNE Psalms |
|---|---|---|
| 1—— | 32-36 | 73-77 |
|  | Ezra |  |
| 2—— | 1-3 | 78-81 |
| 3—— | 3-6 | 82-88 |
| 4—— | 7-10 | 89-93 |
|  | Nehemiah |  |
| 5—— | 1-3 | 94-102 |
| 6—— | 4-7 | 103-105 |
| 7—— | 8-10 | 106-110 |
| 8—— | 11-13 | 111-118 |
|  | Esther |  |
| 9—— | 1-5 | 119 |
| 10—— | 6-10 | 120-130 |
|  | Job |  |
| 11—— | 1-5 | 131-138 |
| 12—— | 6-9 | 139-143 |
| 13—— | 10-14 | 144-150 |
|  |  | Prov. |
| 14—— | 15-19 | 1-4 |
| 15—— | 20-23 | 5-8 |
| 16—— | 24-29 | 9-12 |
| 17—— | 30-33 | 13-15 |
| 18—— | 34-38 | 16-18 |
| 19—— | 39-42 | 20-22 |
|  | Psalms |  |
| 20—— | 1-7 | 23-26 |
| 21—— | 8-13 | 27-31 |
|  |  | Eccles. |
| 22—— | 14-18 | 1-6 |
| 23—— | 19-22 | 7-12 |
|  |  | Songs of Salomon |
| 24—— | 23-30 | 1-8 |
|  |  | Isaiah |
| 25—— | 31-36 | 1-4 |
| 26—— | 37-40 | 5-8 |
| 27—— | 41-46 | 9-13 |
| 28—— | 47-50 | 14-18 |
| 29—— | 51-59 | 19-22 |
| 30—— | 60-67 | 23-26 |
| 31—— | 68-72 | ........ |

(EDITOR'S NOTE: *Facsimile reproduction of the readings published by Dr. Drury as arranged by Dr. Harris. The Introduction is his.*)

The assigned readings I arranged; every student was urged to follow this schedule of Bible readings. The Bible characters are portrayed as natural human beings; their successes and their failures are of real educational value to men of every age.

| JULY | AUGUST | | | SEP. | OCT. | NOV. | DEC. |
|---|---|---|---|---|---|---|---|
| Isaiah | Ezek. | | | Zech. | Luke | Romans | 2 Thes. |
| 27-29 | 9-12 | 1—— | | 1-5 | 9-10 | 1-3 | 1-3 |
| | | | | | | | 1 Tim. |
| 30-33 | 13-15 | 2—— | | 6-10 | 11-12 | 4-6 | 1-2 |
| 34-36 | 16-17 | 3—— | | 11-14 | 11-14 | 7-8 | 3-4 |
| 37-39 | 18-20 | 4—— | | Malach | 15-16 | 9-10 | 5-6 |
| | | 5—— | | Mat. 1-2 | 17-18 | 11-12 | 2 Tim. 1-2 |
| 40-43 | 21-23 | 6—— | | 3-4 | 19-20 | 13-14 | 3-4 |
| 44-47 | 24-26 | | | | | | Titus |
| 48-50 | 27-29 | 7—— | | 5-6 | 21-22 | 15-16 | 1-3 |
| 51-54 | 30-32 | | | | | 1 Cor. | Philemon |
| 55-58 | 33-35 | 8—— | | 7-8 | 23-24 | 1-3 | |
| 59-62 | 36-38 | | | | John | | Hebrews |
| 63-66 | 39-41 | 9—— | | 9-10 | 1-2 | 4-6 | 1-3 |
| Jeremiah | | 10—— | | 11-12 | 3-4 | 7-9 | 4-5 |
| 1-3 | 42-44 | 11—— | | 13-14 | 5-6 | 10-12 | 6-7 |
| 4-6 | 45-48 | 12—— | | 15-16 | 7-8 | 13-14 | 8-9 |
| | Daniel | 13—— | | 17-18 | 9-10 | 15-16 | 10-11 |
| 7-9 | 1-3 | | | | | 2 Cor. | |
| 10-13 | 4-6 | 14—— | | 19-20 | 11-12 | 1-3 | 12-13 |
| 14-17 | 7-9 | | | | | | James |
| 18-22 | 10-12 | 15—— | | 21-22 | 13-14 | 4-6 | 1-3 |
| | Hosea | 16—— | | 23-24 | 15-16 | 7-9 | 4-5 |
| 23-25 | 1-5 | | | | | | 1 Peter |
| 26-29 | 6-9 | 17—— | | 25-26 | 17-18 | 10-11 | 1-2 |
| | | 18—— | | 27-28 | 19-21 | 12-13 | 3-5 |
| 30-32 | 10-14 | | | Mark | Acts | Galatians | 2 Peter |
| | Joel | 19—— | | 1-2 | 1-2 | 1-2 | 1-3 |
| 33-35 | 1-3 | | | | | | 1 John |
| | Amos | 20—— | | 3-4 | 3-4 | 3-4 | 1-2 |
| 36-38 | 1-4 | 21—— | | 5-6 | 5-6 | 5-6 | 3-5 |
| 39-41 | 5-9 | | | | | Ephes. | |
| | | 22—— | | 7-8 | 7-8 | 1-2 | 2 & 3 John |
| | | 23—— | | 9-10 | 9-10 | 3-4 | Jude |
| 42-45 | Obadiah | | | | | | Rev. |
| | | 24—— | | 11-12 | 11-12 | 5-6 | 1-3 |
| 46-48 | Jonah | | | | | Philip. | |
| | Micah | 25—— | | 13-14 | 13-14 | 1-2 | 4-6 |
| 49-50 | 1-4 | 26—— | | 15-16 | 15-16 | 3-4 | 7-9 |
| 51-52 | 5-7 | | | Luke | | Colos. | |
| Lamen. | Nahum | 27—— | | 1-2 | 17-18 | 1-2 | 10-12 |
| 1-2 | 1-3 | 28—— | | 3-4 | 19-21 | 3-4 | 13-15 |
| | Hab. | | | | | 1 Thes. | |
| 3-5 | 1-3 | 29—— | | 5-6 | 22-23 | 1-2 | 16-18 |
| Ezekiel | Zepha. | 30—— | | 7-8 | 24-26 | 3-5 | 19-20 |
| 1-4 | 1-3 | 31—— | | ........ | 27-28 | ........ | 21-22 |
| 5-8 | Haggai | | | | | | |

this life that is worth while. The one absolute requirement should be labor, *especially for the rich.*†

No boy or girl should be allowed to go through college any other way than by work. And by work we mean some sort of labor for which other people are willing to pay money.

One business of education certainly ought to be to liberate the minds of youth from shackles of silly tradition and ancient fraud, which is quite as important as loading the mind down with old things. And one of the most stupendous bunkum ideas in the world is the idea that work is degrading or is only to be done by those who haven't money or wit enough to escape it.

Work is life, and a preparation for life that does not involve work is absurd.[2]

# The Polytechnic Idea—A Home

I could never have built the Polytechnic had I not made it possible for students to work for tuition and board by their labor on buildings and roads, and in the preparation and serving of food, in the laundry, etc. A regular pace of construction work was set up and kept going through the years and not only for normal growth of the school, but for provisions of means whereby students could work for an education. The noble poor are needing our help in every generation. Regular work for all boarding students was always maintained. Training of the *head* and *hand* and *heart* of students was followed to produce in the students a sense of *personal responsibility to themselves, to their fellowmen, and to God,* especially *for the development of their own future home as the greatest institution of this world.*†

The atmosphere of a Christian home was maintained in the college life. It is costly but ennobling. One dining room, with regular times for all to sit down in assigned seats and to wait for the blessing before eating . . . this deepens the home atmosphere and also creates a sense of real value.

## Morning Prayers and Sunday Services Required

For 25 years we held to the following regimen: immediately after the early morning meal came Morning Prayers. Students (and there were 350 students in about one third the size of the present dining room)[3] sat on benches around the breakfast tables with individual Bibles and hymn books in their hands to take part in a half-hour of prayer by students, Scripture selection in unison or responsive reading, hymn singing and to hear a five-minute talk based on explaining the Bible reading for the day. This started the heart off right for a day of abundant living and kept the echoes of hymns ringing along the paths of the campus at all hours of the day.

A plan by which the Bible may be read by students once each year is most profitable and is what I personally have followed since the year 1895.

These assigned readings I arranged; Dr. Philo W. Drury printed them in *Puerto Rico Evangélico,*[4] and every student was urged to follow this schedule of private Bible readings. The Bible characters are portrayed as natural human beings; their successes and their failures are of real educational value to men of every age.

# Chapter 9

## *Growing Pains*

## The J. Will Harris Family Moves

*From the Cozy Two-Story Concrete Manse to the
Moth-Eaten Old House on the Campus, September 3, 1914*

A NEW TERM OF SCHOOL had begun. The girls had moved from the second floor of the old house into McCahan Dormitory. The ground floor was full of girls. The students were moving our furniture from the manse in town into this second floor of the old house. The last oxcart load of furniture had left, behind which Mrs. Harris with Margaret in her arms, Helen and Donald walking by her side, followed up the hill to the old house where we lived for five years till Loma Vista was completed in 1919.

> When I survey the wondrous cross
> On which the Prince of Glory died,
> My richest gain I count but loss
> And pour contempt on all my pride.
>
> Were the whole world of nature mine,
> That were a present far too small;
> Love so amazing, so divine,
> Demands my soul, my life, my all.

The above stanzas express the spirit of devotion which Eunice kindled in my soul daily since our engagement Christmas morning in the home of her parents, Hiawatha, Kansas, December 25, 1900, and sealed in our wedding on the Kickapoo Indian Reservation, May 17, 1905. To *Eunice White*† goes the credit. She made me. I would be recreant if I failed to acknowledge such here. Nothing that I write here can reveal what she has done and accomplished in me, in our home, in our college and among outside friends. She felt deeply what she wrote, in her many, many letters to our friends, in prose and sometimes in verse. She loved everybody, and in some way saw something in everyone to praise and to commend.

Mrs. Harris gathered around our large, round seven-foot-in-diameter dining room table our own family of seven and five or more guests.[1] These visiting friends added greatly to the joys and pleasure of our home life. Our larger family of faculty and students was always invited after the evening meal to shake hands with the celebrated guests, for they were really celebrated individuals, editors, statesmen, educators, authors, poets, philanthropists, industrialists, missionaries and church leaders, who became just common people for the time, who shared their experiences and hopes with us.

Our ranch home in Texas continues occasionally to have delightful and helpful guests, as the one from Mexico, a capitalist, recently wrote: "Our visit overnight in your home was of particular importance because I wanted my wife to enjoy that certain something in the way of a big lift that comes to one from being with you and Mrs. Harris. It certainly registered with her, and as a result we enjoyed it very much."

Her capacity to organize her work in detail and get it done was a real gift. She was responsible for making the menus for the three hundred boarding students and ordering the supplies weekly. She went, on foot, a mile away to the market as many as three times a week before daylight in order to get the best meat and vegetables for the students. She assigned the daily work to 150 girls for six-week periods. She supervised the laundry, the girls' dormitory, the dining hall and kitchen. She appointed chaperones for the girls. She talked daily with individual girls about their spiritual lives and helped them to organize Personality Plus Clubs, etc. She knew just what each girl's reaction to religious living was. She had unlimited patience with everyone but was firm in all things.

On top of all this, she taught our five children the first four grades, in preparation for the fifth grade entrance to our elementary school. She entertained all visitors in Loma Vista. For three years she kept the books of the Polytechnic. She always had charge of our personal expenses and kept our personal books till her strength failed.

Without such a wonderful helpmeet, I could never have succeeded. The Polytechnic Institute would not have survived to maturity had Eunice White not united her soul and body with me to give it birth and to nourish it through all the adolescent years till 1937.

She was small of body but sound of mind, reinforced by the power of the Holy Spirit, which enabled her to do her work and to carry the burdens of life without going to pieces as so many less occupied have done. I wish every husband had a wife of like capacity and Christian willingness to go anywhere and to accept the challenges of life with her husband. On her last day, in mental review of Polytechnic days she said: "I set my face like a flint." Wonderful!

# Jehovah-Jireh

Abraham's conviction . . . "Jehovah-Jireh," Jehovah will provide, was as true and as evident in the years of development of my idea for a school as it was with Abraham of old. The Lord kept us humble and close to the dust from which we are told we came on the way up. Students and teachers lived in the poorest of shacks, sat on board benches in classrooms and wrote on their knees as desks. But we kept adding every year to our enrollment, buying a bed spring and nailing $2 \times 4$ pine strips on the spring for corner posts, calling it a bed for another student. Our experiences in economy and use of money during these hard days developed a love, a fellowship and co-operation day by day as we moved forward. We were down so low that we had only one way to go and that was upward. As long as the spirit and morale of the college increased, there was no stopping of the growth, even in the absence of what is usually considered necessary for a school.

Students helped with younger fellow students. For example:

Antonio Rivera[2] taught in school lower grades and helped us in singing with his flute. He now is Dr. Rivera, head of the History Department of University of Puerto Rico. Nito (now Dr. Rodríguez Quiñones) supervised the manual labor of the little boys and led our morning prayers with his cornet. So did Luis Angel Toro[3] with his trombone. Lorenzo Casiano,[4] a student of mature years, kept the study hall for the boys, directed their religious life and taught agriculture. Robert Jason[5] repaired the old discarded organ given us by a mission school, and pulled the bassos, sopranos, tenors, or altos over their choir rendition difficulties while he played that old organ and sang with the choir. Dr. Jason is now in charge of surgery in Howard University, Washington, D.C. Any student who had a special talent offered his services and accepted added responsibility in helping Polytechnic to make the grade.

In 1914, we had to go forward. Defunct mission schools gave us their desks and books.

Don Ernesto Zapata of Palmarejo on whose land the two remaining buildings of don Cancio's school stood for 4 years was demanding that we move them off his property so that he might plant cane on the half-acre. Don Cancio had given me the buildings in 1910 when his school failed. The Lajas public schools continued to use them after 1910 till they could erect new ones.

Mr. Clarence took our boys over to Palmarejo during the summer of 1914, knocked down the two buildings. Mr. Villard,[6] president of the American Railroad of Puerto Rico, placed flat cars on the nearby siding for transportation of the buildings without charge. Don José Ramírez of Lajas and don José Rodríguez of La Plata loaned us oxen and carts in which to haul the demolished buildings to

Eunice White Harris, life-long companion in faith and service of her husband.

From such a mountain home came, in March, 1912, Polytechnic's
first student (Popo) to live and learn and seek an education.

The boy students help with constructing a dam on the campus, 1916.

The normal school, forerunner of the University of Puerto Rico, as early as 1902 had grounds and buildings much superior to the first buildings of the Polytechnic Institute. (Photo courtesy of University of Puerto Rico).

Typical railroad station and railway, which frequently ran parallel to the highway.

*Above:* One of the buildings (about 1914) donated by don Juan Cancio Ortiz from his school in [Bo.] Palmarejo, Lajas. *Below:* Don Juan Cancio Ortiz (with pickaxe) and members of the faculty with the student body of the Instituto de Agricultura, Artes y Oficios (1907).

Many of the first students came from mountain homes like this.

To this old building I moved, January 10, 1911, the more advanced students from my school downtown (Dr. Harris's own caption).

Founder, trustees, faculty and students in 1912. *First row:* Dr. Harris and don Juan Cancio Ortiz. *Second row:* Dr. Manuel Guzmán Rodríguez, John J. Siebert, Rev. James A. McAllister, Rev. E. A. McDonald, Dr. Edward A. Odell and Dr. Nathan H. Huffman. *Third row:* Antonia Lugo, María Ortiz, Juanita Ortiz, Mercedes Toro, Ana E. Martínez (doña Nená, in charge of dining room and kitchen), and Guillermina Nazario (the only teacher). *Fourth row:* Antonio Lugo, Julio Rodríguez, Leopoldo Ortiz ("Popo," the first student to enroll when school was founded March 12, 1912), Tomás Murphy, Ramón López (house boy and mail boy for Harris family until the retirement of Dr. and Mrs. Harris), Rafael Pérez, Artemio Ortiz and Ramón Ortiz (Monsino).

THE STEPS: MAY GOD'S PRESENCE FOREVER ILLUMINE ALL WHO ASCEND THE STEPS TILL THE END OF TIME (Dr. Harris's own caption).

*Right:* Dr. Harris had left $40,000 in his will for the preservation of The Steps. In 1969 a canopy was erected to protect and preserve them, and the ashes of Dr. and Mrs. Harris placed inside. Part of each year's graduation ceremonies is held here. The trees are the same in both pictures.

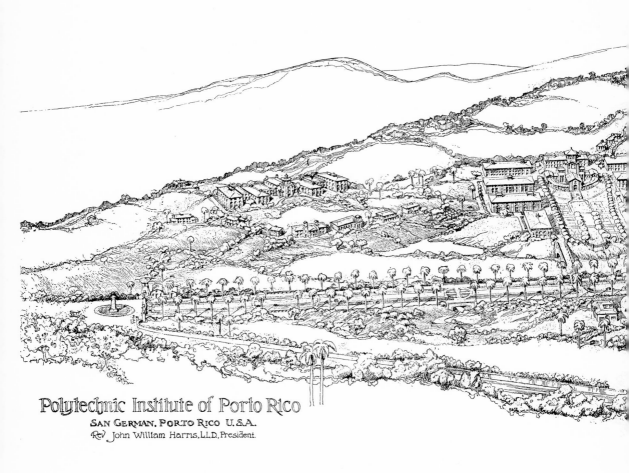

Polytechnic Institute of Porto Rico
SAN GERMAN, PORTO RICO U.S.A.
Rev John William Harris, LL.D, President.

Architect's drawing (1921) for the master plan on which Dr. Harris and the architectural firm of Stoughton and Stoughton had worked for several years.

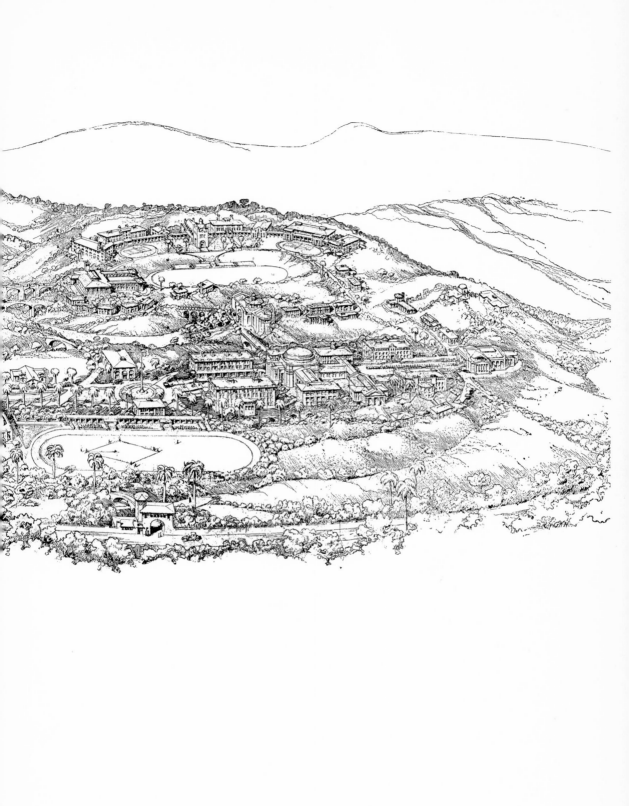

*Above:* Boy's dormitory (date unknown—about 1919) back of where Beverley Student Center is now located: Lorenzo Casiano, Pepín González, Angel Lugo, Félix Casiano, José Rivera García, Erasmo Serrano, Pedro Ruiz, Carmelo Mendoza, Elías Rivero.
*Below:* Morning prayers were regularly held in the dining room until recent times.

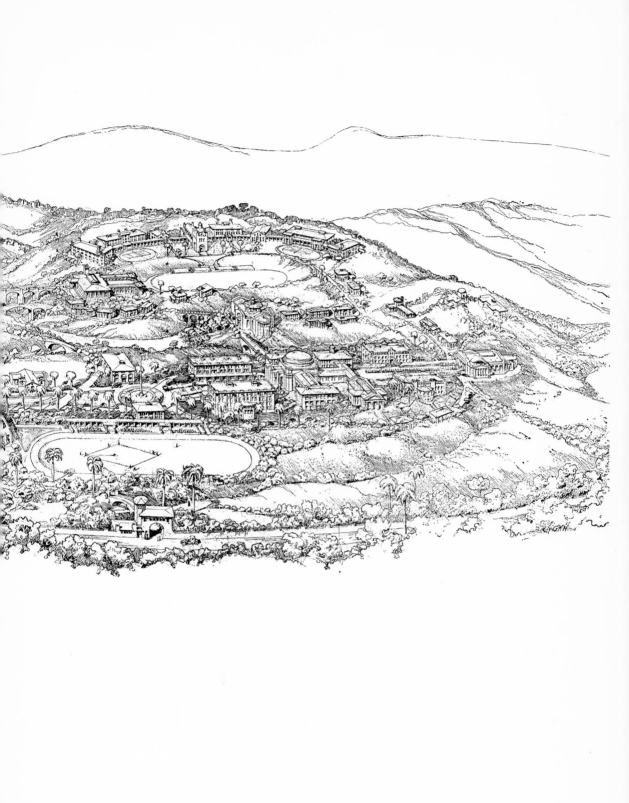

*Top:* The first kitchen of the Polytechnic Institute, 1912.

*Bottom:* The dining shed, 1912. The building alongside was a two-room house where Sra. Ana A. Martínez (doña Nená) and Miss Georgina Villanueva lived.

*Opposite top:* One of the earliest dormitories for boys, later used as the president's office, before the building for which the James family contributed $4,500 in 1912-13. Completed in 1915, it was called Clarence Harris Memorial Hall; now known as Harris Hall, it houses the Home Economics Department.

*Opposite, bottom:* Faculty in 1930: *back row:* Mrs. Mary V. de Harris, Mr. Fred Whaley, Dr. Leker, Dr. Caldwell; *middle row:* María Mercedes Ramírez, Clarence Harris, Mrs. Rachel Akers Palmer, Dr. Boyd B. Palmer, Mr. George Steadman; *front row:* Patria Tió, Lydia Gregory, Dr. Harris, Mrs. Harris, Laura Irizarry.

*Top:* Clarence Harris Memorial Hall, remodeled from the only one of the early buildings still in use, was first a boys' dormitory (1915), later apartments for faculty and now is used for Home Economics classrooms and laboratory. *Bottom:* The Polytechnic Institute faculty, 1918: Seated: Mr. Henry Thomas and Mrs. Thomas, Dr. Harris, Miss Sofía Vivoni, Dr. J. J. Osuna; standing: Mr. Pedro Casablanca, Miss Manuela González, Miss Ursula Nazario, Miss Georgina Villanueva, Miss Buck, Miss Celia Domínguez, Miss Amparo Hernández, Mr. Clarence Harris, Mr. Eduvigis Ramírez.

*Top:* Faculty and student body, 1918-19. *Bottom:* Dr. Leker with trumpet and Antonio Rivera with flute and members of the College Choir: Felipe Toro, Herminio Rodríguez, Gervasio Quiñones, Emilio Acosta, Enrique Adolfo Quiñones, Eugenio Quiñones, Alberto Martínez; seated: Georgina Villanueva, Amanda García, Ramonita Martínez, Carmen Luisa Gregory, Ramonita Rodríguez, Amparo Hernández, Felícita Casiano, Mariana Pagán, Julia Gregory.

*Above:* Cutting firewood was part of the work carried out at the Polytechnic Institute. *Below:* Cane was grown right on the campus; it was a source both of sugar for the school and of some slight income. Phraner Hall is in the background.

*Above:* Dining shed in the 1920s, with Pilar Argüelles at work. *Below:* Another task of students was tending the beehives; the student has not been identified.

*Above:* Boy's dormitory (date unknown—about 1919) back of where Beverley Student Center is now located: Lorenzo Casiano, Pepín González, Angel Lugo, Félix Casiano, José Rivera García, Erasmo Serrano, Pedro Ruiz, Carmelo Mendoza, Elías Rivero.
*Below:* Morning prayers were regularly held in the dining room until recent times.

the railway siding.[7] The buildings were used for a large classroom and for the little boys' dormitory and were, while temporary and inadequate, most helpful for a time. We also received some twenty canvas army cots, a new washing machine run by hand power, an old typewriter, a bellows and an anvil,—all very much needed, from don Cancio's school.

The Colegio Americano, a girls' high school conducted in Mayagüez, was closed down by the Presbyterian Women's Board and gave us their nice school desks and some books.

Then followed the discontinuance of the Aguadilla Presbyterian Mission School, from which we inherited more desks and books.

The Disciples of Christ had erected a fine building near Bayamón, in which they endeavored to build up an institution for orphan boys and other needy children of Puerto Rico. Dr. S. Guy Inman[8] came over to see my Polytechnic Institute. He was the leading spirit in the promotion of cooperation of mission work in Latin America. I walked him up and down the seven hills of Polytechnic, landing on a site I had leveled off for my dwelling, now Hillcrest Campus. Leaning against one of the *cupey*[9] trees, he remarked, *"This school is hitting at the very roots of the solution of our educational problems."*†

His Bayamón school was not making headway. I was asked to go over and attend their conference on just what to do with the Bayamón institution. I went over on the train. They met the train and drove me in a one-horse buggy up the hill, a mile or two to their institution. They decided to sell the building to the Masons and to send their three boys over to me.

A few days later, a weary, smiling young man came up a Polytechnic hill. He had come the hundred miles[10] over the mountainous roads riding his bicycle, on which he had strapped his personal belongings. He pushed his bike up and rode it down hills. It had taken him three days to make the trip of 240 kilometers. His name was Antonio Alers, one of the three boys who were to have come to Polytechnic from Bayamón. Antonio made history that day, for he was the first to ride a bicycle into Polytechnic. Students had usually come on foot, in ox carts or on horseback. Antonio, on account of his superior mode of travel, was envied by all. He was all we got from the Disciples' failure, but was an additional jewel in the very worthwhile increasing number of our students. Antonio was a member of our first high school graduating class.

All the gifts of these defunct schools have perished in the using, except the brand-new anvil from Lajas and the ever-successful Antonio Alers of Bayamón, now Antonio Alers, M.D.[11] of Kentucky.

Why did these schools fail? Certainly not because of lack of anything money could supply. They usually had from the beginning, in Puerto Rico, outstanding and imposing buildings. They were well-supplied with the then modern furniture for schools and also standard books. They had a regular budget, supposedly sufficient for their needs, beyond which they were not allowed to advance. Their teachers were academically well-prepared for work in English-speaking America. Their approach to a cultured Latin American was exotic.

Miss Clara Hazen was a notable exception. She broke away from the Colegio Americano and established the Marina Neighborhood House in the playa of Mayagüez. This work was supported, to a great degree, by local subscriptions, and is still functioning, having now 776 in the Sunday School.[12] She began her work in a lean-to, galvanized-roofed shed with no furniture and little cooperation for a long time. She wrote to friends at home, called on everybody to help her in the work. Her prayers and work brought lasting results. I drew the plans for her first building. Then Mr. Waid[13] made plans for additional buildings. The Lord helps those who help others.

## World War One Comes

World War I struck us very hard. Few people would even consider a gift to my work in Puerto Rico. I went to Washington and secured an endorsement from President Taft, and one from Secretary of War Dickinson and others, because Puerto Rico was then under the Department of War and, ignorantly on our part, was considered incapable of self-government.

I returned to New York and had a conference with H. C. Olin, treasurer of the Home Mission Board. My interview ended by Olin pushing me (literally) out of his office with: "That Polytechnic Institute is just wheels in your brain and will never be anything else." Later he sent a note of apology for his rude treatment of me and my ideas.

I had to economize in every way possible to make my money stretch out to the end of my two weeks' stay in New York City. I had stopped at the Mills Hotel[14] where you pay 25 cents, wait till 10 P.M. to get the cell-like bed and have all things and yourself out of the room by 8 A.M. This did not work, for I had no place to leave my suitcase. I found 50-cent rooms—they called them hall rooms— sometimes they were all enclosed with only a small air hole near the top for ventilation. My suitcase there had permanent quarters. I set aside 50 cents a day for food.

I called on George W. Perkins at 75 Broadway, a member of the Finance Committee of the Presbyterian Home Missions Board, the organizer of the International Harvesting Company, and the man who financed the Bull Moose Party for Teddy Roosevelt. He listened to my story. Then he asked me if I was a missionary of the Home Mission Board. He called up Walter M. Aikman, Chairman of the Finance Committee, Francis S. Phraner, another member of the Finance Committee, and H. C. Olin, Treasurer of the Board, and planned a meeting with them and me for 2 P.M. next day to be held in his office. They decided to ask the Board to take over the Polytechnic Institute under a budget supported by the Board for the duration of the war, and that Harris be charged to raise the budget.

In this I concurred, providing the school would be turned back to an independent board of trustees after the war according to provisions made in the following:

## Proposal of the Polytechnic Institute of Porto Rico to the Home Mission Board of the Presbyterian Church in the U.S.A.

As president of the above-named institution and with the approval of the trustees to have me do so, I do hereby pledge to have conveyed to the Board of Home Missions whatever may be required by the Board of Home Missions, so as to enable that body to accept the complete administration of the Polytechnic Institute of Porto Rico and to carry out the policy for which this school was established, with the understanding that,

1. It is the purpose of this institution to aid youth in securing the best training and preparation possible for life on strong and definite Bible foundations. Good character of the applicant shall be made a requirement for the admission of students.

2. In order to develop a capable, local administrative body in Porto Rico, that a committee of six, all residents of Porto Rico, shall be appointed as the Board's agents in Porto Rico. The president of the institution shall be, ex-officio, the seventh member of this committee. In addition to being an advisory board for the institution, this committee shall act in cases of emergency for the Home Mission Board. With the Home Mission Board as final authority, this committee shall have the general supervision of the institution, the employment and discharge of teachers and the making up of the budget from year to year. One of this committee shall be designated by the Home Mission Board to act as local treasurer of the Institute.

3. It is the explicit understanding that the Home Mission Board will not place the administration of this institution under any other body than the parties to this agreement.

4. When the institution is sufficiently endowed so as not to require the financial help of the Board, the Board shall see that the institution is incorporated under wise management and Christian principles in the uplift of humanity and positive service to the Kingdom of Christ. To this end it is permitted and encouraged that adequate endowment be secured for the different branches of the work. The president of the institution shall be allowed to use all legitimate and approved means in raising funds for increased work and endowment.

/s/ J. Will Harris
President of Institute

19 December, 1913

The reason why I made the above proposal was that the Presbyterian Home Mission Board had often stated its policy to be the promotion of work in the mission fields and the support of that work till the work could walk alone but was not for the purpose of establishing and maintaining work once that work was established. Without friends and any visible support for my school as a private school I hoped that the Home Mission Board would give us support till we could go ahead on our own. Therefore, I made the above proposal to the Board. We were not considered as a Board's school.

The understanding was that I should keep on soliciting funds, which were to be applied on the appropriate budget and on buildings as designated.

Was I expected to keep the school growing? Dr. Dixon, the Home Mission Board secretary, did not expect it. In fact, he wrote me to send away some of the students, not because I was keeping out of debt, but because the enrollment was in excess of the previous year. The extra expense was cared for, however, by increasing the number of students who paid full tuition and board, $10 monthly. After a long discussion, carried on by correspondence, Dr. Dixon agreed to the increased enrollment.

## The First High School Class Graduates

There were five boys and one girl in the class of 1916. My school was not in the highest esteem of the city of San Germán, due at the time to manual labor and co-education, plus the Bible.

The 1916 high school class roll was: Francisco Medina, valedictorian, who entered business; José Gallardo who graduated from Park College and became Commissioner of Education of Puerto Rico; Antonio Alers who graduated from Berea College and is an M.D. in Kentucky,[15] Alberto Martínez who became a Presbyterian minister; Eugenio Quiñones who was an employee in the offices of Guánica Central and María Quintana, the only girl in the high school class of 1916. She became a teacher in the public schools.

## Storms and Travel During Early Days of Polytechnic

Travel, then, was limited to sea-going vessels, time—five or six days to New York and ten days to Galveston, Texas.[16] Now, in airplanes[17] five hours to New York and ten hours to Houston. When a ship left the docks it was cut off from any communication with the outside world beyond the vision of the man in the crow's nest. Now radio and television have annihilated blind sailing of ships. The radio reports the velocity, the advances and the path of the hurricane hours before it strikes your home or ship.

The S.S. *Carolina* of the Porto Rican Line was a long, narrow, old vessel with cabins opening out on the wide promenade deck around the ship. Steamer chairs for passengers to rest, and maybe sleep, certainly to talk with fellow voyagers, lined up against the wall, price only one dollar, six days' duration.

On my last trip aboard the *Carolina,* an unannounced storm appeared a few miles away. Soon the chairs were washing back and forth along the promenade deck, as the wind's velocity increased, smashed in the cabin doors and broke down the railing of the promenade deck as it approached. A prominent Puerto Rican business man [from Yauco], don Luis Dastas, with his American school teacher wife from Ponce, had been given a stateroom on the windward[18] side because he was sick and enroute [to] Johns Hopkins; electric fans had not been invented. After the storm passed, when it was possible to venture out, it was found that their room was soaked and standing in water. Mrs. Dastas, wet and cold, was huddled in a corner by the side of her husband who had died. A tragic incident. A stewardess took her arm and I took the other and walked her around to the semi-dry side of the ship into a dry room. I held a prayer meeting service next day to which all attended in sympathy.

Upon arrival in New York I reserved my passage for the *Carolina's* sailing to Puerto Rico a month hence. The month I spent seeking money for Poly. I was back in New York the day of her arrival and went down to make sure of passage back to Puerto Rico. The papers had large headlines announcing that German submarines were in the waters around the entrance to New York. The big waiting room was filled with friends and families of those arriving on the *Carolina.* The atmosphere was tense and excited as notices were posted. *Carolina* was in the passage where the danger lay. *Carolina* has been attacked. And then the *Carolina* has sunk,[19] survivors are being picked up. Some remained in small boats for three days and drifted into harbors in New Jersey, among whom were Judge Peter Hamilton[20] and his wife and many other well-known people. Ships were not allowed out of the harbor in New York.

I hurried over to the Red "D" Line and saw the president whom I knew. All reservations had been cancelled, only those with urgent need to go would be allowed to ship. Next day twelve people dared to go aboard. First, we had to sign papers relieving the company of all liabilities for death or loss. This was the S.S. *Philadelphia* on which Mrs. Harris and I had gone to Puerto Rico in 1906. The captain was a New Englander who was proficient in swearing as he condemned the submarines.

The *Philadelphia* was the first and only ship allowed to sail that day. The captain, an old seaman, was sure he could outwit the Germans. We sailed from the Brooklyn Pier early in the morning, were not allowed away from the Jersey seacoast. We were ordered to put into harbor at night. During the first day we passed through oceans of dead fish killed by exploding shells from a German submarine. The second day we made Delaware Gap Harbor for the night. The captain went ashore and notified the New York office he would do one of two things—quit the ship or set out to the open sea to Puerto Rico. They told him to use his own judgment.

In the darkness of that night, not a light on the ship, and no one could light a match he set sail due east. We all had to put on and keep on our life-savers. The next morning when we could see each other we looked like a football squad with a mother and two children as mascots! For three days the ship kept a due easterly direction. Then he turned southwest toward Puerto Rico on a straight line about 150 miles east of the Bermuda Islands. We were several days, in fact about a week, overdue and Puerto Rico thought the *Philadelphia* had been sunk. We finally saw Morro Castle[21] in San Juan and the people sighted the *Philadelphia*. Morro Castle walls were covered with people waving flags and cannons firing a welcome as we turned into the harbor around the Governor's Palace to the dock. I never stept on land more satisfying than the feel of Puerto Rican soil. Fortunately, Mrs. Harris did not know I was on the *Philadelphia*.

# Presbytery of Puerto Rico
# Asks for J. Will Harris's Removal[22]

When a person hears what God says and does what God tells him to do he will find all kinds of opposition. It will lighten his load if he will always remember, *All things work together for good to them who love God, to them whom God calls.*† I never answered anonymous letters or bitter criticism.

Had it not been for opposition, the PIPR would have died in birth. When someone wrote a publicized tirade against the Polytechnic, there would always be others who flayed him and called the attention of the Island to Poly's good work. I never did reply. When Padre Angel, Vicar of San Germán, would condemn Poly in his Sunday morning sermon and urge parents not to send their children to Poly, there would be a string of choice young people asking for admission. Had it not been for the misguided hand of the man who planned the complaints against Harris for Presbytery's approval, we would not have had Marquis Science Hall today. Looseleaf books are not allowed in which Presbytery's minutes are recorded. On a recent visit to Puerto Rico in 1952 I wished to get Reverendo Erasmo Seda, clerk of Presbytery, to give me an authorized copy of these complaints. To our surprise the whole record of minutes of the Presbytery that approved the request for Harris's recall had been torn out by an interested party.

A copy of the complaints enumerated and signed by the Chairman of the Home Mission Committee as approved by Presbytery and sent to the Board in New York was slipt to me by a friend. It was hard to forget the charges as stated:

1 That Harris did not keep within the budget allowed him by the Board.
2 That the Board allowed Harris to solicit funds outside of his budget, but denied such rights to the Presbytery.
3 That Harris used money given for specific purposes for other ends.
4 That Harris charged the students more for inferior board per month than was being spent by the directors of the Puerto Rican School of Correction nearby.
5 That Harris made contracts with teachers not having the money on hand to guarantee payment of such contracts.

Dr. John Dixon called a meeting of the staff for consideration of Presbytery's grievances. Dr. Dixon read the charges and asked the staff to request the Board for Harris's recall, that "Harris's head be taken off," were his exact words.

To this, Reverend Dr. Warren Wilson of Rural Department and Reverend Dr. Wm. P. Shriver of the Department of Immigrants objected and moved that a committee be appointed to investigate and report back to the Board of Home Missions.

The Reverend Dr. A. Edwin Keigwin and Mr. Francis S. Phraner, two members of the Home Mission Board, were named to go to Puerto Rico and make a study of the situation. In due time they came and spent ten days in the Polytechnic Institute of Puerto Rico, accompanied by their wives and Mary (Mr. and Mrs. Phraner's daughter). They were guests of Loma Vista, as all visitors were in those days.

They found the books meticulously kept by the principal of my school, Professor Henry F. Thomas, a college classmate of mine and always known as a conscientious, honest, Christian gentleman. The books accounted for all receipts and expenditures down to the last cent, accurately and correctly.

The fourth statement of the five was found by the committee to be: The Polytechnic charged students $4.60 per month while the cost at the Correctional School was $7.50 per month, and that the Polytechnic was serving better food.

The other charges were true, only the implications were wrong.

At the next Home Mission Board meeting in New York, Dr. Keigwin made a most glowing report on the Polytechnic and recommended that Harris be exonerated and be given $75,000 for a science hall. The Reverend Dr. Henry Sloan Coffin then moved that the Polytechnic be placed under a Board of Trustees, independent of the Presbytery of Puerto Rico.

Dr. John A. Marquis, as Moderator of the General Assembly, visited Puerto Rico in 1916, spending several days in my school. He advised me then to draw up a new charter and select a board of trustees for the school. He had been connected with colleges as teacher and president most of his life. He was now elected to become Secretary of the Presbyterian Home Mission Board, which Dr. Marquis led into the present Board of National Missions. I had drawn up a charter to which Dr. Marquis added certain valuable suggestions. I turned it over to William E. Carnochan, attorney of the Board of Home Missions who whipped it into legal terminology, including a *stipulation made by me,*† that the Home Mission Board elect our trustees—which is the only control and official connection with the Presbyterian Board of Home Missions (now the Presbyterian Board of National Missions).[23]

The first Board of Trustees of the Polytechnic Institute of Puerto Rico was dissolved in 1917. I personally had taken in trust, in my own name, title to the property sold to me by Francisco Lagarde in 1912 because the Trustees hesitated to assume such responsibility, and so I continued to hold same, in trust, till the second independent Board of Trustees was incorporated the fourth day of May 1920.

# Chapter 10

## *Accreditations and Recognitions*

OUR ELEMENTARY SCHOOL was inspected by a young man, now Dr. José Padín,[1] who recommended accreditation to the Commissioner of Education. Later the high school was also accredited by Dr. Paul G. Miller, Commissioner of Education,[2] upon the recommendation of Dr. Padín.

The Legislature of Puerto Rico, by Special Act, gave the Polytechnic Institute *legal university standing* † on March 21, 1919. Senator Honorable Juan Angel Tió and Representative Honorable Julio Montalvo[3] were instrumental in the passage of this law.

The following is a true copy of:

### SPECIAL ACT OF MARCH 21, 1919

To authorize the Board of Trustees of the Polytechnic Institute of Porto Rico established in San Germán to confer university degrees, and for other purposes.

BE IT ENACTED IN THE LEGISLATURE OF PORTO RICO:

That the Board of Trustees of the Polytechnic Institute of Porto Rico established in San Germán, upon agreement with the president of the institution and upon recommendation of the different faculties, may grant such degrees as they may deem advisable, and issue certificates and diplomas of ability in determined matters and courses, providing the resources of the said institution shall be such as to enable it to provide the necessary buildings, equipment and professors to give an adequate higher education for the granting of the said certificates, diplomas and degrees, and when the said institution shall have pupils who have finished the courses entitling them to such diplomas and degrees, but no strictly honorary degree shall be granted by said institution unless the grantee possesses the proper literary or scientific knowledge.

Hon. Arthur Yager[4]                                                                July 2, 1919
Governor of Porto Rico
San Juan, Porto Rico

Sir:

I have the honor to acknowledge receipt of H.B. 253, entitled "An Act to authorize the Board of Trustees of the Polytechnic Institute of Porto Rico

established at San Germán to confer university degrees, and for other purposes."

The purpose of this act is to authorize the Polytechnic Institute of Porto
Rico to issue certificates and diplomas. This is the first institution in addition
to the University of Porto Rico to be favored by legislative action of this
kind. Two questions immediately arise: If this measure is approved, will it
form a dangerous precedent? Is the institution worthy of being given public
recognition of this kind?

In reply to the first question, I believe it would not establish any precedent
that may bring harm to the educational interests of Porto Rico in the future.
Naturally every case would have to be decided upon its own merits and not
upon precedent. The amount of real estate owned, the character of the
faculty, the courses offered and other considerations would be the deciding
factors and not the fact that some other institution has been authorized to
grant degrees.

With reference to the second question, I fully believe that the Polytechnic
Institute of Porto Rico deserves recognition as proposed in the bill before
you. The Institute now owns considerable real estate. The secondary courses
have been accredited by the Department of Education. I understand that the
school will receive, within the next five years, the sum of one million dollars
from sources in the United States, for the erection of buildings and endowment for current expenditures. It is true that the Polytechnic Institute does
not have the necessary buildings, equipment and students for college courses
at the present time, but nevertheless, it is perhaps as far along as was the
University of Porto Rico at the time the University Act was passed when not
a single student was enrolled in that institution. I have personally visited the
Polytechnic Institute a number of times. The spirit of the institution is excellent. The teaching corps is well trained and efficient, and, moreover, I find
that all the people who know anything about the Institute have full faith and
confidence in its success. Personally I feel that fifteen years from now the
Polytechnic Institute of Porto Rico will perhaps have more resources than
the University of Porto Rico. The Polytechnic Institute is in a position to
render excellent service to the people of Porto Rico without a cent of expenditure from the public treasury. The Department of Education has already
drawn some of its best teachers from its student body. These young people
have taken the Department examinations with excellent results. I believe the
Institute will establish a Normal Department in the near future, perhaps the
equivalent of the Normal Department of the University of Porto Rico,
which will serve a constituency that cannot and does not avail itself of the
facilities at Río Piedras. The great need for trained teachers is well known to
you, and along this line I believe the Institute will render a most valuable
service. Aside from any mere academic considerations, I believe the Polytechnic Institute is now giving and will continue to give a basic training in
character which is sadly lacking in too many of our schools.

I respectfully recommend that the bill before you receive your approval with the assurance that this measure will tend only to benefit the people of Porto Rico without any expense to them.

Respectfully,
/s/*P. G. Miller*
Commissioner of Education

Thank you, Dr. Miller. Our accreditation has first and always come previously from Heaven.

The Polytechnic Institute is first and last a Christian college. It is so stated in the charter. But the charter's requirements cannot make the college Christian.

Christianity is embodied not in a charter, however well it may therein be expressed, but in life. Each life expresses a part of the whole, but no one life all of the whole.

It is faith in Jesus Christ whose teachings and example are known and embodied in the life of trustees, teachers and students that make a college Christian.

No written requirements subscribed to by faculty and students can of itself make a college Christian. If these requirements are the outgrowth of a deeper inward conviction of the Christian faith expressed in active service for Christ, then the result is a Christian college.

Only so far as we live Christ and try to express that life in service for Him can we expect to build up a school into a really Christian college.

This being true, it becomes us all to try to live an exemplary Christian life. An exemplary Christian life is what this college expects of its teachers and hopes to see developed in its students.

We will not all attain the same degree of faith but we can all show the same spirit of endeavor and interest in the religious services of the institution. By so doing our Christian college will grow into a distinguished service for man.

I have been asked about amusements—what is wrong, what is right. It is impossible to answer these questions. Everything I think and do ought to be measured by me as to its results on me and others as a Christian. Others are going to be measuring me and estimating the connection between what I profess and what I do, and am. A good traffic law of life is "when in doubt turn to the Right." Intoxicating drinks even in social cocktails we all know are unnecessary and perilous.

I have been asked to allow the National Guard to drill in Henry P. Heylman[5] Athletic Field on Sundays. The same request has come for baseball games. Ex-Governor Beverley[6] gave me this advice in regard to such: "*As a college you cannot disregard the Sabbath observance. If you let down in Sabbath observance it will soon cause a breakdown of all other standards that make your school a Christian institution.*"† We need Sunday for spiritual recreation, for the strengthening of our inward man in Christ Jesus. There are six days for ordinary duties. Let us on the Sabbath day find in our social relationship and service that which is in keeping with Isaiah 58:13-14[7] and thus promote the religious life of the college.

Read your Bible prayerfully and carefully and recreations and work will find their rightful places in our busy lives of consecrated service to man and God.

# Chapter 11

## *Building for the Future*

### Master Plan Completed and Approved

MY ENTIRE SPARE time after March 2, 1912, was given to a study of a master plan for the school. For six years I worked alone on these plans. I travelled from New York to the Rio Grande in Texas, studying the campus plans of schools, colleges and universities, to find that no architectural plans had been followed during their early days by any that I visited, some twenty outstanding institutions. Hampton Institute had recently employed an architect and, though in dire need of money, was demolishing a four-story brick dormitory built for Indian boys that blocked the main avenue of the architect's recent master plan. Princeton was wishing for the courage to do the same demolishing work.

I was fully convinced, by this study of old institutions like my own Park College, that a master plan was absolutely essential before a permanent building program could be launched successfully.

Fortunately, I had been required to take a civil engineering course in Park College. I learned how to plan and grade a railroad through hills and deep gorges of Park's surrounding hills, not unlike what I found in the terrain of the Seven Hills of the Polytechnic in Puerto Rico.

I asked D. E. Waid, architect for the Metropolitan Life, who had helped the Home Mission Board with several plans, to help me with a master plan. He was too busy to take on extra work but did give me his card saying: "Take this to Stoughton and Stoughton, who are the finest architects in New York and who are interested in Mission work."

Stoughton and Stoughton were brothers and were the leading architects of that day in New York City, at 96 Fifth Avenue, as the Soldiers' and Sailors' Monument on Riverside Drive attests. Arthur was a college professor of architecture in a Canadian college. Brother Charles William was in the New York offices. I found him all, and more, than Mr. Waid had told me. Charles William had visited China and designed the master plan for Canton Christian College. He also made one for Madura College in India. He asked me for a contour survey of our campus, then went down to Puerto Rico for a study of same on the grounds. He was delighted with the possibilities of our grounds and determined to make it the crowning work of his life—which he did.

It was a long, hard job which Mr. Stoughton and his brother Arthur, during summer vacations, joined me to accomplish. Studies and many restudies were made. Finally, one day, I located Building #2 on the east side of Hillside Campus. After this, I located the other buildings of the different campuses faster than Mr. Stoughton could plot them into position. What fun it was! To get that first building located took me years of study, but the Lord suddenly opened up the whole plan to me. I believe in hard work and definite Divine direction. When we get into tune with doing what ought to be done, for God and man, the Holy Spirit directs us.

The contour map on five foot levels was made by the Guánica Central under the supervision of Mr. William Shanklin.[1] It took three solid months of work to run the lines and to transcribe same on cloth paper. This was a special contribution to help me get the school prepared for advancement. Mr. French Maxwell was now vice president and general manager of Guánica Central. His heart began to soften toward my school, due in great part to Eugenio Quiñones of the class of 1916, who was working in Mr. Maxwell's office and had proved his superior training to Maxwell.

Five of the seven hills were chosen as the natural division into which any master plan had to fit. After locating the building sites individually, we named the five campuses as follows: Hospital Campus, Hillside Campus for boys, Hillcrest Campus for girls,[2] President Hill and the Academic Campus.[3] The Center Line of Academic Campus began in the Auditorium at the east end of Academic Campus, by and across San Juan Street (now Dr. Harris Avenue), down through the center of East Campus and *The Steps,* the Library and Administration Building, on through the West Campus, between the Science Hall on the south and Academic Hall on the north, ending at the Chapel at the head of the Esplanade, where the Flagpole now stands.

Facing the Marquis Science Hall is the Academic Hall for the humanities. These two halls are joined by a colonnade united in front of the Administration and Library Building on the West Campus. The Manual Arts buildings are for woodwork and other industrial machinery, located west of Academic Hall and Chapel, about where the present temporary carpentry shop has a shed. The Chapel is located on the West Academic Campus facing the Library at the head of the Esplanade so as to be centrally accessible to all campuses and to the public for daily and Sabbath worship.

*The Steps* are to be preserved for all time by an iron grating under a covered auditorium for commencements and are a part of the Library and Administration Building.

Stoughton and Stoughton did this work of the plan, almost free, on condition

Mrs. Harris with Dr. Harris in front of their Texas home
shortly before her death and his tribute to her was written.

Another of the buildings donated by Don Juan Cancio Ortiz from his school in [Bo.] Palmarejo, Lajas, and moved to San Germán in 1914.

Typical highway over which Antonio Alers would have cycled the 240 kilometers for three days to enroll.

This first class to graduate, the high school class of 1916, was a real triumph for Dr. Harris. Members were: José M. Gallardo, Francisco Medina, Alberto Martínez, Antonio Alers, Eugenio Quiñones and María Quintana.

*Above:* Panoramic view of the campus about 1923; buildings from left to right are girls' dormitory, Mr. Leker's home and boys' dormitory. *Below:* Marquis Science Hall (1920) in early years, when road ended in front of the building.

*Above:* Three students from the early years: Rafael A. Vélez, Samuel Aparicio, Félix Luis Rodriguez. *Below:* Quarry across the road from Marquis Science Hall from which stone was taken for campus construction. Students have not been identified.

This first college class to enter, 1921, did not graduate, as all left for teaching positions in the public schools at the end of the second year. *Back row:* Rosa Aviles, Samuel Quiñones, Rafael Labiosa, Angel Lugo, Félix Casiano, Héctor Alvarez, Julia María Quiñones; *front row:* Carmelo Mendoza, Edna Lugo, Enrique Rivera, Jennie Jason, Enrique García.

Students making cement blocks for campus construction. The small boy is Donald Harris and the young lady in the elegant hat is his older sister Helen; the student in front of the wall is Florencio Lugo, the others have not been identified.

Loma Vista under construction by student labor (completed 1918) was the first of the permanent buildings in the master plan and Dr. Harris's home until his retirement in 1937.

*Above:* View of Loma Vista and its welcoming porch from across the valley.

*Below:* Mrs. Eleanor Roosevelt with Polytechnic students, unidentified (1935).

*Above:* The Polytechnic Institute 30-piece band with the instruments purchased by
Mrs. D. E. Waid. *Below, left:* Mr. E. P. Mitchell of the New York *Sun Herald* with
members of the Harris family on the entrance porch of Loma Vista (about 1924).
*Below, right:* The Harris family on the steps of Loma Vista: Mrs. Harris, Helen,
Dr. Harris, Donald, Cleland, Robert and Margaret (1922).

*Above:* In the early 1930s Governor Blanton Winship was a distinguished visitor, seen here with: Mrs. Rachel Palmer, Ninía Ramírez, Mrs. Whaley, Patria Tió, Lydia Gregrory, Dr. Harris, unidentified child, Governor Winship, Mrs. Harris, Miguel Angel García Méndez; *back row:* Dr. Palmer, Juan O'Neill, Dr. Leker, Helen Harris, Mr. Dillingham, Dr. Whaley, George Steadman, Laura Irizarry, Cleland Harris, Jesús T. Piñero, Eusebio López Acosta, Juan Angel Tió, Bartolomé Bover, Luis Maldonado, Fanny Carleton, Mrs. Caldwell, Dr. Caldwell, Luis Angel Linares.

*Below:* Governor and Mrs. Muñoz Marín visited the campus during the presidency of Dr. Edward Seel and Mrs. Seel (1947-55). *Back row:* Mrs. Seel, Mrs. Lucy Vélez, Lester Vélez, Dr. Ismael Vélez, Mrs. Muñoz Marín, Governor Luis Muñoz Marín, Gustavo Adolfo Ramírez de Arellano, Dr. Seel, Mr. and Mrs. Rubén Sánchez; *front row:* Iris Vélez, unidentified boy, Miriam Castro, Margarita (last name unknown), Alice Gómez and Noemí Ruiz.

Cooking the daily rice and beans over *carbón* (charcoal)
on a cement stove (Pilar Argüelles, B.A. 1930).

Forestation, planting the mahogany trees that grew into Los Caobos,
the delightful Mahogany Hill (early 1930s).

*Above:* Student body with one of the [Bo.] Palmarejo buildings in the background.
*Below:* Women students, 1914-15: Amanda García, ———— Cordero, unidentified,
Ursula Nazario, Amparo Hernández, ———— Hernández, Ramonita Martínez
(Mona Marti).

*Above:* Women students, 1916-17. *Below:* Men students, 1916-17.

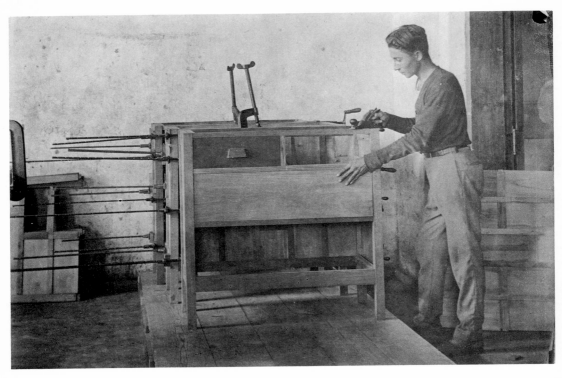

*Above:* Woodworking shop with Florencio Lugo at work on finishing a piece of furniture. *Below:* Carpentry shop where students made furniture and similar work under the supervision of Antonio Padilla.

Student group, 1921: *back row:* Félix Rodríguez, Oscar Rodríguez, Félix Casiano, Arnold Petersen, Isidro Hernández, José M. Rodríguez Quiñones (Nito), Pedro Olivari, José A. Luciano, Abelardo Pérez; *second row:* unidentified, Helen Harris, Ramonita Acosta, Miss Richards; *third row:* Antonio Rivera, Crispiriana Nazario, Felícita Casiano, Olga Rivera, Consuelo Butterbough, Ana L. Alvarez, Grace Jason, Paquita Serrano; *front row:* Amparo García, Rosa Nazario, María González, Carmen Burgos, Aidita Montoya, Rafael Vázquez.

Costello Hall, built in
1925 with funds from
the Gillespie-Costello
families, to be used as
a guest house. It is now
the Music Department.

View from the porch of Costello Hall across the valley
at the time of its building and for years after.

that they be given the architectural work to do. To this the trustees agreed, giving Stoughton a written and signed contract. They were paid for the master plan and all constructed buildings up to 1937. All other work, which included elevations of buildings, bird's-eye view of campus, drives, etc., was free. The drives, bridges and landscaping were drawn into the master plan for ease of communication and beauty of scenery and economy of construction.

Stoughton and Stoughton gave us elevation prints of all the buildings located properly on the contours, one above the other, tying the distinctive groups into one whole picture of design (an adaptation of Greek Renaissance to modern usage)—a symmetrically balanced college grounds and campuses. Elevations of a hundred buildings were drawn to scale for present and future demands by Stoughton and Stoughton, representing thousands of dollars in labor, freely donated by the architects. *I left the blue print copies in the closet of my office when I retired in 1937, and some of the original drawings, plus the contour map of the whole campus.*† Some of these were salvaged by a true and daring employee, from a pile of rubbish back of Science Hall before the match was applied by orders of the administrator.

*Our master plan is so designed as to allow the gradual development of the college.*† The buildings, as are needed, may be erected for 600, 1000, 2000 or more students. When the last building is completed in the distant future, the whole will appear as a perfect painting, of one architectural design, with every building of the same style of architecture located and standing in its proper place. This is a wonderful talking point to those of large means who desire to leave a memorial that is to be permanent, beautiful, useful and in keeping with a general plan.

Every building hitherto erected (and there is at least one on each campus) has been a memorial building which appeals to sentiment of the giver to honor some person with a lasting memorial. The *inside plans* and *arrangements*† of every building should be adapted, by wise and experienced architects, to the needs of the rapidly changing times for interior arrangements such as air-conditioning, etc., as well as for conformity to the more rapid changes of science and comfort. *Let the* style *of architecture and the original plotted location of every building be retained.*† This will make every succeeding generation of students feel an increasing love for their Alma Mater.

Every building and site is the result of years of study and restudy. I hope that this master plan may be adhered to strictly, as to *locations of buildings and architectural style.*† The interior must be kept up to sane but modern needs of advancing new demands, throughout the years. This deserves repetition often, and especially, to every incoming president, and new trustee.

Remember always that, while you are erecting for a definite present need from time to time, you are also slowly erecting buildings of an institution for the ages to come. Spare not money and give much serious thought in making every addition fit in and be a part of the *master plan*.† Instead of three-story dormitories, it may be found that a twelve-story one is even better. The site of buildings and style of architecture should always be retained as established by Stoughton and Stoughton in 1920, accepted and approved at the time by the Board of Trustees as the *master plan for all future development*.†

Without this master plan I could never have interested large givers in the Polytechnic, such as the Carnegie Corporation.

I called on Mr. Leffingwell,[4] president of Carnegie Corporation, also president of Morgan & Company, at One Broad Street. Mr. J. P. Morgan, Jr., came by as I was showing the elevated drawing in colors to Mr. Leffingwell. With one arm around my shoulders and the other around Mr. Leffingwell, Mr. Morgan studied the master plan carefully, asked questions and remarked, "That is the finest master plan I have seen. Next time I am in Puerto Rico, I will go and see the grounds." Unfortunately, death knocked at his door before Mr. Morgan, Jr., returned to Puerto Rico. President Beverley has this copy I showed Mr. Morgan.[5]

## The Completed Buildings

The first building of the master plan was erected on President Hill. The building was given by Mrs. Mary Copley Thaw[6] and the Misses Mary R. Tooker and Gertrude Tooker, *as a home for the founder and president and for the future presidents*.† It was called Loma Vista and designated on master plan by letter *A*. Miss Mary Tooker (now Mrs. Heylman) later gave $1,000 more to add a bedroom upstairs by my study. Total cost—$6,500.

Marquis Science Hall, *B* on master plan—West Campus, given by the Presbyterian Home Mission Board at a final cost of $85,000. I named it in memory of the Reverend Dr. John A. Marquis, Moderator of the Presbyterian General Assembly, General Secretary and reorganizer of the Home Mission Board into a union of several boards now known as the Board of the National Missions of the Presbyterian Church, U.S.A. He was also trustee and secretary of the Polytechnic.

Phraner Hall, letter *C* on Hillside Campus, given by Mrs. Caroline M. Phraner (at a cost of $60,000) in memory of her husband, Francis S. Phraner, first treasurer of the Polytechnic till his death.

Keigwin Cottage, letter *D* on President Hill, in honor of our first board president, Reverend Dr. A. Edwin Keigwin, given in the will of his wife to our college. Cost—$6,000.

Roberts Cottage, letter *E* on President Hill, (cost $6,000) given in memory of Mary Roberts, the wife of the Reverend Dr. William Charles Roberts, Moderator of the General Assembly and General Secretary of the Home Mission Board of the Presbyterian Church, by her daughter, Mrs. Mary Roberts Miller.

Arturo Lluveras, letter *F* on President Hill, is in honor of the first Puerto Rican to make a sizable donation of $5,000 to the College.

Goodyear, letter *G,* entrance to Hillcrest Campus, (cost $7,000) and Atwater Cottages, back of Hillcrest Campus, letter *H,* (cost $5,000) are memorials given by Mrs. Anna Costello Ropes.

Costello Hall, letter *K,* at entrance of Hillcrest Campus, was erected in honor of their grandfather, by his three grandchildren, Olivia, Bertha, and James C. Gillespie. Cost—$25,000.

Gillespie Cottage, letter *L,* at entrance to Hillcrest Campus, given by our trustee, the Reverend Dr. James P. Gillespie. Cost—$6,000.

Elias D. Smith Cottage, letter *M* on President Hill, given by his daughter Mrs. Jessie Smith Hamner. Cost—$6,000. Mr. Smith invented a heating system and thus made it possible to erect high buildings with heat appliances.

Borinquen Hall, letter *N* on Hillcrest Campus, given by many, principally residents of Puerto Rico. Cost—$60,000.

Casa María was so named by Captain Heylman in honor of his wife, Mary Tooker Heylman, and erected by student and hired labor for Captain H. B. Heylman and Mrs. Mary Tooker Heylman. This house is not on the master plan and was intended to become "a home for Dr. and Mrs. Harris when they retired from the college."[7]

Veve Cottage, (cost—$5,000) letter *V,* just back of Hillside Campus, left in the will of Dr. Santiago Veve of Fajardo, to the college, as a friendly farewell and with his best wishes.

Dairy Farm Building, letter *W,* given by Captain H. B. and Mrs. Mary Tooker Heylman. Cost—$3,000.[8]

Clinic Building, letter *X,* given by Edward S. Harkness. Cost—$5,000.

Clarence Harris Hall #2 East on Hillside Campus. Cost—$5,000.

                                                        December 18, 1917

My dear Mr. Harris:—

Kindly accept my thanks for the copy of plans for the Polytechnic Institute, as well as for your kindness in showing me your plant during my recent visit to San Germán.

I am more and more impressed with the excellent work you are doing in your school. I do not know of any other secondary school in Porto Rico where students are doing their work with a greater degree of thoroughness, willingness and cheerfulness than in the Polytechnic Institute.

You will be interested in knowing that in the examinations held for teachers' licenses at the close of last summer session, the highest grades were attained by two young people from your school.

Your plans for the future exceed by far any plans made by the Board of Trustees of the University of Porto Rico. You have the faith and the vision. May you be successful in getting the funds necessary to carry out your plans to a full realization.

Very cordially yours,
/s/ *P. G. Miller*
Commissioner of Education

# Chapter 12

## *Loma Vista and Its Functions*

### The President's House

LET ME TELL YOU FIRST how I got the money for Loma Vista . . . the *first* permanent[1] building. I was now staying in the Twenty-third Street YMCA, New York, because it was convenient, cheap and spiritually uplifting. Mr. Stoughton had drawn the plan and elevation of Loma Vista. I went to Pittsburgh. Mrs. Mary Copley Thaw invited me to her home for tea. She was always interested in colleges and missionary work. She looked at the size of the living room, 20′ × 20′. "I will give you $500 for this president's home as it is. If you will promise to add 10′ to it, making the living room 20′ × 30′, I will give you $1,000." That is what I agreed on the spot to do, and she gave me her check for $1,000. I could not interest others in Loma Vista. After calling on many rich people in Pittsburgh, I returned to New York to Twenty-third Street "Y" to pray for courage and to rest over the night. I found a letter there from Eunice with this poem quoted for my benefit:

I cannot do it alone;
The waves run fast and high,
And the fogs close chill around,
And the light goes out in the sky;
But I *know* that We TWO,
Shall win in the end . . .
    Jesus and I.

Coward, wayward and weak,
I change with the changing sky,
Today, so eager and bright,
Tomorow, too weak to try;
But HE never gives in,
So we TWO shall win . . .
    Jesus and I.

(*Author unknown*)

Next morning I went out to the home of Mr. Nathaniel Tooker, a sugar man of East Orange, N.J. He had sent for me when I was a senior in Princeton to come into Dr. Dixon's office at 156 Fifth Avenue to see him. I liked him. He tried to get me to go to Caparra Sugar Mill in Cuba as his missionary. I could not then see it. I wanted to go to the Southwest, get married to the best girl I ever knew and build a college for poor boys and girls in the Southwest.

When I arrived at his home, the maid told me he had died, but that his two daughters lived there. The older would come in on the afternoon train from a visit to her sister, Margaret, in Pennsylvania. I told the maid I would return at 4 P.M.

I knew no one in the town. Under such circumstances, I usually went to grave-yards to read the words of those whose folks could afford a gravestone, to read such as:

> Friend, I was where you are.
> You will be where I am.

Another big tombstone in Princeton with the name Aaron Burr, nothing else worthwhile could be written about him. A much later epitaph came with the auto:

> He speeded to an early grave
> Never to enjoy the time he saved.

At 4 P.M. I was back at the old home of Nathaniel Tooker. Sat down to wait for Miss Mary R. Tooker, his daughter. The Lackawanna train was an hour late. She came and apologized for the ink stains on her fingers. She had written letters over the bumpy railroad. She listened to my story and had me stay for dinner. I was hungry, living on a 50 cents per day diet. Her nieces, nice little girls, sat down with us. Miss Tooker picked up a big fork and then a long knife and cut generous portions of the big spiced baked ham. Just like her, she was liberal in portions served and gave me a double portion. After supper, or it was dinner, as she called it, I talked a while and she told me of her interest in China and India. As I left she said she would consult her sister Gertrude, as they usually acted as one, and let me know. The next day or so, I had a letter with two checks, one signed by Miss Gertrude for $3,000 and another from her for $1,000. She said she would give me more later, which she did and continued to do manifold to her last day.

Loma Vista was the first permanent building erected by the students with money *designated specifically by the donors, as the home for the president of the college.*† Here, after five years in the old house, the family of the founder and first president lived for nearly two decades.

Loma Vista sets forth the *architectural style to be followed in the erection of all buildings*† of the master plan, designed by Stoughton and Stoughton. The style *which they adopted was a blending of the Greek-Renaissance*† into the adapta-tion of modern usage, which style was *approved and adopted by the board of trustees as the approved master plan in 1920.*†

Loma Vista is large and commodious, imposing and attractive, with a 210 foot porch, 10 to 14 feet wide, extending around three sides. It has six bedrooms, five baths, a reception room 20′ × 30′, so made by Mrs. Thaw's suggestion and money. The second-story bedroom was added later and paid for by Mrs. Mary Tooker Heylman. Loma Vista was constructed by student labor of reinforced concrete at a cost of $6,500.

Loma Vista was built *not just for a president's home; the IDEA was to invite influential people, not for weekends, but for weeks on end.*† Here came George D. Selden, president of Erie City Iron Works, and spent five weeks. He returned home, made a new will including PIPR, expecting to sign it next morning, but died that night. Captain and Mrs. Heylman were part of our family for months, and steady benefactors of Polytechnic. Our hearts were gladdened when our guests extended a day into many days' sojourn with us. The *object* of Loma Vista is to acquaint our friends with the work and life of the Polytechnic Institute. While not a castle, Loma Vista is nevertheless a beautiful home in keeping with ideals of the future college, such as to make even Fifth Avenue residents comfortable, and desirous of helping in the development of our college into *the* "University of the Antilles."

It worked, as the several buildings attest, built as memorials of loved ones whom visitors wished to honor.

Many of the world's great men and women have entered Loma Vista for the night's stay or for a month's rest with us. It was a personal pleasure for Mrs. Harris and me, and a blessing to the college thus to make friends and to deepen the interest of our friends in the work we had undertaken. They were all too many to enumerate here by name. Many you knew, among whom were:

The soft speaking, motherly Mrs. Mina Miller Edison, who never retired at night until her great inventor husband, Thomas A. Edison, had worked out from five to sixty experiments for his laboratory assistants to prove the next day. Mr. and Mrs. Edison always watched the Old Year out and the New Year in. She came to Loma Vista to spend her first vigil alone after Mr. Edison's death on October 18, 1931. She sat on the flat roof of Loma Vista just outside her apartment with a vacant chair by her side that December 31, 1931, in memory of him who lighted up the world's dark and perilous nights for all mankind. She hoped to catch an audible greeting from Mr. Edison. She also believed that the departed in Heaven followed close contact with our life on this earth. Both I know to be established facts, now, in my own life.

Mr. and Mrs. Edward S. Kelley, of Kelley-Springfield Tire fame, came to see us twice.

Missionaries, like Rev. Dr. Waddell of Brazil, who introduced the navel orange to the U.S.A.; the Reverend Dr. John A. Mackay of Peru, now president of Princeton Theological Seminary and also past president of our Board of Foreign Missions; Reverend Dr. S. Guy Inman, specialist in Latin American affairs, who kept us in touch with mission work in Latin America.

United States senators and congressmen, like Senator Hiram Bingham; yes, even Eleanor, the President's wife,[2] popped in on us, for three days' push and rush of investigation into Puerto Rican rural life. She liked it and insisted President Roosevelt spend a night with us.[3] Governors of the Island came with motorcycle policemen leading the way. One time fifty places were set at the banqueting tables in the sala of Loma Vista, for a touring party of prominent people headed by the Governor, led by three motorcycle policemen.

They were all usually sent on their way by a farewell of the 300 singing students led by the band. Dr. Keigwin, that silver-tongued king of the pulpit, recalled frequently the Keigwin and Phraner goodbye at Loma Vista steps.[4]

Roswell Miller, Jr., our New York treasurer, rode Ranger (my Texas horse) up the front steps of Loma Vista onto the balcony, while his wife, Margaret Carnegie Miller (the only daughter of Andrew Carnegie) twirled a lasso in true Texas style, in roping at her bronco buster. They performed well.

Dan E. Waid, chief architect of the Metropolitan Life Insurance Company, who had no time to make our master plan, walked around on the porch of Loma Vista with mouth open in amazement at what his eyes saw and ears heard, saying, "I never thought it was like this." Mrs. Waid immediately gave us new brass instruments for the thirty-piece band.

Mr. E. P. Mitchell, chief editor of the *New York Sun Herald,* often visited us for a week's stay in Loma Vista. President Villard, of the American Railway, placed his private coach at the disposal of Mr. and Mrs. Mitchell for Mr. Mitchell's first visit to us. Other trips were made yearly in his Model T Ford— named by him "Joseph" because it had so many brothers!

On one of these visits, as we walked and talked on the porch of Loma Vista, Mr. Mitchell remarked that he would try his hand at a line or two for the Poly-technic in the *Sun Herald*. I took his suitcase to his car and he left soon for New York. I sailed on the same boat with him. He introduced me to Mrs. Roswell Miller, Sr., and family, fellow passengers on the *Borinquen.*[5]

Two weeks later I was sitting in the reception room of the New York Arts' Club on Gramercy Park, where a friend entertained me for a weekend. Mr. Fleming H. Revell, Sr., a brother-in-law of Dwight L. Moody,[6] and trustee of PIPR and head of Fleming H. Revell Publishing Co., called on me as he was leaving the Club, giving me the Sunday morning edition of the *Sun Herald* containing an editorial by our good friend E. P. Mitchell.

This editorial was a priceless contribution to my school, and at that moment was worth more than money to me. This was a *fruit of Loma Vista* † hospitality, and the beginning of a friendship that deepens with gratitude from my heart as the years go by. Gracias, Amigo Mitchell. For Christmas 1924 Mr. Mitchell sent me a copy of *Memoirs of an Editor,* his autobiography, and on the fly-leaf graciously wrote me his last word:

# The Sun
## AND
# THE NEW YORK HERALD.
### FOUNDED 1833-1835.

NEW YORK, SUNDAY, MARCH 21, 1920.

THE SUN-HERALD CORPORATION,
Publishers, 280 Broadway.
Frank A. Munsey, President.
Ervin Wardman, Vice-president; Wm. T.
Dewart, Vice-president and Treasurer; R.
H. Titherington, Secretary.

### The University of the Antilles.

Perhaps the most significant fact just now in the progress of Porto Rico is the swift and somewhat astonishing development of a great institution for the higher education, both academic and technical, near San German, in the southwestern part of the island. In one of the most beautiful hill surrounded sites which the imagination can conceive—a tropical version of Williamstown, Massachusetts, with a climate that without irreverence may be described as heavenly—there is growing with tropical rapidity the future University of the Antilles, the school at present known as the Polytechnic Institute of Porto Rico. Its destiny is as obvious as its history is amazing. It promises to be for the long future the source of culture and the central seat of the liberal arts not only for Porto Rico but for the other Antillean islands and for a considerable part of Latin Central and South America.

It happens that it was just one year ago to-day that the Legislature of Porto Rico conferred upon the existing school at San German the full university functions. Under the auspices of the Presbyterian Board the school had been opened seven years before with a single student on its rolls.' Under the direction of the Rev. J. W. Harris, a Texan of large vision, indomitable energy and a very remarkable practical faculty for realizing ideals, it has already become a university in the true sense, occupying a campus of one hundred and twenty acres, with an adequate scheme of future physical development already matured by the architects to whose aesthetic perceptions New York owes the Soldiers and Sailors' Monument on Riverside Drive; and it is affording through competent professional teachers a thorough education, both academic and technical, to nearly three hundred students of both sexes. The promise of the institution and the quick recognition of its importance to the future of the Caribbean peoples is shown, perhaps better than in any other way, by the circumstance that nearly four times as many students as are admitted are turned away from San German because of present lack of housing facilities.

The plan of the Polytechnic Institute of Porto Rico, that is to say, the University of the Antilles of the future, contemplates buildings which will accommodate 1,200 boarding students and their teachers, at a cost of $2,000,000, and an endowment of $6,000,000 for the same. Among all the college and university drives now on, and their name is legion and their respective claims are indisputable, none is urged more worthily than this from down amid the royal palms. Certainly none appeals more directly to sympathetic imagination alive to the possibilities of Latin American development, and concerned, for reasons either of philanthropy or of American patriotism, or, again, of enlightened selfishness, that Porto Rico shall have every opportunity which northern good will and generous northern pockets can afford.

To my friend,

Dr. John William Harris, Devoted servant of God and humankind, and the most useful man in the Antilles.

With cordial regards,
*Edward P. Mitchell*

*Loma Vista was designed for this very service: to welcome, instruct, and make people want to have a share in the work.*† Now in 1955 prominent visitors to Puerto Rico have increased to an astounding number—Loma Vista should stand in reception line to all. All invited guests, in fact all prominent people, should be invited and should always be entertained in Loma Vista *in the home of the college president*† where they can be made comfortable and feel at home in the center of campus life. Thus, they will see the campus on all sides, and drink in the college spirit as they hear the gleefully exhilarated students singing, laughing and talking. The visitors will be encouraged to help abundantly when they come to know and feel the student life, and get acquainted with the president and faculty, on the long strolling porch of Loma Vista.

If the trustees of the Polytechnic Institute wish to keep a stream of money flowing through the years into the erection of new buildings, roads, equipment and endowment; if the trustees wish to make it possible to continue to help the richly endowed poor youth into a training for Christian leadership of the Island, then they had better require the president to live in Loma Vista and give him extra money for the entertainment of influential people *in Loma Vista*† in everyday style of family life (not banquets), *not in Costello.*† Casa María is a solitary, restful and comfortable home of Puerto Rican scenery, but not a place for getting strangers into close contact with college life and purpose.

## Loma Vista's Function Illustrated

Loma Vista was the gateway and Mrs. Eunice White Harris held the key that opened the doors to the hearts of guests who came in as invited strangers and left as cooperative friends of Polytechnic during the years I was begging money from people. No, I did not beg a cent, I simply told what we needed to carry on the work of developing Christian character and a sturdy faith in our students of Polytechnic. I wish I had time and space to tell you many such pleasant experiences during the otherwise difficult work of founding and developing a college. Here are some illustrations and results:

The Hon. don Manuel Camuñas was the first prominent native son of Puerto Rico who came in person and investigated the objectives and work being done in the PIPR. We asked him to be the Commencement Speaker for the H. S. Class of 1917.[7] He, with his friend Dr. Miller, mingled with students and teachers for a couple of days. Then he made the most eloquent appeal, in Teatro Sol,[8] on Commencement night for the hearty support of the Polytechnic Institute of Puerto Rico. He was convinced that Polytechnic was striking at the very roots of the solution of Puerto Rico's social and economic problems.

The next night he was the speaker at the A&M College[9] in Mayagüez and gave the same address of an hour's duration, holding up PIPR as the example of the kind of educational training the Island most needed.

When he returned to his offices in San Juan he sent the following report of his impressions of our work to the San Juan daily paper, *La Democracia,* of June 5, 1917:[10]

There is in San Germán a jewel unknown to many outside of that district—a Polytechnic Institute, worthy of note both for the way in which it came into existence and that in which it is working out its high aims. It is situated in the country at the entrance to San Germán.

Agriculture is taught in a scientific and practical way, and the now seventh and eighth primary grades and the four high school grades are taught in accordance with the plans of the Insular Department of Education, as are also the fundamental sciences for an industrial career. The teachers in the sciences are university graduates and the instructor in agriculture is an experienced agriculturist of the Island.

The founder and director of this school, Mr. J. W. Harris, was a minister of the Presbyterian Church in San Germán, and left that work to undertake this educational work with admirable devotion and self-sacrifice. He raised funds in the United States and bought more than one hundred acres of land in San Germán; he found teachers, erected most modest wooden buildings, and thus began in 1912 the instruction of a dozen or so of young men and women, and for which Don Juan Cancio Ortiz, now living in Mayagüez, gave some old school buildings formerly occupied by his secondary school in Lajas.

Mr. Harris has little by little enlarged the sphere of this altruistic work; its fruitful activities have gone on multiplying from day to day until now more than one hundred and forty students of both sexes, the greater part of which live on the campus, are receiving instruction. The wooden buildings have been increased but there have also been erected larger buildings of concrete for dormitories, one for each sex, with spacious, well-ventilated rooms, which the students are now occupying, although neither of the buildings is yet completed because of the lack of sufficient funds and the high cost of materials.

Mr. Harris has a large and comprehensive plan in which all the edifices necessary for the completion of the work have a place, such as classroom buildings, dormitories, laboratories, workshop, domestic science hall, and homes for teachers—in a word, to cover all the needs of the great educational plant. He goes on building little by little as the resources at his disposal will permit.

It must be taken into account that seventy per cent of the students are poor boys and girls who can pay nothing, while the tuition even of those who pay something is very moderate. The Institute is helped somewhat by the products of the farm.

It is most wonderful! The students work with their own hands, plows and hoes, cultivating the land under the direction of the teacher of agriculture. They themselves have graded and paved the macadam road opening up the grounds from the main government highway to the school. They themselves have done the work on the buildings so far constructed, taking part in the construction of concrete blocks and in the work of carpenters, masons and painters, under the direction of the teacher and director of labor, Mr. Clarence Harris.

All this has been accomplished by the great willpower of this extraordinary man, and Mr. Harris will no doubt succeed in carrying out his splendid project. "Where will you get the money for the carrying out of your ideal?" I asked him. "Oh," he answered, with all the faith of a believer, "I will hunt for it."

The Commissioner of Education, Dr. Paul G. Miller, who accompanied me, left highly impressed with that work. Public men ought to seek an opportunity of knowing that superior man and that most interesting school. The young people of both sexes who live there study joyfully in an atmosphere of delightful happiness.

*Manuel Camuñas*
Commissioner of Agriculture

# Chapter 13

## *The New Charter and By-Laws of 1920*

CERTIFICATE OF INCORPORATION AND BY-LAWS

OF POLYTECHNIC INSTITUTE OF PORTO RICO

"We, the undersigned, citizens of the United States, of full age, namely, Francisco P. Quiñones, Charles F. Darlington, A. Edwin Keigwin, Roswell Miller, Fleming H. Revell, John William Harris, Mary R. Tooker, James H. Post, John A. Marquis, Henry S. Coffin, Francis S. Phraner and John E. Berwind, desirous of associating ourselves for the purpose of establishing an institution of learning, as herein provided, under and pursuant to the provisions of Sub-Chapter I, Chapter XVIII of the Code of Law for the District of Columbia,[1] hereby certify, as follows:

FIRST: The name or title by which such institution hereby incorporated (hereinafter referred to as the Institution) shall be known in law is "Polytechnic Institute of Porto Rico."

SECOND: The management of the Institution and the management and disposition of its property and affairs shall be vested in fifteen trustees (subject to enlargement or diminution of their number as hereinafter provided), who shall constitute its Board of Trustees. The names of those who shall constitute its first Board of Trustees are as follows:

(1) The following who shall hold office until the third Tuesday of April, 1921, or until their successors are elected as hereinafter provided, namely: John A. Marquis, Henry Sloan Coffin, Charles F. Darlington, John W. Harris and William E. Carnochan.

(2) The following who shall hold office until the third Tuesday of April, 1922, or until their successors are so elected, namely: Wilton Merle Smith, Fleming H. Revell, William Albert Harbison, Mary R. Tooker and Francisco P. Quiñones.

(3) The following who shall hold office until the third Tuesday of April, 1923, or until successors are so elected, namely: A. Edwin Keigwin, Francis S. Phraner, James H. Post, John E. Berwind and Roswell Miller.

With the exception of those above named for the terms above named respectively, the Trustees of the Institution (including successors to those above named, upon the expiration of their respective terms of office or upon their ceasing to be trustees by reason of death, resignation or otherwise) shall be elected from time to time by the Board of Home Missions of the Presbyterian Church in the United States of America for such terms as said Board of Home Missions may determine. The number of the trustees of the Institution may be increased or diminished at any time and from time to time by said Board of Home Missions, and in case of an increase the additional trustees shall be elected by said Board of Home Missions. Said Board of Trustees of the Institution may adopt and from time to time alter By-Laws, which, subject to the provisions herein contained, may prescribe the number of trustees necessary to constitute a quorum, which number may be less than a majority of the whole number, but not less than three; and, for convenience of administration, may provide for the delegation by any of the trustees of his powers to another trustee, who at any meeting may represent and vote and act for the delegating trustee within the terms of the authority given to him by the latter, with like force and in all respects the same as if such delegating trustee were personally present, and may provide also for the place or places for holding meetings, which may be held in Porto Rico, Washington, D.C., New York City, N.Y., or any other place in the United States of America. Subject to the provisions herein contained such By-Laws may contain any and all further provisions which may be proper and suitable and which the trustees may prescribe for the administration of the Institution, the management, regulation and control of its affairs and property, the election of its officers, and other matters pertaining to the accomplishment of its objects.

THIRD: The objects for which said Institution is organized are to maintain and perpetuate the institution now known as "Polytechnic Institute of Porto Rico," to carry on and advance the work in Porto Rico which it has heretofore carried on there; to develop youth of both sexes mentally, morally and physically through regularly accepted studies in liberal and practical arts and sciences, the study of the Bible, which shall be used as a textbook in the work of all its students, and the performance of manual labor by students domiciled at the Institution, thus to produce well-rounded character, resourceful, independent and of sturdy Christian faith; and to that end to receive and make use of such funds as may be given to it by will or otherwise or as may be turned over to it by said Board of Home Missions or other body at any time and from time to time, and upon such terms and conditions, consistent with the provisions hereof, as may be imposed by said Board or other body in connection with such receipt and use of said funds, and to make the resources and organization of the Institution available to said Board or other body for the purpose of accomplishing the objects, or any of the objects, herein expressed; to confer upon such persons as may be considered worthy such academic, technical and honorary degrees as are usually conferred by similar institutions, and subject to the provisions herein contained, to do and perform all things necessary, proper, suitable or convenient for the maintenance, support, administration and advancement of said Institution or incidental thereto. Said Institution shall be evangelical in principle, adhering to the Scriptures of the Old and New Testaments as the main foundation of its life and ideals. Its teaching shall always be in accord with that of the evangelical churches concerning the fatherhood and sovereignty of God, the deity and atonement of Jesus Christ, the person and work of the Holy Spirit and the Bible as an authoritative revelation from God stressing the fundamentals that unite Christians and not teaching sectarian or controversial views.

FOURTH: The Institution is to have forthwith departments of elementary, secondary and higher academic instruction; and, as its resources increase, it is to be of the rank of a college or university. The particular branches proposed to be taught are those usually offered in the Liberal Arts and Scientific Courses of the best Colleges and Secondary Schools in the United States of America, among them the following, namely: English Language and Literature, Ancient and Modern Languages and their Literatures, History, Pure and Applied Mathematics, the Physical Sciences, the Social Sciences, the Holy Bible, Philosophy, Psychology and Ethics, Education and Teacher Training, the Fine Arts, Oratory, Physical Culture and Hygiene, Stenography, Book-keeping and Business Training, Agriculture and Engineering. Professorships corresponding in number and designation to the branches above enumerated are to be established and also, in course of time as the resources of the Institution increase, additional professorships in Theology, Law and Medicine and the usual courses offered in graduate and technical schools.

FIFTH: The Institution, subject to said Sub-Chapter, shall have power to accept and hold real and personal property given, devised or bequeathed to it by will or otherwise in any way given or turned over to it regardless of the amount thereof, provided, however, that, except in cases where the terms of the gift, devise or bequest otherwise expressly prescribe, all of the funds and property of the Institution of every kind shall, in case of its dissolution, or in case or so far, if at all, as they shall cease to be used for purposes and objects herein set forth, become and be the property of, and vest in, the Board of Home Missions of the Presbyterian Church of the United States of America, to be used and administrated by said Board of Home Missions for the furtherance of its educational work in Porto Rico, preference to be given, however in such use and administration thereof, to the work of educating students of Porto Rican birth and parentage, but subject, in the case of special trust funds, to the trusts in respect thereof.

IN TESTIMONY WHEREOF we have hereto set our hands and affixed our seals, this 4th day of May, 1920.

*Francisco P. Quiñones* (L.S.)
*Charles F. Darlington* (L.S.)
*A. Edwin Keigwin* (L.S.)
*Roswell Miller* (L.S.)
*Fleming H. Revell* (L.S.)
*John William Harris* (L.S.)
*Mary R. Tooker* (L.S.)
*James H. Post* (L.S.)
*John A. Marquis* (L.S.)
*Henry S. Coffin* (L.S.)
*John E. Berwind* (L.S.)
*Francis S. Phraner* (L.S.)

Office of Register of Deeds,
District of Columbia

This is to certify that the foregoing is a true and verified copy of the Certificate of Incorporation of the "Polytechnic Institute of Porto Rico" and of the whole of said

Certificate of Incorporation, as filed in this office the 6th day of May, A. D. 1920.

In Testimony whereof, I have hereunto set my hand and affixed the seal of this office this 6th day of May, A. D. 1920.

*R. W. Dutton*

Deputy Recorder of Deeds, D. C.

(Seal)

## BY-LAWS POLYTECHNIC INSTITUTE OF PORTO RICO

### ARTICLE I

### *Seal*

The corporate seal of the Institute unless and until changed by the Board of Trustees shall in general consist of a circular disc upon the outer edge of which shall be the words "Polytechnic Institute of Porto Rico."

### ARTICLE II

### *Meetings*

1. There shall be an annual meeting of the Board of Trustees in the City of New York on the second Thursday of April in each year at 156 Fifth Avenue, at three o'clock in the afternoon, unless the President of the Board shall designate a different hour and place for the meeting, and in that case it shall be held at the place and hour designated. It shall be the duty of the Secretary to give by mail to each trustee two weeks' written notice of such meeting.

2. The President shall have power to call a special meeting of the Board whenever deemed necessary and must call such meeting upon request of three members. When such a meeting is so called a notice of two weeks in advance shall be sent to each member, stating the objects for which it is called, and the time and place at which it will be held.

### ARTICLE III

### *Quorum*

Seven Members of the Board of Trustees shall constitute a quorum for the transaction of business; and at any meeting at which as many as five trustees are present in person, and of which and the purposes for which it is called, written notice of as many as fourteen days has been given to each trustee, trustees not personally present may be represented by a trustee or trustees personally present at the meeting to whom the absent trustee or trustees may have delegated their power by a written proxy; and such absent trustee or trustees having given and being represented at the meeting by such a proxy, shall be counted as present and as part of the number required for a quorum, and, through the trustee or trustees so personally present holding such proxy or proxies, may vote and act with like effect and in all respects the same as if present in person within the authority conferred by the proxy.

## ARTICLE IV

### *Officers*

The officers of the Board of Trustees shall consist of a President, a Vice-President, a Secretary and a Treasurer and such other officers as the Board may from time to time designate. The officers of the Board shall be elected at the annual meeting to hold office for one year or until their successors are chosen.

## ARTICLE V

### *Committees*

There shall be the following standing committees elected by the Board at each annual meeting:

1. Executive Committee which shall consist of seven members of whom the President of the Board shall be Chairman and shall exercise such powers and transact such business as the Board may assign to it.

2. Finance Committee which shall consist of seven persons whose duties shall be to devise ways and means for promoting the financial interest of the institution and to recommend to the Board from time to time such financial policies as may seem best for strengthening and developing it.

3. Faculty and Curriculum Committee which shall consist of three or more members whose duty it shall be to cooperate with the President of the Institute in developing the needed courses and securing qualified teachers.

There shall also be appointed by the President of the Board of Trustees:

1. A Library, Museum and Auxiliary Committee of seven members to be chosen from the Board or the Ladies Auxiliary, or both, whose duties shall be as their name suggests.

2. A Nominating Committee which shall prepare a complete list of nominations for all offices and standing committees for the annual meeting of the Board; but this does not exclude nominations from the floor.

The President shall appoint other Special Committees as the needs of the Institute may demand. The duties and powers of such Special Committees shall be fixed at their creation.

## ARTICLE VI

### *The Management of the Institute*

The Board shall elect the President of the Institute. An affirmative vote of at least two-thirds of those present at that meeting, either in person or by proxy, shall be necessary for a choice. The President of the Institute shall employ and dismiss, subject to the approval of the Faculty Committee, anyone connected with the Institute in Porto Rico, and shall be held responsible for the proper conduct of the Institute.

## ARTICLE VII
### *Amendments*

These By-Laws or any of them may be altered, amended, added to, or repealed at any annual meeting of the Board, or at any other meeting of the Board, provided notice of the proposed alteration, amendment, addition or repeal shall have been given in the notice calling the meeting at which action is to be taken, but no such notice shall be required for the temporary suspension of a By-Law.

What a set-up! . . . in Objectives and Personnel for an eight-year-old Elementary and High School breathing in the air of the *"future University of the Antilles"* as we were later christened by E. P. Mitchell, editor of the *New York Sun Herald*. Of this number of original trustees, God has crowned all but Roswell Miller II and J. Will Harris.

May God deal gently and give unfaltering convictions to those who shall, through the centuries, take their places as trustees of Polytechnic Institute of Porto Rico under God for a greater, bigger and better college of evangelical Christian service to mankind.

As individuals and as a united group, there never was a more loyal, faithful and interested Board of Trustees with the insight and vision of an Isaiah, who upheld me with their prayers and council and financial support, who opened their homes to me as well as their hearts, and to whom I am, with my college, eternally indebted.

Their names should be engraved on a bronze tablet and later, when the Library and Administration Hall are erected, that tablet should be placed in the reception room of same, and also impressed upon the hearts of trustees, presidents, faculty, and students, as they were: trustees of vision and reality in the days when the Polytechnic was only a *dream* to most people.

> Give me men to match my mountains,
> Give me men to match my plains;
> Men with empires in their purpose,
> Men with eras in their brains.

This I found true in my Board of Trustees, whom I personally selected, organized and had incorporated the 6th day of May A. D. 1920.

I

The Charter states that meetings of the Board of Trustees "may be held in Puerto Rico, Washington, D.C., New York City or any other place in the U.S.A."

The By-Laws state that the annual meeting is to be held "in the city of New York on the second Thursday of April in each year at 156 Fifth Ave., at three o'clock in the afternoon unless the president of the board shall designate a different hour and place."

I composed this Charter of 1920 and By-Laws; were I to write them to-day,* thirty-five years later, I would state in the By-Laws, Article II, that the annual meeting of the Board of Trustees is to be held in the Polytechnic Institute on the date to be decided upon by the Puerto Rican resident trustees; and that the meeting shall continue for two days in order to acquaint trustees with the actual life and work of the Institution before any business is transacted or approval given to proposed budget and program of the Institution.

II

Further, I would today change Article V, Section 2: The Finance Committee shall consist of seven persons, "five of whom to be members of the Board of Trustees—all to be residents in or near New York City, whose duties shall be etc., etc.

These two changes I now present were considered by Dr. Marquis and Dr. Coffin, my counsellors in the drawing up of the Articles of Incorporation and By-Laws. Dr. Marquis suggested that we wait till the institution became of age, when such would be necessary. At that time the institution was young, and too far from New York for members of the Board of Trustees to attend annual meetings, and there were few Puerto Ricans qualified who would be willing at that stage to assume responsibility.

Puerto Rico is now of age. Deep down in the heart of every Puerto Rican is the desire and urge to assume the responsibility and direction of everything that lifts the people of Puerto Rico into their own highest field of service for the welfare of man and the glory of God.

III

Ten years ago Puerto Ricans were allowed to choose their own political freedom.[2] They voted overwhelmingly for their Commonwealth within the U.S.A. in which they have [as] complete freedom as any State in the Union, plus many

* Date of writing is 1955.

exceptional advantages. Everything has been placed in the hands of Puerto Ricans with no further U.S.A. supervision or control of their political freedom as citizens of the U.S.A.[3]

An editorial in *Life,* March 15, 1954. . . . "Thank Heaven for Puerto Rico" and the Report of Chase National Bank [4] states that Puerto Rico's increase in living standards during 1942-1952 *"Tops That Recorded Anywhere in the World for the Decade."*

*Puerto Rico Is Now of Age.*† I hope now to see Polytechnic Institute of Puerto Rico directed with a Board of Trustees all residents of Puerto Rico, except the members of the Finance Committee which will be residents of U.S.A.

The announcement by the Board of Trustees that these changes are approved will cause rejoicing and encourage every graduate and ex-student of PIPR, who will become alive and achieve, under God, marvelous physical, spiritual, economic life in PIPR in the education of the Head, the Heart and the Hand of all.

## Don Francisco P. Quiñones

I chose don Paco (Francisco P. Quiñones) as one of the charter members of the Board of Trustees. Don Paco lived on his sugarcane plantation at Filial Amor, near the PIPR. His library was large and was what attracted me to him. He moved his residence to New York and became the first native son of Puerto Rico to become a trustee of PIPR.

On May 10, 1920, he wrote the following to *El Tiempo,* San Juan:

On Tuesday May 5, 1920, the Rev. John William Harris organized the Board of Trustees of PIPR which was incorporated duly in Washington, D.C. He has overcome innumerable difficulties through the strength and energy of his character. He has erected in San Germán a school beginning with boys and girls, now men and women, who are now showing the Island the value of their training in PIPR.

Mr. Harris has taken the second step in the permanent establishment of his school by organizing and incorporating the Board of Trustees for his school. I have been given the honor of becoming one of the incorporators as trustee. We held our first session today.

As you understand, the members of this Board are men of vast experience and practical knowledge—such men as John E. Berwind and James H. Post, whom Puerto Ricans recognize as financial leaders.

Of course I was asked about the attitude of Puerto Ricans toward the U.S.A. There have been certain doctrines advocated by a few who do damage to the advancement of the Island.

What Mr. Harris is offering to Puerto Rico is of first importance and we should cooperate with him with all our energy and good will, uniting our shoulders with those of Mr. Harris in his work of helping our youth of both sexes through the knowledge and habits there acquired, that they may be an honor to their Patria and to the students as well.

Let us lay aside our differences, be they political, religious or what not, in order to cooperate with this great man in the formation of future generations for Puerto Rico.

I thank you, Sr. Editor
Su atto. amigo y SS. SS.[5]
*Francisco P. Quiñones*

# Chapter 14

## *Fund-Raising*

## Historical Letters[1]

THE FOLLOWING LETTERS printed over the years on a single sheet—sometimes postal card size with a statement of our needs on the reverse side—were mailed to wealthy individuals able to give financially and to interested friends always glad to pray for us as step by step we moved upward and onward toward our goal. This is the way we prepared people for helping in the development of our school.

Most of these copied here were written in the first years of the Polytechnic life and give an inner history of objectives. A constant stream was mailed out. These first ones may be of more permanent value than the later ones as an insight into early historical growth of our college and are here reproduced.

Each letter carried this heading.

### THE INSTITUTE
### *An Occasional Letter to Friends of*
### *The* POLYTECHNIC INSTITUTE OF PORTO RICO *Inc.*

On the reverse side of each of The Institute letters, something like this always appeared:

### *Our Immediate Necessities Are*

| | |
|---|---|
| Three homes for teachers, | Laundry, |
| Residence Hall for one hundred girls, | Woodworking Shops, |
| Residence Hall for one hundred boys, | Waterworks, |
| Dining Hall, Kitchen and Bakery, | $15,000.00 for purchase of adjoining properties. |

The above needs are so urgent that it is impossible to say which we ought to have first. The teachers' homes must be erected before September 1921, if we are to keep efficient teachers.

[ *106* ]

*1912*

| | |
|---|---|
| *Our Field* | Latin America. Nineteen Republics and Porto Rico. Population 60,000,000. |
| *Our Purpose* | To help these nations out of spiritual darkness into the Gospel light and out of material idleness into the industrious march of the Twentieth Century, by a thoro Christian training in the practical arts, sciences, Bible and a liberal education. |
| *Our Plans* | To give every student who will work for it a full course in his chosen lifework, and to send out men and women to impart their knowledge and vision to their fellowmen, to uphold right and to establish justice. |
| *Our Means* | This is a purely charitable institution and we depend on the Lord's stewards for our money, on you. This is an institution being built up by students and we depend entirely on student labour for our work. Every dollar given to this work helps to provide work by which the students support themselves. |
| *Our Location* | Porto Rico is the most easterly of the larger Antilles, and taking the Polytechnic Institute of Porto Rico as centre, a semicircle marked by a radius of 1200 miles from northwest south will reach twelve of these nations representing 48,000,000 people. We have all the privileges and blessings of American citizens and most moderate tropical climate. |

For further information address,

Rev. John William Harris, President,

Box 66, San Germán, Porto Rico.

*1912*

This school proposes to place in reach of every boy and girl of the Island a thoro education. Young people go to the States to study. Where one goes to the States, a hundred are forced to stay in Porto Rico for lack of means.

The Institute has a self-help department in which a limited number of students may work and acquire an education. This department must be enlarged to accommodate all earnest, worthy young people, who have no means, yet are willing to work to gain an education.

All students work. Those who have no money work $4\frac{1}{2}$ hours per day.

Others who pay $4.00 per month, work 3 hours per day.

Those who pay $8.00 per month, work 2 hours per day.

Those who pay $10.00 per month, work $1\frac{1}{2}$ hours per day.

Those who pay $12.00 per month, work 1 hour per day.

Work is honorable and all boarding students must spend part of every day in some service, principally tilling the ground. "A good hard day's work will put feathers in any old bed."

There is a threefold reason for the work department in Porto Rican schools. First, the students must learn that the man who toils is an honorable man because he is doing an honorable service. All honorable service should be done by honorable men. The man who follows the plow or swings the hammer is doing an honorable service and is insofar an honorable man. Which conclusion is never reached by the present youth of Porto Rico. Secondly, most youth have no means other than their own physical strength of acquiring an education. These must be given a chance for they are going to be the governors, the law-makers, the preachers, the producers of industrial and spiritual forces of the Island. Thirdly, hard, faithful work develops character, the kind of character that stands like an oak in the storms, struggling on for righteousness and truth, and prosperity. They are not waiting a chariot, but they would like to have a passageway through the forest of ignorance in which their lot is cast.

THE WHITE HOUSE, WASHINGTON

February 18, 1913

My dear Mr. Harris:

I have been much interested to learn of your efforts to establish a Polytechnic Institute in Porto Rico, and I congratulate you on thus adding to the existing educational advantages of the Porto Rican youth.

Sincerely yours,
/s/ *Wm. H. Taft*

Wars, rebellions and general discontent will continue in Latin America until the right kind of men are found to direct the industrial, civic and religious life of these tropical lands. This direction *can never be permanently done from without. The people themselves must be trained to do it.*† This will take time.

Not many are fit for the leadership of men, in anything but war, without a Christian education. The education of the youth is the surest and most economical way to get results. If we are really praying for the peace, prosperity and purity of tropical America, let us then give these youth an opportunity for a Christian education. Money generously invested in a wise program of Christian education of the youth of these lands would build up nations and insure them to the Kingdom of God.

The Polytechnic Institute of Porto Rico aims to fit youth, familiar with the conditions of life here, for a consecrated service in the industrial, civic and religious life to the end that Christian principles may be cherished and strengthened till righteousness and honesty become the motive in life. It can be done. And will be done.

November 4, 1930

It was my desire, when founding this institution, to give to the educational work of Porto Rico new ideals and improved methods leading to a maximum utility, something concrete to be copied and incorporated into the public schools. For eighteen years I have talked and urged the necessity of combining with the regular public school course an extensive and intensive industrial training. Three years ago, my friend, Hon. J. B. Huyke, then Commissioner of Education for Porto Rico, opened the first public school which combined work and study, and called it a Second Unit.[2] Today Governor Roosevelt[3] and Commissioner of Education Dr. Padín, are extending the idea as fast as time and means permit. I was in part paid for my years of service in reading in *El Mundo* of November 1 the following statement made by Ex-Commissioner of Education Hon. J. B. Huyke:

> It is impossible to deny the Polytechnic Institute the glory of having been the first institution that gave the greatest emphasis to manual labor, introducing it even in the college courses. "Work and study" was its motto. *From it we copied. From it other systems* † which try to give to the educational work its maximum of utility, *shall copy.*† Commissioner Padín has taken great interest in the work of the Second Units, where manual labor and study receive equal attention. The idea is being carried out. It is an act of justice to acknowledge Dr. Harris's vision. He has been the most energetic and enthusiastic pioneer.

Our graduates are helping in these Second Units. I will write you next week of their work in one of these schools.

## Fund-Raising Campaign for $500,000

I proposed in 1921 to the newly organized Board of Trustees the securing of $500,000 for buildings and endowment. The members of the Board had been selected by me from those who had encouraged me and were able to help me develop my school into a college which could boast as yet only a high school standing with one year of college.[4] They heartily approved the $500,000 drive for funds. I, of course, had to raise it with their blessing.

Application was made to the Carnegie Corporation for a grant of $250,000 on condition that we raise a like sum. Dr. William S. Learned of the Carnegie Foundation for the Advancement of Teaching was sent down to Puerto Rico to make a study of the educational work of Puerto Rico. He is not only an educator but a Christian statesman. Mrs. Harris in her forthcoming book, *The Steps,*[5] quotes Dr. Learned's full report on the Polytechnic to the Carnegie Corporation of January 3-7, 1923. I wish to quote just a sentence or two from that juicy report: "It is the only private institution with a logical and comprehensive plan for thorough education. *Its religious feature is strongly emphasized but is not overdone, and generates a school atmosphere that is wholesome and invigorating.*† The industrial aspect of the school is both of great benefit to the Porto Rican youth and makes it possible to provide for large numbers of poor students. The founder of the school has visions of a future . . . If they materialize, the Institute is destined to perform a significant international service." Our sincere thanks to Dr. Learned!

Later Dr. Henry S. Pritchett, President of the Carnegie Corporation, made a report to the corporation in December, 1923:

## Polytechnic Institute of Porto Rico

The people of the United States are absorbed in their domestic problems. They give *little* thought to their obligations toward the peoples who have been brought under the government of the Union through the treaty with Spain in 1898.

If there is any one of these problems that should appeal directly to the conscience of our people, it is that of education in Porto Rico. This fertile, densely populated Island is destined, both geographically and by reason of its relations to other Spanish-speaking nations of the Caribbean, to play an important role as an outpost of the United States and as an instrument in the development of the islands of the Caribbean and of the nations of Central America.

During the past year the Corporation caused an examination to be made of the present educational situation on the Island. This examination showed that, outside of the governmental activities with respect to education, the Polytechnic Institute, founded in 1912 at San Germán, Porto Rico, has had a notable development and is offering a form of technical training greatly needed by the people of Porto Rico. Beginning with an enrollment of twelve students, it teaches now a body of 375 boys and girls drawn from Porto Rico, Santo Domingo and the Virgin Islands. It has established itself as the only private institution on the Island with a logical and comprehensive plan for a thorough education. The academic work of the Institute begins where the rural schools end, approximately at the fifth grade of our public school work, and continues through the second collegiate year. The teaching is of good character, though greatly handicapped by the lack of suitable equipment. The high school department particularly gives a sound training under good teachers and admits by certificate to American colleges.

Partly with the object of training the Porto Rican in manual pursuits and partly in order to maintain and develop the school as cheaply as possible, the industrial feature of education plays a large part. Three hours of each student's day are devoted to profitable and varied labor under good supervision. In this manner over fifty percent of the labor cost of new construction is met without direct payment of service. The attitude of the general public in Porto Rico toward the method and program of the school has been transformed from one of indifference or distrust to confidence and support.

The Institute is controlled by a board of trustees who reside in the United States. They are chosen by the Board of Home Missions of the Presbyterian Church. The school is supported wholly by student fees and voluntary contributions.

With its present physical equipment, the school cannot accommodate half of the students who seek admission, and those who are admitted work under great disadvantages through the lack of suitable libraries, laboratories and housing facilities. In order to provide for these needs, the trustees of the school have entered upon a three-year program which involves the raising of the $500,000, to be used partly for buildings and partly for endowment.

The trustees of the Corporation, at their meeting in April 1923, voted to appropriate to the uses of the Polytechnic Institute of Porto Rico a sum not to exceed $250,000, over a period of three years, to be used in the erection of necessary buildings and in endowment, provided that for each payment by the Corporation an equal amount shall have been secured by the Polytechnic Institute from other sources toward the three-year program as projected by the Institute, and provided further that at least one-half of the total amount paid by the Corporation and secured from other sources by the Institute shall be set aside as permanent endowment.

The expenditure of income from the endowment of the Carnegie Corporation is, by the terms of the trust, restricted to the United States, with the exception of a portion of the income that may be spent in the British Colonies. The grant just noted is the first expenditure which the Corporation has made in any part of the United States outside of its continental area. *It is the hope of the trustees that a genuine interest in the educational progress of Porto Rico may grow up on the part of the citizens on the mainland of the United States.*† In such a process of education lies our great hope, not only for the happiness and well-being of the people of this wonderful Island, but also for that sound understanding of our institutions which will make their inhabitants Americans in the sense of intelligent and devoted citizenship.[6]

The campaign was on. We were given three years from April 1923 in which to raise our portion. Every time we secured $25,000, Mr. Roswell Miller, Jr., our treasurer, reported same to Dr. Pritchett, who in turn deposited a like sum from the Carnegie Corporation to our credit. That was Mr. Carnegie's method of making every dollar produce another dollar. It is a fine method for all concerned. It added to his gift by doubling it. It made the recipient appreciate every dollar received. It aroused interest of others in the proposed work. It doubtless has led others of large means to require similar conditions along with large gifts. By January 10, 1925, we had raised $260,000. The two largest gifts to this amount were made by Mrs. Caroline Stone Phraner: $60,000 for Phraner Hall; and the Gillespie Costello families, through the efforts of Reverend Dr. James P. Gillespie, three homes for teachers: $50,000 for Goodyear, Atwater, Gillespie, and Costello, our guest hall.

# A Dinner of Thanksgiving at 9 East 90, Mr. and Mrs. Miller's Home

When we had gone over the top, Mrs. Margaret Carnegie Miller invited her mother, Mrs. Andrew Carnegie, over to 9 East 90 Street for an impromptu dinner and thanksgiving in celebration of our triumph. The centerpiece on the dining-room table was a large hand-painted gold dollar mark on a green background, dated above "January 10, 1925." On the right side of this sign was $500,000. Below the sign were two words, "The End," the artistic and clever idea of Mrs. Carnegie Miller for a welcome victory.

Nothing in my life brought such financial gratitude and rejoicing to my heart as this "The End," except it be that last $300 in payment for the 100 acre site for my college in January 1912. I cannot recall the menu of that thanksgiving family dinner celebration of victory on January 10, 1925. I cannot forget the family there assembled to give thanks that night at 9 East 90 Street, New York City. Dede, the oldest child, though only half past four in years, joined us in our rejoicing dinner. The radiant smiles of our hostess, Mrs. Roswell Miller; the-I-told-you-we-could-do-it cocksureness of Mr. Roswell Miller, our treasurer; the beaming satisfaction in the face of Mrs. Carnegie; the angelic voice of Dede as we rejoiced around "The End" as a united family in which I was allowed to share was an experience I shall ever cherish. It was the celebration of an achievement, a realization of a goal, won by prayer and persevering efforts, a *"Thank you, God, for everything."* My gratitude is now deepened by memories. Memories of the oldest and youngest who sat around that family table; of Mrs. Carnegie and Dede, whose vacant chairs remind me of their sunshine and readiness to enter into the joys and hopes of others, the one whose fourscore years was ever a benediction to all fortunate enough to have known her, the other for a short time like an ever increasing brilliancy of a meteor stopt suddenly in its path. They left something more than material things in their spiritual victories in Skibo Castle, Scotland. A meditation by Edgar A. Guest comes to me now in those beautiful lines of:

## Out of This Life

Out of this life I shall never take
Things of silver and gold I make.

All that I cherish and hoard away
After I leave on the earth must stay.

Though I have toiled for a painting rare
To hang on my wall, I must leave it there.

Though I call it mine and boast its worth
I must give it up when I quit the earth.

All that I gather and all that I keep
I must leave behind when I fall asleep.

And I wonder often what I shall own
In that other life when I pass alone.

What shall they find and what shall they see
In the soul that answers the call for me?

Shall the great Judge learn, when my task is through
That my spirit had gathered some riches, too?

Or, shall at the last, it be mine to find
That all that I had worked for I'd left behind?

Mr. and Mrs. Carnegie held what God had allowed them to accumulate as trust funds. The way they employed their possessions marches on down the pathway of life enriching and encouraging the poor to make the most out of life, and also the rich to give their wealth wisely for the uplift and development of mankind. This thought and love for others has now extended around the world. A wealthy Chinese, out of his appreciation of what Christ has done through missionaries and Christian workers for China, gave a million dollars to the Presbyterian Foreign Mission Board to provide, in America, homes for retired mission workers from China, and another million for a similar service to retired Chinese workers in China. Even here in Texas, where I am now writing this, foundations of millions of dollars are yearly increasing in number for the advancement of humanity on earth. Such was not true when Mr. Carnegie set forth his revolutionary idea of the use of money, and how to perpetuate it in service for man and God.

And now appears in a recent number of the *New York Times Magazine* the cheering words of Arnold J. Toynbee, the historian. Like the prophetic vision of Isaiah quoted by the Master in Luke 4:18,[7] Toynbee announces what Edison often discussed with his friend Henry Ford. I quote: "Can we guess what the outstanding feature of our twentieth century will appear to be in the perspective of 300 years? My own guess is that our age will be remembered chiefly neither for its horrifying crimes nor for its astonishing inventions, but for its having been the first age since the dawn of civilization, some five or six thousand years back, in which people dared to think it practicable to make the *ideal of welfare for all*† a practical objective instead of a mere utopian dream."

The offer from the Carnegie Corporation of dollar for every dollar I could raise, brought hearty response from Christian people. It was a *Godsend*† to us. Institutions are like children . . . their necessary needs are demanding; beyond a supply of necessary needs, money perverts the integrity and fidelity of ennobling *objectives*.† I thank the Carnegie family, the Corporation and the Foundation for their support of my college during the years.

**FOUR HUNDRED
PARK AVENUE**

*Mrs John S. Kennedy encloses her cheque of $1000. 00 to Dr Harris for the Polytechnic Institute at Porto Rico in response to the appeal made by her friend Mr. Carnegie*

*Dec. 14ᵗʰ 1924*

EDITOR'S NOTE: *This letter is a facsimile that Dr. Harris included in his manuscript. Since it was a social custom at the time of the letter to use the third person in all but the most informal correspondence, it is not known whether this note was written by Mrs. Kennedy herself or by a social secretary.*

## The Giver and Her Gift

The most gracious Giver and Gift during the $100,000 campaign in Puerto Rico for the Polytechnic was doña Antonia Díaz, widow of our friend and neighbor don Ulises López. Her home was just across the street[8] in a big Spanish-style house with banisters across the front porch. With one elbow and hand on the top of the balcony rail doña Antonia's face beamed with a high look of joy as she stood beckoning me to come over.

The entrance to her house was a small door in the large heavy wood portón by the side of the house leading through the patio of gorgeous colored shrubs and fragrant flowers to the main door of the house. Doña Antonia asked me to have a seat by a table on which she placed a canvas pouch. She put her hand into the pouch and brought out a handful of polished shining silver dollars, piling them in ten dollar stacks, as she counted 10, 20, 30, . . . 500 silver dollars! She put the fifty stacks back into the pouch and handed it to me, saying in her low, cultured voice: "Lo siento que es tan poco. ¡Ojalá que fuere mil veces más! ¡Que Dios bendiga su magna obra en bien de nuestra juventud!"* I stood up to leave. She walked with me to the door. Putting her arms around my neck, she kissed me on each cheek as only an appreciating, understanding mother knows how.

> Yea, this in her was the peculiar grace,
> That before living she learned how to live.

* I'm sorry it's so little. Would that it were a thousand times more! May God bless your great work for the good of our youth!"

# Chapter 15

## *The First College Class, 1927*

DURING THE REMAINING YEARS from 1923 to 1937, our construction work was continuously carried on. The newly-equipped carpenter shop with its $20,000 machinery turned out doors, windows and mahogany furniture for all the buildings. This was done by students under the direction of don Antonio Padilla with Popo as an assistant. Our college enrollment increased year after year till we had sufficient students for a full four-year academic course in liberal arts.

In June 1927 [twelve] young men and eleven young ladies had completed the required course for the standard A.B. degree, which the Puerto Rican Legislature had in 1919 authorized the Polytechnic to grant.

Academically, this was the greatest event in the history of the Polytechnic. At the same time (1927), the elementary school was discontinued. If my memory now serves me right, all financial obligations pending by any member of that first graduating class were cancelled in celebration of the event and in appreciation of the fidelity of the members of the class.

The first Baccalaureate Sermon [was] delivered on the Sunday morning (June 24, 1927) of Commencement Week by the President of the College, Dr. John William Harris.

*Text:* Joshua 1:11 "You are to pass over this Jordan, to go in to possess the land, which Jehovah your God giveth you to possess."

### *The Land of Promise*

The school days of Israel had ended. They had been under the direction of Moses forty years. They had left Egypt a bunch of slaves. Now they are a trained people. In their school with Moses they had learned the necessity of obedience, the value of humility, the reward of intelligent service, the power of unity and the wisdom of honoring, worshiping and believing the true God.

Instructed in the law, disciplined in obedience, industrious in service with a conscious realization of God's presence, prepared them for their land of promise. In the text of today they stand on the banks of the Jordan and Joshua says, "You are to pass over this Jordan, to go in to possess the land which Jehovah, your God, giveth you to possess."

**1927 Graduating Class**

*Bottom row, left to right:* Rosa Casiano, Carola Borreli, Mrs. Harris (Dean of Women), John William Harris, president and founder of the college, Professor Carmelo Mendoza (Class Sponsor), Lucy Frank, Laura Irizarry, Mario Milán.
*Second row, left to right:* Amanda Marty, Trinidad Acarón, Carmen Rosa Guzmán, Delia Teresa Toro, Luisa Monsegur, Felícita Casiano, Ursula Ramírez. *Third row, left to right:* Luis Nieves, Rafael Labiosa, Domingo Sepúlveda, Alfonso Prats, José M. Rodríguez Quiñones (Nito) (highest honor student). *Fourth row, left to right:* Julio César Biaggi, Calixto Vázquez, José H. González Cardona, Juan Antonio Nazario, Pedro P. Casablanca (Dr. Harris's caption). [Angel Lugo, who entered in 1921, was also awarded his degree with this class. Ed.]

1927 GRADUATING CLASS

*Bottom row, left to right:* Rosa Casiano, Carola Borreli, Mrs. Harris (Dean of Women), John William Harris, president and founder of the college, Professor Carmelo Mendoza (Class Sponsor), Lucy Frank, Laura Irizarry, Mario Milán.
*Second row, left to right:* Amanda Marty, Trinidad Acarón, Carmen Rosa Guzmán, Delia Teresa Toro, Luisa Monsegur, Felícita Casiano, Ursula Ramírez. *Third row, left to right:* Luis Nieves, Rafael Labiosa, Domingo Sepúlveda, Alfonso Prats, José M. Rodríguez Quiñones (Nito) (highest honor student). *Fourth row, left to right:* Julio César Biaggi, Calixto Vázquez, José H. González Cardona, Juan Antonio Nazario, Pedro P. Casablanca (Dr. Harris's caption). [Angel Lugo, who entered in 1921, was also awarded his degree with this class. Ed.]

*Above:* Among the many activities held to celebrate the first graduation of college students was the crowning of a May Queen and King, Laura Irizarry and Mario Milán, both members of the graduating class. *Below:* Not only was 1927 a year to be celebrated because of the first graduating class. The 1927 men's basketball team swept the Island. The championship was a surprise to all the other contenders but a source of great pride to the Polytechnic. Team members were: José M. Gallardo (coach), Manuel García, Rafael Bonilla, Eduardo Vales, Rafael Sánchez, Juan Martinó, Juan Nazario, Rosendo Quesada, Calixto Vázquez; *front row:* Zoilo Monteverde, Rafael Ferrer, Elías Fernández, Sixto Forestier, Miguel Ponte.

Faculty and staff, 1927: *Seated:* Patria A. Tió, Mary Barlow, Julia Quiñones, Zelmira Biaggi, Lidia Quiñones, Mrs. James C. Gillespie, Mrs. Rachel Akers Palmer, Mrs. Mary T. Heylman, Mrs. Eunice W. Harris. *Second row:* José M. Gallardo, Capt. Henry B. Heylman, Dr. J. W. Harris, George Steadman, James C. Gillespie. *Standing:* Boyd B. Palmer, Rafael Labiosa, George Gillingham, Edward Akers, Carmelo Mendoza, Pedro P. Casablanca.

Panoramic view of campus.

*Above:* Dining hall under construction by the students. *Below:* Completed in 1947, the dining hall was called The Commons. It now houses the Art Department.

*Above:* These two Jerseys were Dr. Harris's special pride and were always called by their own names: Doña Evelina and don Jersey. Dr. Harris is beside doña Evelina and Ramón López beside don Jersey. *Below:* Dr. and Mrs. Harris (seated) surrounded by their children: Cleland, Helen, Donald, Margaret and Robert (1934).

Special farewell to Dr. and Mrs. Harris on their leaving Polytechnic Institute in 1937 by members of the community. *Front row:* Pedro Casablanca, Mrs. Harris, Dr. Harris, Mrs. Morris, Dr. Jarvis Morris (who succeeded Dr. Harris as president of the Polytechnic Institute), Mrs. Isabel Cristina de Alvarez, Hernán Alvarez and Antonio Rivera.

*Opposite above:* Marquis Science Hall, a recent view.

*Opposite below:* Beverley Student Center (completed in 1963) was named for James R. Beverley, early promoter and unstinting benefactor of Polytechnic Institute/Inter American University.

*Left:* María Dolores Mercado and Pilar Argüelles at work at the laundry tubs. *Below:* Borinquen Hall, girl's dormitory, 1928.

*Opposite above:* Lamar Women's Dormitory, adjacent to Borinquen Hall. *Opposite below:* Dr. Leker (faculty); Dr. Huffman (trustee), and Dr. Morris (president, Polytechnic Institute) at ceremony of investing Mr. Beverley with the honorary degree in 1941.

Airport farewell to Dr. Harris on his last visit to the Polytechnic, March 1956: Carlos Vélez, Mr. Font, Angel Saavedra, Margarita Capriles de Rivera, Lucy Frank de Font, Amanda García de Irizarry, unidentified, Israel Planell, Dr. Donald W. Harris, Dr. J. Will Harris, Rev. Isidro Díaz, Margaret Harris and her daughter, unidentified, Moneleo Tomasini, Helen Harris de Artau, Juan G. Soto, Ana de Rodríguez, Vicente Santiago, Axa P. Jusino, Dr. José N. Rodríguez, Guillermo Artau. (Probably the last photo taken of Dr. Harris in Puerto Rico.)

Leopoldo Ortiz (Popo) with his daughter Abigail Ortiz, principal of the Yauco Senior High School until retirement in 1973, and his grandson, who also studied at Inter American University.

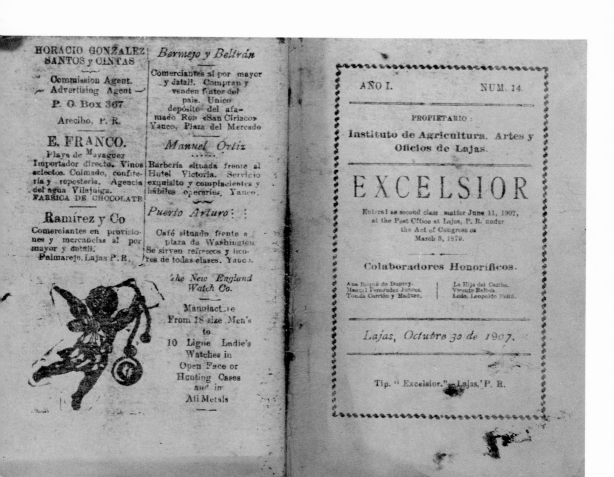

AÑO I.                    NUM. 14.

PROPIETARIO:
Instituto de Agricultura, Artes y
Oficios de Lajas.

EXCELSIOR

Entered as second class matter June 11, 1907,
at the Post Office at Lajas, P. R. under
the Act of Congress of
March 3, 1879.

Colaboradores Honorificos.

Ana Roqué de Duprey.          La Hija del Caribe.
Manuel Fernández Juncos.       Vicente Balbás.
Tomás Carrión y Maduro.        León Leopoldo Feltó.

Lajas, Octubre 30 de 1907.

Tip. "Excelsior." Lajas, P. R.

First and last pages of the paper published by the
Instituto de Agricultura, Artes y Oficios (1907).

*Above:* Casa María, built in 1931 by Capt. Harry and Mrs. Mary Tooker Heylman for use of Dr. and Mrs. Harris on their retirement. *Below:* Capt. and Mrs. Heylman seated on the porch of Casa María, which Dr. and Mrs. Harris never used.

In a like manner we are assembled today to prepare for the crossing over this week into the promised land which Jehovah your God has given you of the Class of 1927 to possess. We have been in the wilderness, developing from raw material an educational institution best fitted to the needs of Puerto Rico. There have been hardships, sacrifices on the part of teachers and students alike. Through these experiences God has been teaching us to obey, to be humble, to be diligent, to respect the rights of others, and in it all to cultivate the conscious presence of God as the center of our life.

Our one desire, as your instructors, has been to prepare you for living a practical independent, Christian life with high ideals and clear visions of your future possibilities in the service of God and man. To do this it is necessary to have, during all time, as leaders in the classrooms, in the industrial department, in athletic life and in the social direction, men and women of unimpeachable character, teachers of integrity, high ideals and sturdy Christian faith so as to present a clean, clear-cut example for the students to follow.

Most of you are to become teachers. Remember it takes a Moses in the teacher's chair to develop a Joshua or a Caleb out of the raw material seated in the students' desks. The response from the Joshuas and Calebs is in direct proportion to the interest the teacher takes in his class. The greatest lesson the student learns is not what he finds in his books but what he sees in his teacher. You may forget even the name of some of the courses you studied but you will never forget the kind of teacher you sat under for a semester.

You have reason for deepest gratitude for your teachers. I trust that you will not soon forget what you learned from your books, and that you will always be encouraged to do your best by the remembrance of the lives of your teachers, their weakness to avoid, their strength to embody.

You will turn this week from your teachers to find your way through the land of promise which Jehovah your God has given you to possess. Some of you may become great teachers, doctors, lawyers, preachers or leaders in science, art and industries. Take a look at your Promised Land.

Geographically, it is a big world into which you are going. Were you to walk through the land of promise, you could hardly do more than touch the fringes of it, during a lifetime. And that is about all a great many people do . . . walk through to see without taking hold, and at last to die without accomplishing very much. YOU are to go into and to develop your inheritance, whatever your work may be, make it a better land in which to live, for everybody.

Look for a moment at that promised land, Puerto Rico, Santo Domingo, Cuba, and on south to that great continent of undeveloped resources, its unexplored mountains and valleys. In this South American continent you could place the United States of America in great stretches of territory where are found only wild animals and Indians. Out there is waiting a work for your brave soul to do . . . a land to be cultivated, towns to be built, churches to be organized and Christian homes to be established. I could wish you nothing better than that you find your place in that unoccupied continent of South and Central America. Some of you will go to the other great continent to the North of us. There you will find the land under intense cultivation, the natural resources harnessed, capital and labor organized, and you will hear the whirling wheels of factories from shore to shore. The people there are not satisfied with good enough, but spend money and energy to make things better, to save a little time, to increase production and incidentally, to better mankind. You who go North should help to make this unheard of development into a more efficient Christian service for all mankind the world round.

And there is Africa with its beautiful lakes and wonderful waterfalls exceeding [those of the rest of the] world, with rivers for navigation and rich soil from sea to sea, populated with races of men who have not realized that they are human beings. This too is part of your promised land.

What a world before you to be taken for Christ's Kingdom! You cannot possess it all. You will have to find your place and there stay. If you will follow on day by day you will find that God has the best place prepared for you . . . not the easiest but the best for you.

In Baalbek there is the largest carved stone in the world, lying near the Sun Temple. It has never served its purpose because it never found its place among the other large stones though sixty feet long and seven feet square. Its destined place was in the Sun Temple. It was a finished product for thousands of years; it never reached its destination. And *you,* though you have culture, education and ability, you will, like that large and beautifully carved stone of Baalbek, be of no benefit to man or to yourself unless you find the place God, your Creator, has provided for you. You are not a stone, but a living soul. The responsibility of finding the place God has provided for you is *your responsibility.*†

Then what is required of you? Certainly you cannot become idlers and waste your time. You are to continue to better, to enrich your life as you go on into your land of promise. Abraham Lincoln said, "I will study and get ready and maybe my time will come." It did come but he was sixty years old before he entered into his promised land. Again Lincoln says to us, "You are not bound to win but you are bound to be true. You are not bound to succeed but you are bound to live up to the best you have."

To make your life tell for the most, to fit you for that place, and to be ready to take the place God has from all eternity prepared for you, you must be:

1. A person of Integrity . . . unbroken completeness . . . uprightness of character and soundness of heart . . . trued up and steeled through by the grace of our Lord Jesus Christ. Have you studied the expression . . . Integrity of Character? I like the mathematical expression of an Integral . . . the function of variables that remains constant. A man of integrity is the man moving steadily on, bumping as it were over variables, moving steadily on to higher ascending planes of usefulness, but here quite unlike the mathematical series of infinitessimals, man moves on by infinite bounds to higher planes of service, because man cooperates with his Creator, by choosing and resolving under God so to do.

2. To possess your promised land for which God has created you, you must live a life of consecration . . . a dedication of integrity to noble ends. It is a life with no ravels hanging down; a life that gathers the odds and ends and the apparently useless things and binds them together into one strong rope. It is a life that brings the sun-

shine through the rifts from beyond the clouds and casts it over the paths of his fellow men; a life that gathers the snow from the mountain peak to cool the fevered brow of the sick; it is a life that in a handshake or a smile passes the warm sympathetic currents of feeling on to comfort another, to encourage and to uplift a brother. Such a life is the result of an unconditional surrender of your life to God. This will make you love more, think deeper, pray oftener, work harder and finally will lead you to the place God has prepared for you to live the most useful life on this earth.

3. You must also be a consistent, intelligent, faithful and persevering worker. "A good hard day's work will put feathers in any old bed." Ruskin declares: "There is no law of right that consecrates laziness." Faithful continual endeavor is the price of success. The continual flow of water over Niagara is not only eating away the hard stones but digging a deeper pool for water below. The constant breezes have covered up ancient walled cities under mounds of dust, because the inhabitants thereof isolated themselves from other men. There is no substitute for hard work intelligently directed.

A worthy objective usually begins in a small way. It will remain small if you lie down on your job.

Young people of the class of 1927! Do not go from place to place looking for a bigger work, a larger field of service. Any real worthwhile work that needs someone to do it, however shallow at first, will lead you at last to an ever-increasing field of service till one day you will find yourself out in the front among the leaders of the world's great work. One of the world's great leaders, Dr. Cleland B. McAfee, shouts back today from his vantage ground in Heaven to us who follow:

> It is great to be out where the fight is strong,
> To be where the heaviest troops belong,
>     And to fight there for man and God!
>
> O, it seams the face and it tires the brain,
> It strains the arm till one's friend is Pain,
>     In the fight for man and God.
>
> But it's great to be out where the fight is strong,
> To be where the heaviest troops belong,
>     And to fight there for man and God!

The place where God wants you most is a place involving sacrifice. If you succeed without suffering it is because some one has suffered before you. There must be a Gethsemane in every life and for some there will be a Calvary, in the fight for man and God. To the one who is interested in his work there is sure to come much sacrifice and suffering. These are counted as incidentals but sometimes are very painful. They are stepping stones for a higher work. "God will look you over not for diplomas, degrees and medals, but for scars."

4. The promised land requires *faith* in God. God's work for us always appears impossible at the beginning. That is what it should be to force us to our knees. The man who wants to wait to see the last turn in the road on the other side of the moun-

tain before he starts to climb upward on this side will never reach the goal. I sat in a fireman's seat on a great mountain-climbing locomotive attached to the train of forty carloads of coal in Missouri one day. Another like engine was in the rear. Before us, there was an unseen end of ascent over the divide. Orders came to move forward. I looked at the steam gauge . . . "Only enough to get started," I remarked to the engineer. I rang the bell. The engineer opened the throttle. It seemed to me he let out what little steam we had. The fireman kept shoveling in the coal. The engine puffed and pulled. One mile passed and the gauge was slowly going up. Two miles and then three miles. We could then see the divide a couple of miles ahead. The old engine quivered and strained as though it had life and could feel the load. With steady hand, the engineer fed the steam to the engine, and he seemed to breathe with it, as it slowly moved forward. The engineer looked at me and smiled when we reached the divide with steam shooting out on all sides. The engine had increased in power by running. Young people, start out today with what you have. You too will make the grade.

I like to think of you going out in the way the sun came out this morning. The sun wore a bright crown and robe to replace our shroud of night. He shook his brilliant plumes of light and they fell in splendor over the mountain tops, turning the dew drops on grass and tree into shining diamonds. He kissed the clouds of dawn and they became mountains of silver and gold; he stencilled the over-arched temple of the heavens with curtains and tapestry of thousands of rainbows. He came on down to earth driving the smoke and fogs ahead of him till we here on our campus could see clearly the Cerro Gordo's grandeur across Río Grande[1] and the gorgeous flamboyans here and there over our campus. His appearance silenced the croak of frogs and opened all the stops of nature in the woods to accompany the oratorio of the innumerable birds in their anthems of peace and praise.

So may your lives, young people, like the morning sun, become an expression of God's love and thought to all mankind, taking with you light for darkness, beauty for weeping, and harmony for discord, wherever you may go.

You are now to go out from this your home, but you are not going alone. You are taking our hearts and prayers and love with you. And, remember, our dearest and best Friend and closest Companion, Christ Jesus our Lord, is going with you always, and the Holy Spirit will teach you what you shall say and do as you begin to "possess the land which Jehovah your God giveth you" this day. God bless and keep you to the end.

# Chapter 16

## *The Lindbergh Resolution*

BE IT RESOLVED BY THE HOUSE OF REPRESENTATIVES, THE SENATE OF PORTO RICO CONCURRING:

To confer upon Charles A. Lindbergh the representation of The People of Porto Rico as bearer of the following:

MESSAGE FROM THE PEOPLE OF PORTO RICO
TO THE PEOPLE OF THE UNITED STATES,
ENTRUSTED TO COLONEL CHARLES A. LINDBERGH [1]

Colonel Lindbergh: Porto Rico welcomes you. Our first Governor, Juan Ponce de León, one of the glorious adventurers that accompanied Christopher Columbus on his second voyage, sailed from our shores in quest of the fountain of youth and discovered Florida. Ponce de León was the conqueror of our fair Island by the force of arms. You will return to your native country from Borinquen along the same route as our conqueror, and like him, you have conquered Porto Rico by the force of the prestige of your name, by the glory irradiating from the mighty adventure that you, as the knight-errant, conqueror of space, have accomplished.

Welcome to our Island, Colonel Lindbergh; welcome to the only place under the shadow of Old Glory where the discoverer ever set foot. Welcome, worthy son of the American Eagle. Welcome, Lone Eaglet. The good wishes of Porto Rico will go with you to the land of the brave and the free; and to your country, and to your people, you will convey the message of Porto Rico, not far different from the cry of Patrick Henry: "Liberty or Death." It is the same in substance, but with the difference imposed by the change of times and conditions. The message of Porto Rico to your people is: "Grant us the freedom that you enjoy, for which you struggled, which you worship, which we deserve, and you have promised us." We ask the right to a place in the sun—this land of ours, brightened by the stars of your glorious flag.

*José Tous Soto*
Speaker, House of Representatives of Porto Rico

Antonio R. Barceló
President of the Senate of Porto Rico

Following quotation taken from *Porto Rico Progress* [2] February 9, 1928:

## *"Didn't Mean Separation"*

The joint letter to Dr. J. W. Harris, president of Polytechnic Institute, San Germán, [by] Antonio R. Barceló, president of the Senate, and José Tous Soto, speaker of the House, was in reply to a communication from him asking for a clear statement of their meaning of "freedom and liberty" contained in the Lindbergh message. Dr. Harris said he wanted a message that could not be misinterpreted.

Dr. Harris was moved to action by the receipt of a cable from Fifield Workum, of New York, trustee and chairman of the finance committee of the Institute, tendering his resignation from both posts after having read the Lindbergh message. Mr. Workum cabled he would use his influence to have financial assistance of the Institute from the United States withdrawn.

Before any letters were exchanged three members of the board of trustees of the Institute—Mrs. Roswell Miller, Jr., of New York, Chief Justice del Toro,[3] and Dr. Harris—called on Governor Towner[4] Saturday to get from him such information as he had regarding the legislative message and to learn its exact meaning. The Governor is reported telling them he knew nothing of the message and asked that they get him a copy. He said he would talk to Mr. Barceló and Mr. Tous Soto and find out what they meant. In the meantime Mr. Tous Soto had requested Dr. Harris to write him asking for the information desired. This Dr. Harris did at once and Monday the Senate and House leaders were busy drafting a letter in reply.

The reply to Dr. Harris was submitted to Gov. Towner, although the Lindbergh message had not been. The letter to the Governor transmitting the Harris letter was not made public.

The resignation of Mr. Workum from the Polytechnic Board followed the publication in the States of the message given to Col. Lindbergh. The message was cabled in full to the Associated Press and released for publication in New York at the time it was delivered to Col. Lindbergh here.

In his letter to Mr. Barceló and Mr. Tous Soto, Dr. Harris said:

Dear Sirs:
   I received a cable from the chairman of our Finance Committee who is a member of the law firm of Simpson, Thatcher and Bartlett of New York City, which is as follows:
      Harris, Polytechnic Institute,
      San Germán.
      Read message to Lindbergh American influence being resented. Tender my resignation Trustee and Chairman Finance Committee. Will use best efforts withdraw American financial assistance. Continuing enthusiastic support of you personally. Please publish this in school.
                                             Workum.

This is an expression of what probably others feel in my Board of Trustees. As you know we have asked the Carnegie Corporation for $1,000,-000. This request will probably be considered during the next few days. Unless this impression of resentment by Porto Rico can be cleared up it will bring fatal results to our school and possibly to the whole Island.

Will you please state clearly in terms which cannot be misinterpreted just what is meant by "Liberty and Freedom" asked for in your message? Does it mean political separation from the United States as an independent republic? Or rather does it mean a sovereign state of the Union?

Thanking you for your consideration, I am

Yours truly,
*J. W. Harris,*
President

The Harris letter to President of the Senate Antonio R. Barceló and Speaker José Tous Soto and their explanatory answer were read Monday at the Alianza Directory.[5]

Barceló's and Tous Soto's messages to President Coolidge, to the Pan-American Conference and to Lindbergh were unanimously indorsed.

EL PRESIDENTE DE LA CAMARA*
SAN JUAN DE PUERTO RICO

Dr. J. W. Harris, President
Polytechnic Institute of Porto Rico,
San Germán, P. R.

My dear Doctor Harris:—

We are answering your letter of this date. The message of the People of Porto Rico to the People of the United States entrusted to Colonel Lindbergh by the Legislature of Porto Rico at the joint session held in his honor does not need any explanation. It is self-explanatory. Its meaning is plain. Porto Rico wants her internal sovereignty; that is to say, the same that the Continental States enjoy, but with the power to retain, as at present, all public revenues derived from sources on the Island to meet her public needs which are greater than those of any State because we are performing now the task of centuries.

We are not asking for international or absolute independence. We do not want to sever the ties of a common flag and a common citizenship. We acknowledge and accept the sovereignty of the Union as defined in the Constitution, that is to say, the powers vested in the Federation by delegation of the States themselves. We want the national tariff, but with power vested

---

* Speaker of the House.

in our local Legislature to reduce, with the approval of the President, said tariff on foreign raw food staples in order to lessen the cost of living for our laboring classes, and to increase, also with the approval of the President of the United States, the schedules on agricultural products of our soil not protected by the tariff and not produced in the Continental States, in order to prevent the importation of inferior goods into Porto Rico and their exportation as Porto Rican products. We want the guarantee of life, liberty, equality, justice and property of the Federal Constitution, that we fully enjoy now, in spite of the fact that the Great Document has not been extended to Porto Rico, because of the Bill of Rights contained in our Organic Act. We want to preserve the American institutions and systems that we ourselves have adopted in our laws; we aspire to a perfect friendship and close brotherhood with our fellow citizens of the States. Even we do not resent not being an integral part of the Union, in spite of our American citizenship, according to the decisions of the United States Supreme Court. But we aspire also, and above all, to the government of our people, by our people and for our people; that is to say, to a republican form of government. That is, certainly, American freedom. That is the freedom that we ask in the message of the People of Porto Rico entrusted to the messenger of goodwill sent to us from the People of the United States. In the terms of the message: "The freedom that you enjoy, for which you struggled, which you worship, which we deserve, and which you have promised us." For this reason we state: "Our message is not far different from the cry of Patrick Henry. It is the same in substance, but with the difference imposed by the changes of times and conditions." We mention the cry that he dared to raise, not against his English ancestry, but against "taxation without representation" and against the "guiding hand of governors appointed by the Crown"; we refer to it as an echo of your history, appealing to your national pride, not in a hostile attitude, not in an angry mood, but as a friendly notice to your people, to the American People, that we are neglected from the standpoint of our political aspirations and of our economic needs; that our voice is not heard, that you have forgotten that our progress in all the paths of human endeavor is far ahead of that of many of our sister Latin Republics of whose independence you feel so proud and are prone to maintain.

It is inconceivable that we would take advantage of the courtesy of the Governor in acceding to our request for a special session of the Legislature to render homage to Colonel Lindbergh and hand him a message containing petitions which may imply a severance of ties of Porto Rico from the United States, or which may be construed as inimical to American ideals. Such a thing would mean a discourtesy to Porto Rico's guest and a lack of consideration to our Governor.

As regards our present political aspirations, we shall state in very few words that these are the following: Complete self-government including the right to elect our own Governor; as to the future the majority party has reached a conclusion as a compromise, between the conflicting solutions of statehood and independence that this matter must be left to be solved by the coming generations according to the best interests of both the people of the United States and the people of Porto Rico.

As regards statehood, permit us to say that if Congress is ready to grant us statehood, no doubt the people of Porto Rico will feel deeply the honor of becoming one of the stars of your glorious constellation. There are some of them that have sprung from the same origin, the same stock that we are. This is a matter that should be placed before our people for its decision. But what are the chances of statehood for Porto Rico in the light of the utterances of your statesmen and the silence of your political platforms? When collective citizenship was urged upon Congress by President Taft, the request was accompanied by the statement that citizenship did not imply any future promise of statehood. For these reasons, and many others, we are not now urging statehood. If you think it is better for your national interests not to admit us into the Union, we will abide by your decision; but it is up to you to be true to your history and institutions and to devise a scheme of government for Porto Rico that will harmonize your dignity, liberty and happiness and ours. We will cooperate with you to find the way to the solution of the problem. But do not misunderstand us; do not be misled by the enemies of our noble aspirations as a people. Do not pronounce the word "disloyalty" to describe the deepest sentiment in the hearts of men: Love for the freedom of the country in which his cradle was rocked by the hands of a loving mother.

Your letter has been a surprise to us. We cannot understand how the message of the Legislature can be construed as a plea for international or absolute independence. It is the same as our message to President Coolidge, transmitted also to the Pan American Conference, not because we look to it for redress or remedy for our inferior political condition, but because the President himself offered to the Conference the relief for that condition, that is to say, plain home rule; and for that reason we feel entitled to obtain the endorsement of the Nations of our own origin to the words of the chief magistrate of the nation in order that he may apply them to the sick man at home. In the said message the words "internal sovereignty" were changed by news agencies into "international sovereignty," entirely changing, of course, the meaning of the statement. We shall not be surprised to find that the present message also has been mutilated or misquoted. That will explain the alarm voiced in the cable received by you. We trust that you will acknowledge that there is no reason for alarm or uneasiness. We voice a truly American sentiment which is imbued in the minds and hearts of all our school children by the study of your history, and which is also a natural sentiment deeply rooted in the hearts of human kind.

In conclusion let us answer with dignity that part of your letter wherein allusion is made to the question of money by saying: that had we had in mind the asking of independence for Porto Rico, the loss of one million dollars or of untold millions of dollars to all the institutions of Porto Rico, will not deter us in the least.

Yours very truly,
*José Tous Soto*
*Antonio R. Barceló*

HURRAH! For SOTO and BARCELO . . . Prophets of the COMMON-WEALTH! [6]

# PART IV

# Addenda

# Chapter 17

## *The Brookings Report*

### Quod Erat Demonstrandum

THE Q. E. D. for Polytechnic's main objective had arrived in the graduating Liberal Arts College Class of 1927. There was now no question in my mind but that, under God, Polytechnic would continue to grow. I wanted to go to Texas and duplicate the Polytechnic in Southwest Texas. I asked Dr. José J. Osuna, once head of Poly's Bible Department but then head of the Educational College of UPR, if he would accept the presidency.[1] He said after some study that he would like to have a competent appraiser make a study of Poly. To this the trustees agreed and sent down Dr. Dean S. Fansler of the Brookings Institute of Washington, who made the following report:

The Board of Trustees
Polytechnic Institute of Porto Rico
156 Fifth Avenue
New York, New York

Gentlemen:

In accordance with your request for an impartial report on the desirability of continuing the Polytechnic Institute of Porto Rico, and for recommendations looking toward a better adjustment of the institution to the educational and social conditions of the Island if it should appear worthwhile to continue the school, I have the honor to submit the following observations. These judgments are based on an inspection of the Institute itself; on a study of its past record as revealed through official data; on conferences with faculty members and representative graduates, conferences with distinguished educators not connected with the Institute and conferences with various prominent business and professional men of the Island; and on a personal acquaintance of twenty years with problems arising from the superimposing of American educational ideas upon Spanish culture.

It may be said at the outset—and it can hardly be said too strongly—that the Institute should continue. Nearly everyone with whom I spoke had words of praise for it. No one was uninterested or antagonistic. There were differences of opinion, to be sure, as to what the school should try to accomplish educationally, but all were agreed that it would be a real loss to the Island for its work and influence to cease.

## Some Opinions as to the Place of the Institute in the Educational Program of Porto Rico

There is still room in Porto Rico for almost all types of education: much room for certain types, very much less for other types. For instance, there are now many more engineers, lawyers, and teachers than the Island with its present resources can absorb. It does not differ greatly from the United States in this respect. On the other hand, nearly half the children of school age have no access to the schools, and a high percentage of the elementary schools now open work in double enrollment. The chief reason for this deplorable situation is the financial inability of the government to furnish the needed equipment and instruction, though the very able Commissioner of Education has done all that can possibly be done with the available resources. Another reason is the impoverished condition of the people themselves, which makes it impossible for many families even to clothe their children, let alone furnish bus fare to and from the school centers. For it must be remembered that about 80% of the population of Porto Rico is rural: To care for even the primary school population, many additional small scattered centers of instruction in the barrios are needed. A single centralized institution like the Polytechnic could do practically nothing to relieve this situation.

The very high mortality between the eighth grade and the high schools the government has attempted to reduce through its continuation schools. Junior high schools might be a partial solution of the problem, but here again the problem is one for the state, not for private institutions. As for the high schools themselves, they seem to be sufficient in number and carefully enough distributed to accommodate all who are qualified and who wish to attend. This year the Polytechnic Institute, wisely it seems to me, is closing up its secondary department. San Germán has now a good insular high school. Moreover, it seems to be sound educational practice to keep secondary schools and colleges entirely separate in respect to campus, faculty, administration, and social interests. It is preposterous to attempt to fit the identical discipline to the eight years of adolescence and early adult life from the first year of high school to the last year of college. In its long, gradual but steady growth from a one-room shack with a few primary pupils to a collegiate institution with a physical equipment second to none in the Island and a college alumni list of about two hundred, the Polytechnic Institute was not able to make the desirable separation of the high school department from the collegiate. It now appears that many of the intramural problems and difficulties at the Institute in the past arose from the fact that it tried to be both a high school and a college at the same time. It is to be expected that with all its energies directed toward a single goal, the Institute will be spared in the future such enervating and wasteful disorders as the strike of 1930.[2]

In answer to the question, "What should be the objective of the reorganized Polytechnic?" a number of persons (three of them members of the faculty of the state university) have said in effect, "The Polytechnic should emphasize arts and trades: the Island needs skilled workmen such as mechanics, carpenters, furniture-makers, masons, needle-women, cooks and plumbers. The Institute started out to prepare for these trades; it ought to go back to its original purpose." But it seems to me that this demand is not altogether ingenuous. It is very true that Porto Rico does need a few representatives of all these crafts and trades; but where the public is either unable or unwilling to pay adequately for skilled labor, there is little incentive on the part of students to enter upon even a two-year course of preparation. Moreover, it would seem to be the obligation of the state to furnish this minimum industrial training. (Incidentally it might be remarked that the name, Polytechnic Institute, is largely misleading. The Polytechnic never has been really a technical or industrial school, and during the last five years less of one than earlier in its history. Just as so many state agricultural colleges in America have lately been renamed, so the Board of Trustees might carefully consider the advisability of renaming the Institute. A new name would at least spare the administration the embarrassment of being considered in certain quarters directors of an industrial school specializing in the handling of bad boys.) Furthermore, the inauguration of comprehensive courses in the manual arts and trades would involve expensive special equipment that might be used only a few years at most. A privately supported institute like the Polytechnic could hardly afford to enter upon such a special and possibly temporary educational program—a program that could not be considered seriously as a basis for re-organization. Again, these industrial units, to be efficient and to adapt themselves to local needs, should be placed at various points through the island and in or near the large cities, not centered in one utterly unindustrial town like San Germán. It is to be remembered, also, that Porto Rico is agricultural and in no sense industrial: a very limited number of trained artisans and mechanics is all that can be absorbed for many years to come. It is reasonable to suppose that the new school of arts and trades already established at the University of Porto Rico in Río Piedras will be able to fill the demand for workers of this sort.

From other persons comes the suggestion that the Polytechnic might well be reorganized as a junior college. This development also seems to me unnecessary and unwise. The public and private high schools are now turning out more prospective college material than the state university can take care of adequately, and the Polytechnic as a junior college would simply be one more feeder for the upper years of the university, which already maintains pre-legal and pre-medical courses, in addition to large schools of agriculture and engineering. In Porto Rico the loss between high school and college is very much less than in the United States. Nearly fifty percent of the high school graduates in Porto Rico continue their education in the government university. Many others enter colleges in the States. The demand for higher educational opportunities in Porto Rico is increasing and is insistent.

## The Investigator's Opinion

It is my personal opinion, as it is that of a number with whom I have talked, that the Institute should be continued not as a grammar or high school or even a junior college, but as a Christian college of liberal arts directed on broad humanitarian lines, endeavoring to establish and maintain strong departments in those fields in which the state university is weak. The Polytechnic already enjoys the reputation of awakening and fostering in its students a sense of community duty. It is generally admitted, I believe, that it has turned out graduates with a strong sense of social obligation based on a well-developed moral and spiritual sensitiveness. The Institute should no less have as its objective the training of highly intellectual, scholarly leaders. There is as much need in Porto Rico as elsewhere for tolerant, earnest, highly-educated patriots. The Institute would be performing an enduring service for the Island if it should offer a carefully selected curriculum of genuinely cultural courses for a selected group from which to develop real community and state leaders. (It is not without significance that the Spanish language, having no equivalent for the word "leader," has in Porto Rico adopted the English word, spelling it *líder*.) The Institute has already prepared not a few for unselfish service to their communities: it is unthinkable that it should withdraw now from that endeavor.

But the Polytechnic must strengthen its faculty and its curriculum if it expects to be recognized as an institution of higher learning. Two conditions that have been chiefly responsible for the falling off in attendance at the Institute latterly have been the lack of an experienced, highly trained permanent faculty and the lack of recognition by colleges in the United States of work done in Porto Rico. The second condition results in part from the first; the first, in part from the lack of funds to carry on the work efficiently. But mere money will not provide the most suitable faculty for a school like the Polytechnic. The new teaching staff should be recruited with skill and care. This will be the task of the new president, who should have behind him sufficient financial support to enable him to offer his new faculty reasonable assurance of permanency of tenure.

It appears, however, that lack of money has not alone been responsible for the all too frequent faculty changes. Not only has there been too much paternalism on the part of faculty toward students, but too much on the part of the college administrators toward faculty. There has been too much fussiness over unimportant details, too much busy-ness about the mere mechanism of running the Institute. There are, moreover, too many officers and committees for a faculty of twelve. It is suggested that the entire internal organization be simplified. To mention only a few points: the office of vice-president seems unnecessary; the duties of the dean as conceived at the Polytechnic appear to overlap those of the president in certain respects; most of the committee work could be handled by the faculty serving as a committee of the whole. In other words, the teaching staff should be encouraged to devote all its energies to the business of teaching and to inspiring in students the zeal for self-education—which is research. With regard to compensation of the faculty, an effort should be made to approximate (in money and such perquisites as living quarters, electricity, table supplies from the school farm, etc.) the salaries paid at the University of Porto Rico. If the cost of living at San Germán is appreciably less than at Río Piedras, that fact might possibly be considered in drawing up contracts; but a little superiority in salaries, however small and even nominal the excess may be, often gives a tremendous superiority in institutional reputation. No salary in Porto Rico educational work, however, is unduly large.

The curricular organization, as has been said, needs careful scrutiny. While one prime immediate objective will be to secure accreditation with American colleges, nevertheless the Institute should not be satisfied with offering only the stereotyped, traditional courses. In this era of the "New Deal" there should be provided facilities for distinctive work. To avoid narrow intra-departmental specialization, the system of group-majors might well be adopted. A divisional rather than a rigid departmental organization would promote freer intellectual intercourse among faculty members and a broader, more completely integrated program of studies for the student. Those responsible for drawing up the new curriculum may be interested to have their attention called to recent utterances of two of our most illustrious college presidents. Three years ago President Butler of Columbia wrote, "Narrowly limited specialization beween mounting walls of closely restricted interest, knowledge, and skill will not do. That way lies the path to the academic graveyard." In his last annual report to Harvard University, President Lowell, speaking of certain latter-day trends in higher education, mentioned four that have been significant not only at Harvard but elsewhere. These trends, he said, have been toward a less vocational objective, a greater correlation of knowledge, a recognition of the principle of self-education, and stimulation of more vivid intellectual interests. I believe that the new Polytechnic should so draft its course of studies and its requirements for graduation as to keep pace with these trends.

Without particularizing all the details, I would suggest that the academic work might be grouped under five divisions: 1) languages and literature, 2) the mathematical sciences, 3) the natural sciences, 4) social studies, 5) the fine arts. There seems to be an especially rich opportunity for contributive work in sociology, politics, and government; in Latin-American history and archeology; and in the folklore and traditional literature in Latin America. Other rich fields that lie open are music and dramatics (a college traveling little theatre would be a distinctly worthwhile novelty) and painting and design—especially design (there is a pathetic paucity of original native design in needlework, pottery, and basketry of the Island). Good journalism is a modern subject of study (the Porto Ricans are omnivorous newspaper-readers, but the journalism displayed in the papers I saw was feeble and uninspiring. Moreover, insular newspapers in English are practically non-existent). Then creative writing comes to mind (I am told that Porto Rico has produced no fiction of any distinction, though the Island teems with interesting situations and material). Some of these fields have never been explored in Porto Rico; others have been only superficially surveyed. With opportunity for intensive and extensive instruction in all of them, there is certainly no excuse for the Polytechnic's being merely just another small college of the conventional type. It could, with the right effort expended, become distinguished. The plant is there, the time is ripe, and this is a crisis in its life.

Vocational interests, which the Polytechnic has always stood for, should be retained and insisted upon; but these interests, I think, should be definitely modified toward the more aesthetic. For the resident students at least I believe that for the four undergraduate years one hour a day of chosen manual work might well be a requirement for graduation. In order that this work might have a real educational value by orienting students for life interest, the program of assignments should be worked out carefully in advance. In other words, the course should be progressive and not haphazard. Its aesthetic appeal should be emphasized. The work should be made vital. A criticism has been expressed that in the past the Institute has laid undue stress upon the academic aspect of education, and has not realized that its manual activities might be organized into educative processes. In a college of liberal arts the chief value, it seems to me, of this extra-curricular manual activity—whether it be bookbinding, horticulture, cabinet-making, pottery-making, or printing is that it throws students together under less formal conditions than the classroom; it teaches them the need of working together; it appeals to their native gregariousness; it shows them the dignity and satisfaction of making a beautiful or useful object by bringing the joy of actual creation; it quickens their reactions and increases their dexterity; it gives them a pleasant and profitable "avenue of escape."

In time, perhaps very soon, there will be a demand in Porto Rico for a graduate school of superior qualities. The state university at present offers graduate work in the department of Spanish Studies, but in no other, I believe.

Material for research of all kinds is abundant in Porto Rico and in Latin America. If the Polytechnic can be placed in the enviable position where, independent of political favor and prejudice, it has economic security and is free to develop its own life under a scholarly president and a distinguished faculty (small though that faculty may be at first), I am convinced that it will grow steadily both as a college and as a graduate school. There is no reason why, under these conditions, it might not become the leading American school for the study of Latin-American cultures and relations. This consummation would be a very happy one, welcomed, I am sure, by all scholars and universities in the United States.

## *Immediate Needs of the Polytechnic If the Proposed Objective Meets the Approval of the Board of Trustees*

The prime requisite, then, to attain the status of an acceptable college, is an additional permanent income of at least $37,500 (representing additional endowment of approximately $750,000). This amount together with the present permanent income and the annual additions from tuition, fees, room rent, board, sales from the farm, etc., is thought sufficient to maintain a college of two hundred students. $37,500 is a small sum, especially these modern days. It is hardly credible that that amount would guarantee the life of this unique institution; yet it is estimated, and correctly, I believe, that it will. $37,500 is a little more than half the amount that one of our middlesized Eastern colleges spends annually on its English Department alone. With that permanent additional income a small but superior faculty could be secured, and the requirements met for full recognition from a standard accrediting agency in the United States. It seems to me essential that the Polytechnic secure this accreditation with American colleges if it is to maintain its own personality, enjoy a life of peace with its neighbors, and attract and hold a superior student body. Thanks to the untiring activity and generosity of its friends of the past, the Institute has now a physical plant that will serve it at little expense for many years to come. Practically the entire amount of money derived from permanent funds could be used, and should be used, for salaries of administrative officers and teaching staff, for increasing the library, and for student scholarships. Though independent the Institute could work in complete harmony with the state university. The two institutions would supplement each other and co-operate in exploring the various fields of their particular interest. There need be no fear that the Institute will not do its part if it goes forward under the guidance of broad-minded scholarly men of high purpose.

## Summary and Recapitulation

There is room and need in Porto Rico for a superior Christian college of liberal arts that will stress equally the ideals of community service and high scholarship. With adequate financial support the Polytechnic can be made such a college.

The new president-elect, Dr. Osuna, is a man of highest scholastic training, of lofty principle and engaging personality, and of broad and successful experience as an administrator and teacher. He appears to me in every way qualified to direct the institution understandingly. I believe that the Board of Trustees should do all in its power to secure Dr. Osuna's early acceptance of the post, and plan to have him assume office by January 1, 1934, at the latest. In order to obtain his acceptance of the presidency I am of the opinion that the Board would need to be in a position to assure Dr. Osuna that the permanent endowment necessary to enable him to carry out his program will be forthcoming.

Without in any way wishing to pass judgment on the qualifications of the present administrators and faculty at the Polytechnic, I feel that it would be wise for the Board to support the incoming president in all his recommendations for change in personnel. I have only the warmest and kindliest feelings toward everyone I met connected with the Institute. My reception at San Germán was cordial and friendly; every effort was made to enable me to learn the facts and to hear opinions. Still I feel that the best interests of the Institute and of the people it is to serve require that the new president be given every chance to develop his own ideals. I had many pleasant conferences with Dr. Osuna, and I believe that his hopes and plans for the school are substantially the same as those herein recommended.

The Faculty and Curriculum Committee of the Board should hold itself ready to cooperate freely and intelligently with the president of the college in developing desirable courses and securing the most suitable faculty. The Committee should, however, I believe, be willing to accept the president's judgment and recommendations, for on the president's shoulders rests the responsibility for the success of the college. The relationship between president and faculty is intimate and reciprocal: their association together can produce the desired results only in an environment of closest harmony, and of unity of endeavor through complete understanding and candor.

I believe, finally, that the time has come to change the name of the Institute, to represent more exactly its purpose and aims.

Respectfully and faithfully yours,
/s/ *Dean S. Fansler*

August 9, 1933


## *A Perennial Word to Trustees and Faculties*[3]

In 1906 I came to San Germán and have lived nowhere else in Puerto Rico. Soon after arriving I was convinced that the great need was a Christian College combining education with practical experience in work. In my *first* charter for this school, secured in 1911, I expressed our objective as a Liberal Arts College. When I, with the help of Dr. Marquis, wrote our objectives into the *second* charter of 1920 it was specifically stated that the Institute was to become a "Liberal Arts College." I am more than rejoiced now that, after careful study in the field by Dr. Fansler, my early objectives have been recognized, approved and clearly outlined in his report as the best objectives for Puerto Rico.

Dr. Fansler recommends not a reorganization but a strengthening, not a knocking down but a making sure of our standards long ago lifted up. He would have us do what as trustees we were originally organized to carry out, viz., "To maintain and perpetuate the institution now known as the Polytechnic Institute of Porto Rico. . . . The particular branches proposed to be taught are those usually offered in the liberal arts and scientific courses of the best colleges and secondary schools of America" (Arts. 3 and 4 of the Articles of Incorporation). Read Articles 3 and 4 and see to what you are therein committed to carry out when you became a member of this board and faculty.

I outlined in 1914 a program of complete development calling for $10,000,000 endowment. Someday that amount will be realized.

Donations, tuition and student labor provided six-sevenths, or $60,000, every year to balance our budgets. I have only one time asked the trustees as a body for a contribution for current expenses and that was for $800 in December 1933. I have never asked the trustees to raise the money of our yearly budget. Every year we faced bankruptcy. I recognize and fully appreciate the noble and sincere support of the trustees and the generous gifts from some of the trustees who have always helped along with other friends in making it possible for us to operate without accumulating debts, by *means of student labor.*†

You have the picture of this college with its general plans of ninety buildings, model athletic field, etc. Picture it as it is today—the seventeen modern buildings nestled down on the seven hills on 200 acres of land covered with 100,000 *capá* trees, 15,000 mahogany trees, thousands of mango trees and hundred of palms with an occasional flamboyan in fiery red; its beautiful scenery of mountains, valleys and ocean beyond and colorful skies above; its dairy of pure-bred Jerseys, its poultry and its vegetable gardens. Your heart rejoices in this physical set-up.

I would have your heart rejoice in something more important than these things above mentioned. I do ask you to take up in your arms today the crying demands of this college and help us to attend to the demands of students and faculty.

Our freshman class is large. We have had to turn away scores of applicants. The Lares High School alone had fifteen students of as fine and pure blood as ever flowed from Castilian palaces, whom we could not admit. We had room for them but no remunerative work in 1934 to offer, for which they asked and needed to help pay their expenses. I ask you to let students like these lay their heads heavily on your heart as you think of their needs.

In 1930 Mrs. Harris and I had gone to Philadelphia to see a specialist for Robert, our fourth child, who in later years passed on to Heaven, and to seek financial support for the college. As usual, I remained some time in search of donations. Dr. Akers [4] sought us out and told us of the student strike against Dean Leker in which the students had shattered the glass of every window in Phraner Hall and refused to go to class. We took the first boat back to find a group of students shouting for me to remove the dean. I asked Judge Pedro Rodríguez[5] of San Juan to make an investigation for cause, if any, for criminal prosecution of the strike leaders. I also asked the parents to come and help us in the solution of the troubles. Most of the students had opposed the strike and those having taken part in the strike were sent home. Strikers were readmitted by paying all damages done to property and signing a statement to abide in the future strictly to the rules of the Institute. They returned. Parents made payment in full and the students did the work on replacement. Peace again reigned for all time.

The college faculty griped under having to observe high school rules, and *rightly so,*† but so long as there was a high school with all students and teachers under one roof and living on one campus together, we could have only one set of rules. The high school furnished us our revenue to pay expenses for many years. In 1933 the need of a high school had diminished and it was abolished for every reason but financial. Our college students come from families of most limited means or no means at all in many cases.

A college faculty, like a church choir, always has some member who knows that what he thinks is right and that it is the way the college should travel. The fact is that before a college is out of the diaper stage in years, both administration and student body along with the faculty is unpredictable at times. I simply mention this as a matter of record. An employee, not a member of the faculty, knew that I found this unpredictable employee in an embarrassing situation. This employee decided that the best way not to be exposed was to get rid of me. So with two or more faculty members the letter of complaint against me was sent to the Board of Trustees in New York in such a way as not to cause an investigation on the field in Poly. Only Mrs. Harris and I knew the real causes, outside of the parties concerned. For the good of PIPR and of the two concerned, we let the complainers go at the end of the year and took it all on the jaw standing. The trustees withdrew financial responsibility by cancelling all contracts as of June 1932, during the world financial crisis. The faculty had to assume the responsibility, suffer the losses as they have come and rustle for students' fees with which to pay 40% of their salaries. These faculty members are not finding fault. I repeat this so that you may grasp the situation and appreciate what they are doing for the college. No one who loves youth, and especially the Puerto Rican youth, would do or could do other than what our faculty is doing to help them. They are giving of their own best thought and strength plus 60% of their rightful salary. These loyal ones in Puerto Rico were sweating as if it were drops of blood to keep the doors open as a school. And they did it! They conquered! Our college enrollment is 20% above last year's enrollment. Our freshman class of 53 students is larger than last year's class at this time. These figures indicate Puerto Rico's reaction to the 1930 student strike and recent actions of disgruntled teachers.

There is only one way out and that is to increase our endowment sufficiently to meet our needs, as Dr. Fansler recommends in his report. This must be done before we can talk business to any sane man.

Dr. Padín, Commissioner of Education in Puerto Rico, is a man of integrity, Christian integrity, who enjoys the respect of all Puerto Rico. You may be surprised to know that before Dr. Fansler's report was made, Dr. Padín stated to me definitely that he wanted to teach in the Polytechnic Institute if, and when, another is appointed Commissioner of Education. Dr. Osuna has told me also that he was ready to accept the Board's offer if it is supported with necessary means for life and development of the college. With Dr. Osuna and Dr. Padín in this school, and funds to support our program, the immediate leap forward would be marvelous.

My friends, Dr. Fansler's report presents no new factors but clearly emphasizes the already known objectives as expressed in our charter and to which we as Trustees are legally subscribed and to which we have given our word to Dr. Osuna that we would support. "He that putteth his hand to the plow and looking back, is not fit for the Kingdom of God."

We have a healthy, growing pink-faced baby in our arms. It is crying loud for nourishment. Shall we throw it into the Ganges and flee back to our homes free of all responsibility, or shall we nourish the child and suffer with it in its growth to manhood and service for man and God?

Let us consider Dr. Fansler's report weighing carefully two words he used, "scholarly" and "Christian." They should be united in one character but are too often separated, especially by those commonly known as "scholarly." We do not want a Harvard, Yale, Princeton or Columbia transplanted to Puerto Rico. We would like to have their scholarly standards united with devout Christian lives. We do not want a philosophy of life to take the place of religion. Basic ground is in Christ's teaching. The scholars are too often given to theories. We need, first of all, a faculty whose life is based on Christ as each member has by prayer and Bible study arrived at a practical solution of life's problems. I shall be ashamed that I ever founded this school, if it ceases its objective and active endeavor to build up all the students in the positive faith in Christ; if theories and philosophies and sectarian views take the place of God's Word in and out of classroom; if the emphasis is not first of all on the development of well-rounded Christian character of students.

To accomplish this we must make sure:

1. That every new president is a man who is thoroughly, not only a Christian, but a man who will hold his faculty true to Christ, and lead the campaign for $10,000,000 which I mapped out for us in 1914 and Osuna now proposes to you in 1934.

2. That contracts are signed only with employees who are active, evangelical Christians and who place Christ first in their scholarly service as a means for developing character in students.

3. That the Bible shall be used as a textbook in the work of all college students, as our charter states.

History will be made here today. The door of opportunity has been opened to the first College of Liberal Arts in Latin America under definite evangelical leadership in service, a forerunner of peace to man and glory to God. The door has stood open now since 1927 as our classes graduate with B.A. degree. It can only be stopt if self falls into the door. It will become a permanent reality of scholarly Christian service if the Christian principles we are seeking to establish in the College are allowed to rule in our actions and deliberations as Trustees and Faculty.

/s/ *J. Will Harris,* President

December, 1934

## Later [1955]

Dr. Osuna accepted the presidency of PIPR. He met with the Board of Trustees in a restaurant in New York City and read his ten page program for PIPR which the trustees breathed in as good, but when Dr. Keigwin asked him, "Dr. Osuna, just how are you to raise this $10 million?" Dr. Osuna replied: "Not how am I but how are you to do it?" This was the last straw that broke the camel's back. The Board of Trustees had not from the beginning of 1911, and this new Board of 1920 had never, undertaken to raise money. Dr. Marquis expressed the Board's part in budget-raising in these words to me at a Board meeting in Room 706 of 156 Fifth Ave.: "Harris, you have your budget approved and ready to go. If you stay within that budget I will kick your pants. If you come up at the end of the year with a deficit I will be the first to kick your pants." I had always done it and I was the one as president to raise the money with the Board's blessing. Osuna was willing to lead in raising his fund but he expected the Board to see that it was raised. The Board gasped and backed down. We there lost Dr. José J. Osuna — and our great opportunity to go forward. We could easily have had, by 1955, 3,000 students and dormitories in which to house them, had Osuna taken over.

# Chapter 18

## *Interesting Characters I Met*

### *During the Years I Was Riding*
### *My Boss's Big Ideas and Roping in Money*[1]

A GENERAL IMPRESSION made on me while soliciting is that the rich man is handicapped because there is nothing he cannot buy and still be rich. The rich is usually deeply interested in anything that will advance the integrity of man—of all men. He has the money but does not have the time to investigate personally the appeals of human needs. Most rich men are lonesome people, for money separates even friends. The wealthy man is bombarded for financial aid from every worthy and many unworthy causes, till he wonders in time if there is such a friend as once in boyhood days he had imagined. Dr. Henry Sloane Coffin once told me how he had invited his old roommate of college days in Yale, Edward S. Harkness,[2] for lunch. Harkness had been a more or less regular contributor to my Institute in Porto Rico, but I could never get in to talk with him. He was shell-shocked and came to expect or suspect that all people wanted with him was to get money. After Dr. Coffin and Mr. Harkness had finished their lunch, he asked Dr. Coffin, "Henry, what do you want of me?" On being assured by Dr. Coffin that he did not seek a contribution—it was only a friendly meeting—Harkness remarked that this was the first time in years he had been invited to have lunch without being asked for money.

Wealthy people are very busy people when they are home. That is why I always stand when calling, and make my calls short. I walked in on a Wall Street banker one day. It was the noon hour and he was sitting alone. I introduced myself, told him my business, showed him some pictures while I was telling my story. He never smiled nor said a word but interjected with "uh huh" and literally ousted me with his "uh huh," without ever opening his mouth. The only person like that I had ever met.

Rev. Dr. Charles Wood of the Covenant Church of Washington, D.C. and Mrs. Wood spent the night with us in the Old House. As he left he gave me $5.00 for a new house about which I had talked and invited me to come see him in Washington and he would give me his card to some rich people. He gave me a card to Herbert Hoover, then Secretary of Commerce. Mr. Hoover was very nice, made me lay off my coat, put his feet up on his desk and offered me a cigar! As he smoked he told me all about his experiences with the fine missionaries in the Orient in early days. Asked me a jillion questions about Polytechnic. Things were just going fine. He asked and I showed him how I was going to raise $150,000 in ten $15,000 gifts, etc. The smoke then thickened as he said that he had just yesterday told President Coolidge he would continue at his post while Coolidge was President and then he expected to get out and make some money. His salary did not begin to support him in Washington. But he said he would put me in touch with a man who had ten dollars for his one. He rang the Secretary of War, John W. Weeks, and made an appointment for me to see Mr. Weeks immediately.

Over to Mr. Weeks's office I trotted in my boots, was admitted and seated. I told him the same story. He told me he was a sick man and had at the most a year to live, that his daughter had just pumped him the day before for a $30,000 donation to some good cause but said that he could put me in touch with a man who could give me ten dollars to his one. I was lifted ten times ten to a level of a hundred-fold. I was making progress fast in getting into the circle of big pockets of gold. He called up Mr. Andrew Mellon, Secretary of the Treasury. Mr. Mellon was in New York. Weeks said, "I will see him at the next Cabinet meeting and get you an appointment." Sure enough, I got the telegram in New York and took the train back to Washington. You know Mr. Mellon was a little, skinny man with a rather large mustache—looked like Dr. Henry Van Dyke.[3] I did not upset him, for he had often been touched before. He asked me to call again on my return from Chicago. I did so a week later. I had an appointment to see Mr. Coolidge at a certain hour, and, do you know, when I called up Mellon, he set the same hour. I called up the secretary to the President, asking to be excused. Mr. Mellon delayed a few minutes and his secretary told me how financially troubled Mr. Mellon was at the time. It looked as though he would have no letup for some time to come. Mr. Mellon owned a big distillery worth some millions and a sealed up warehouse full of whiskey. In all about $10,000,000 in a bottleneck, and that he would gladly take $3,000,000 for it all. Since I was not in the market, I simply expressed my sympathies, just as the bell rang for me to enter Mr. Mellon's office. There he sat complacently. I secretly wished he would let me relieve him of his troubles of that distillery and warehouse. I would gladly carry that burden by taking it from his shoulders. He talked a long time to me and very nice, said he had his accounts checked thoroughly by his advisors and that he was just not able to give me $15,000. If he could call me back now he would gladly give me even his bonded warehouse of sorrows. So ended my first financial run on Washington.

No, no, it did not end. Later I saw Mr. Coolidge, who smiled but said very little to me. That night it snowed all night and next day. I felt it was a good time to find people at home after the dinner hour the next night. Someone had given me the name of an editor and owner of one of Washington's big daily papers. I got on a streetcar and rode to the end of the track, got off and walked about a mile through snow out to this country estate. Every time I got out of the road I would lunge up to my waist in snow. It was some walk I took to relieve another poor sinner of his money. I never did know if the person at the end of the road was a he or a she, for I never got inside. The butler simply said there was no one at home. That was before I had learned what "not at home" meant. It was a good thing I did not understand for I might have sat down and waited till he got home, as I did on seeing General Charles H. Sherrill enter his house on East Fifty-seventh Street, New York. The butler told me nicely that the general was "not at home." I waited a block away to see. Sure enough, in a short time out stepped General Sherrill with his cane and attendant. We would always watch and wait on the ranch for the big, wild steers and catch them when they came to water. I finally caught Sherrill one day in Washington. He wasn't a mean man to meet at all. In fact, quite contrary, for he was an elegant and genteel man.

Dr. Marquis gave me the name of a woman, wealthy in railway stock. I picked up my briefcase and pictures and took the train for Clinton, New Jersey. Dr. Marquis had told me to pray that no one came in while I was there. She was an elderly lady, living frugally in a frame, two-story house with a maid as housekeeper and cook. A jewel of a woman in personality and cheer. It had snowed again, which I took as a good omen for my immediate trial to see this saint all alone. The train had a snow plow ahead of it, pushing the snow off the track. We were an hour or two late in getting into Clinton. It was a little village where Mrs. Ralph C. Vorhees lived in peace. The snow was deep and wet as I mushed through five blocks of scattered small homes to the home of this woman who had given, and was still giving, wisely, to the Presbyterian colleges west of the Mississippi. I could see by the smooth snow that no one had called on her. I rang the little twisting door alarm. She came to the door and asked me in. There I sat and warmed my feet at her fireplace, told her my story. Her heart was set in the West and she wanted to know why I had not built my college out in Texas. She out-talked me; at last, I got out and back to New York City, after a very pleasant hour with Mrs. Vorhees.

When I had first planned to visit New York at the beginning of my solicitations for money, a reporter on a big paper in New York came to Puerto Rico and told me about a man by the name of Carnegie. He had, just before leaving New York, sat at a dinner table by the private secretary of that man. He was an intimate friend of the secretary and the reporter promised to take me right in to see Mr. Carnegie. I was green enough to swallow all. When a cowboy told you where he could rope in an outlaw mustang in Texas, he really knew what he was talking about. I came to New York and was invited by this reporter to lunch down near the Post Office building. He ordered tripe, and since I was from Texas, insisted on my taking tripe too. I consented, not knowing what tripe was. The big black waiter came back with two servings balanced on a big tray on the tips of his fingers.

I have butchered lots of ruminants on the ranches of Southwest Texas. I wished I was back there at this time. Smell brings back memories and you don't have to try to recall to see all the past. This was a New York plate, sumptuous and tempting to the hungry man who did not know what he was eating. Not so with me. I knew the smell before I saw that honey-combed tripe, the second paunch of a cow. This was my first down, and twenty yards to go. This was the portion we tossed over the fence to jabalinas and coyotes. Let's get on up to 2 East 91 Street, to have a long talk about my college with Andrew Carnegie. He pushed a button. A boy dressed in blue and striped trousers came to the big iron doors faced with heavy glass. Took my well-wisher's card, and seated us in that little room to the right of the entrance. The reporter was prompting me just what not to say, etc. I was all set to see and shake the hand of the Mighty Steel King, when the same door bell boy came back with the card saying that Mr. Bertram was sorry but could not see the reporter! We parted, and my head was still puzzled on the kind of intimate friends one had in New York.

I called on ex-President Theodore Roosevelt in *The Outlook Magazine* offices in New York to get endorsement for my school in Puerto Rico. George W. Perkins gave me his card to Teddy. He had recently been in Puerto Rico with his daughter Alice, who smoked and rode horseback astride, to the consternation of Latin-American mothers. He was much interested and asserted that if he were President he would surely give me a letter of highest endorsement. Then he put his arm around my shoulder and walked with me through that large waiting room to the elevator, exclaiming loudly, "Doctor, I can't do it. I just can't do it." This certainly put fears in the heart of the long line of people waiting to see him. His son, Teddy, Jr., was a chip off the old block. I visited in his home in the Governor's Palace in Puerto Rico, and sat around his dinner table with intense interest listening to Mrs. Roosevelt's accounts of hunting tigers in India from the backs of elephants. All the Roosevelts I knew, including Franklin D. and Mrs. Roosevelt, were bundles of energy that rushed like a fire department through daily life.

Mr. and Mrs. Edward S. Kelly, of the Kelly Springfield Tire Company, and son, Oliver S., came to see us in Loma Vista. He was mayor of Springfield when the city decided to put in a sewer system. A little German youth came to work digging sewer ditches with pick and shovel. Mr. Kelly noticed how industrious this youth was. He advanced the day laborer to boss of a gang and later transferred him to the Kelly Springfield Rubber plant. After a few years Mr. Kelly sent this youth, Harvey S. Firestone, on to represent the Kelly Springfield Rubber Company in Chicago on a salary of $2,500 a year and gave him some stock in the company. Harvey worked and saved, and one day a letter came asking to be relieved. He had saved up enough money to start in business for himself in Akron, where he attracted Mr. Ford's attention and you know the rest of the story.

Mr. Kelly asked me to visit them in Ohio. He lived in the country and drove a Model T Ford, always. His wife had a Cadillac. Later I learned Mr. Ford always drove a Model T. Mr. Kelly gave me letters to Harvey S. Firestone and Henry Ford, both real friends of Kelly.

I called on Mr. Firestone. He was a little man with a kindly smile, about an inch or two higher than his big roller type desk. Also met his son, Harvey, Jr., and was taken out to lunch by Mr. Firestone's secretary and returned in time to catch the train to Detroit.

Mr. Ford had no office hours. Mr. Liebold, his secretary, said that some days he did not get to the office and seldom remained longer than to give the necessary-for-action verdict. He was usually in the factory or trying out a tractor, or the new brakes on the Model T, or driving the Model T on an inspection tour all over the 10,000-acre vegetable gardens adjoining the offices. A day or two before I arrived, he had turned his Model T over as he twisted the wheel suddenly to get in that left turn from the highway to his house back there in the woods. Mr. Kelly said Mr. Ford would certainly give me a million dollars if I could get him to visualize what I was doing in the Polytechnic. Instead of a million, he asked me to send him 25 of my boys to take the apprentice schooling he was offering to a thousand students from all over the world. I went with the principal of his Apprentice Trade School to lunch where all the heads of the departments usually found Mr. Ford at the head of the table to eat and to talk over problems. Any institution that grows does so through the wise solution of daily problems in conference with those in charge. He paid my boys $6 daily and they finished the two years required course in less than 20 months. Mr. Ford wrote me a letter that they had excelled the Chinese and German boys who had always carried off the honors before.

Mrs. Roswell Miller, Sr., had given me a letter to Mr. Cyrus McCormick of Chicago, and also another letter to a wealthy lady, Miss Blaine, daughter of a Vice-President,[4] James G. Blaine, her friends. They received me most cordially. I stopped in for a day with my friend Dr. Kellogg[5] of Battle Creek, who had preached for me at Guánica for three months. And thus my home was wherever night found me on the way to some man or woman able financially, or with personal prestige, to become my co-partner. A great life! They were all so willing to be of service and encouraged me. One little woman with a smile and spirit of conviction, encouraged me with, "Will, don't you give up. You will come out on top, sure." This was Mrs. Adah Brokaw McAfee, wife of J. E. McAfee, Secretary of Home Mission Board, whom I knew in Park College and watched her take the highest honors of the graduating class. A wonderful bundle of life. Everybody seemed to think my Boss would see me through in some way. The following unsolicited letter to the President of the United States is a fair sample:

EXECUTIVE MANSION
PORTO RICO

San Juan, Porto Rico
October 26, 1922

Hon. George D. Christian
Secretary to the President
Washington, D.C.

My dear Mr. Secretary:—

This note will be handed to you by the Reverend Dr. John W. Harris of Porto Rico. Dr. Harris is a noted Presbyterian minister and is President of the Polytechnic Institute of Porto Rico. He has been here about sixteen years and has built up a very remarkable institution, the largest on the Island. I would like for you to have a little chat with him and, if possible, the President and the Secretary of War. Dr. Harris is really a very unusual man and so regarded generally in Porto Rico, and all of you will find it a pleasure to have a few words with him. He is the kind of a man the President of the United States would really appreciate.

Thanking you in advance for anything you can do for him, I remain

Yours very truly,
/s/ *E. Mont Reilly* [6]
Governor of Porto Rico

All the above experiences I have narrated with the thought that such may encourage others in their development of Polytechnic. I attempted to call on everybody who was financially able to help in my work. That does not mean that all gave. I have never counted noses, but I daresay 95% of my calls were failures. Some were big failures, like that of my application to Mr. James N. Jarvie for a million dollars.

Dr. Marquis was lunching every Thursday with Mr. Jarvie and helping Mr. Jarvie to write out his will. Mr. Jarvie set up "The Commonweal Fund" of $27 million at this time. Dr. Marquis was General Secretary of the Board of National Missions and also Secretary of my Board of Trustees. He was a very intimate friend of mine who advised me in many things. I wrote a note to Mr. Jarvie, who was a trustee of PIPR, so as to reach him the following day, Wednesday afternoon before the Thursday luncheon with Dr. Marquis. This note was a request for a million dollars for endowment for the Polytechnic. I had not informed Dr. Marquis. Next day after the lunch Mr. Jarvie produced my request to Dr. Marquis and asked his opinion. Dr. Marquis told me the discussion between him and Mr. Jarvie as follows: "Mr. Jarvie asked me for my opinion on granting your request for a million dollars for endowment. I objected to it on the grounds that in the history of other colleges in America, none has had such a rapid development during the founder's life and regime as you have had. I was afraid it might ruin your young institution. I also told Mr. Jarvie that you had been able to get the backing and support of many wealthy families and also of the Carnegie Corporation, which assured a reasonable growth of the Polytechnic during the years. Mr. Jarvie then rejoined: 'But I have put him down for it. What will we do with the amount?' I replied: 'You know you have a request for a YMCA in Jerusalem which would be a fine thing for all, or a part of that amount.' " (To Jerusalem went part of my million dollar request.)

The reasons Dr. Marquis produced against further endowment floored me, weakened me dreadfully; doubly so because he was a real friend and thought he was doing what was best. To this day I cannot see Dr. Marquis's point of view. Maybe I am dumb.

# Chapter 19

## *Things to Remember*[1]

NOW that most of the first people to show their love and interest in the Poly-technic Institute of Puerto Rico are in Heaven looking down upon us who carry on, I am sure if they could speak to you, it would be:

1. You have a Charter under the federal laws of the District of Columbia to guide all your acts in the chief objective of the school. The Board of Trustees is an independent body, chosen to perpetuate the work begun in 1912 and to de-velop same. To safeguard the work and life of the Polytechnic Institute of Puerto Rico from any and all diversion of funds and purposes, and at the request of its founder, John William Harris, there was incorporated in its Charter that the Board of Home Missions have the power to elect the trustees, and if the Institute ever fails or is diverted from its original objectives as stated in the Charter, said Institute shall return to the Board of Home Missions.

2. The Charter requirements are that *all domiciled students perform manual labor.*†

3. That the Bible, as *an authoritative revelation from God*† stressing the basics and fundamentals that unite all Christians, be the textbook for all students.

4. That highest standards of classroom work of teachers and students be main-tained.

This is a big job to keep going into an ever-increasing number of faculty and students and larger resources for maintenance during the years, with everyone from president to janitor unconditionally surrendered to and dedicated to doing his best in a united institution for the glory of God and good of man.

Remember also the following:

That its scope of service is to all mankind in service and love, as I printed in 1915, as follows:

### *A Word About the Polytechnic Institute of Porto Rico*

Let it be once and forever understood that this institution does not seek to serve any particular division of the Christian Church. The church is universal or catholic. Unfortunately, the particular sect that is commonly known as the Roman Catholic is the most uncatholic of all the sects. The division into sects is a human division, the result not of God's purpose but of narrow vision and selfish thinking of man. The Polytechnic Institute wants to throw itself on the side of the great union effort of all

Christians into one democratic organization, an ecumenical church of the people, by the people, and for the people under the leadership and direction of the Holy Spirit. This union can never come around doctrinal standards nor traditions. The great commission, "Go ye therefore, and teach *all* † nations, baptizing them in the name of the Father, and of the Son, and of the Holy Ghost: teaching them to observe all things whatsoever I have commanded you, and lo, I am with you always, even unto the end of the world," is the great compelling command, obedience to which will unite all Christians into one bond of brotherhood and liberty under God in Christ Jesus. This school aims at this very goal.

We want to make this the greatest school in Latin America for the development of *Christian Character.*† It can be done and therefore ought to be done. To make it such is not only my duty but your duty, because we are working not for any particular denomination, however great a service that might be. We are working together for the glory of God and for the good of man in the advancement of Christ's Kingdom.

The Polytechnic Institute of Porto Rico offers its most hearty co-operation as a Porto Rican institution in the advancement of every good cause and worthy object in Porto Rico. It seeks to develop liberal, democratic, but real Christian character. Our ideals are not only great buildings and a large enrollment. That is only a means to the end. Our ideals are centered in the lives of the youth. Our purpose is to send out strong men and women; empowered to dare to attempt the impossible thing in life; to develop young men and women too great to live for themselves, "reliable and trustworthy." We all belong to the Universe under God.

How like our Pledge to the Christian Flag of recent years:

"I pledge allegiance to the Christian Flag, and to the Saviour for whose Kingdom it stands, one Brotherhood uniting all mankind in service and love."

"This is my Father's world."
"Lead on, O God of Might."

May God bless you.

*J. Will Harris*

# Chapter 20

## *Hats Off to Puerto Ricans*[1]

PUERTO RICO, AS A WHOLE, through its government and its people as individuals and corporate bodies, once they understood the purpose and the work of the Polytechnic Institute, not only praised the objectives of my school but helped me in every way possible to realize its ideals.

A very poor family in the barrio of Santa Rosa rented us its sala for one dollar monthly, in which Guillermina taught 30 children while we were erecting the concrete house on the opposite side of Javilla Street.

Don José M. Acosta later sold me an acre back of the Presbyterian Church, facing the railway, where I prepared to build my college.

Don Enrique Rossy, mayor of San Germán, offered me a better site, the old Cuartel, a large building with tiled floors and large native beams for upholding the roof used as barracks for Spanish soldiers and later for American soldiers. He also offered to secure 20 acres adjoining. He was blocked.

Don Juan Cancio Ortiz offered to give me his defunct school in Lajas as a site for my school. This offer was accepted in September and abandoned in November 1910.

Don Francisco Lagarde offered to sell me 100 acres known for centuries as the Hills of Santa Marta, hills on which the Polytechnic Institute is now located.

When we were functioning, don Francisco Lagarde, a wholesale merchant, provided provisions for faculty and student needs for several months yearly while I raised the money to pay salaries and food.

Mayor Julio Montalvo invited the mayors of the other 76 municipalities for dinner in the Institute to get them acquainted with our work in the school.

When the city saw that our school could not advance without ample supply of water, San Germán voted bonds and installed the Water Works. They went further and, in a deed of contract, signed officially by both San Germán and the Polytechnic Institute and filed in the records of the Registry of Deeds of San Germán, in which the Polytechnic gave the land for the reservoir and the right of way for the water mains and the city, in turn, gave us perpetual use of all water, in excess of what the city and the Polytechnic needed for consumtpion, to be used for irrigation of our vegetable gardens and school farm. This was not waste water but all water coming down by gravitation from the mountain intake after the reservoirs were filled. The flow was never to be cut off.

The Legislature approved a bill exempting the Polytechnic from all taxation for 99 years, which was approved by the Commissioner of the Department of Interior, don Manuel [Victor] Domenech, and signed by the Governor.² This Joint Resolution was introduced by the Hon. Miguel Angel García Méndez in the 12th Assembly and 3rd Legislature of Puerto Rico, March 21, 1931, and follows:

[J. R. No. 60]

## JOINT RESOLUTION

TO EXEMPT THE POLYTECHNIC INSTITUTE OF PORTO RICO, THE LANDS USED BY SAID INSTITUTION, THE BUILDINGS OCCUPIED BY IT, ITS BELONGINGS, ITS HOUSES FOR TEACHERS, AND ITS ANNEXED DEPENDENCIES, FROM THE PAYMENT OF ANY TAXES WHATEVER, AND FOR OTHER PURPOSES.

WHEREAS, It is a well-known fact that the Polytechnic Institute of Porto Rico is an educational institution wherein a beneficial work is done for the welfare of the Porto Rican youth and where educational experiments are carried out for the benefit of the Island, without any cost to the Government of Porto Rico;

WHEREAS, Said institution has been progressively developing due to the continuous efforts of its president, Mr. Harris, and of its other trustees or directors, and it has attained a high classification as an educational institution, which should be a reason for legitimate pride for the people of Porto Rico;

WHEREAS, Said institution has been carrying out a building program which is already out of proportion to the proceeds derived from interest on the endowment fund, and has provided students and teachers with good buildings and adequate equipment and furniture for their educational needs, without collecting rents of any kind;

WHEREAS, Almost one-half of the students, enrolled therein have to be assisted by the Institute from the interest on the endowment fund, in order to enable them to continue their studies;

WHEREAS, The agricultural work and the care of cattle within the grounds of said institution is done by the students for the benefit of same, and the machinery therein is not used by contractors, but by the institution itself in the construction of buildings and of school furniture, thereby developing in the students a real vocational spirit for doing industrial work;

WHEREAS, The law now in Porto Rico limits the exemption from taxation to lands the area of which does not exceed five *cuerdas* and where buildings are erected for the use of educational institutions, and the Polytechnic Institute of Porto Rico owns lands the area of which exceeds by far the area thus exempted from taxation by law;

WHEREAS, If the said institution were to pay taxes to the Treasury of Porto Rico a great number of poor students to whom this institution has given generous help would not be able to finish their education, which would mean a limitation of the disinterested sphere of action of the above-mentioned institution, which is doing a work beneficial to the Porto Rican youth with an annual average enrollment of 405 students.

NOW, THEREFORE, *Be it resolved by the Legislature of Porto Rico:*

Section 1.—From and after July 1, 1931, and for a period of 99 years, the educational institution known as "Polytechnic Institute of Porto Rico," its school buildings, lands belonging to said institution, houses for teachers and students, garages and all other property and belongings of said institution located in the *barrio* Sabana Grande Abajo, in the city of San Germán, Porto Rico, are hereby exempted from any tax whatsoever. All such tax receipts as the Treasurer of Porto Rico shall have prepared, or may prepare for the fiscal year 1931–1932, in connection with said property, are hereby declared to be null and void, and the Treasurer of Porto Rico is hereby directed to cancel the above-mentioned receipts if they are being prepared for collection.

Section 2.—This exemption shall become ineffective immediately that the said institution for any reason alters, whether temporarily or definitely, the educational purposes to which it is devoted, in which case, it shall be subject to pay in full all taxes for the fiscal year or years in which such alteration may take place; *Provided.* That in such case the Treasurer of Porto Rico shall recover the proper taxes under the laws in force.

Section 3.—The application of section 291 of the Political Code now in effect is hereby limited under the provisions contained in the preceding sections, and all laws or parts of laws in conflict herewith are hereby repealed.

Section 4.—This Act shall take effect ninety days after its approval.

*Approved, May 7, 1931.*

The Legislature also passed a Special Act of March 21, 1919, authorizing the Polytechnic Institute to confer academic degrees for such courses as the Polytechnic may develop. This was introduced by Senator Hon. Juan B. Huyke, and Representative Hon. Julio Montalvo of San Germán, with the co-operation of Hon. Antonio Barceló, president of the Senate and Hon. Senator Juan Angel Tió of San Germán.

The Polytechnic feels also forever indebted to Puerto Rico and especially to Honorable Juan B. Huyke, ex-Commissioner of Education,[3] for having approved our Manual Labor Plan as was adopted by the Department of Education in the second units. It started after Commissioner Huyke (the first native Puerto Rican to fill the chair of Commissioner of Education of Puerto Rico, whom I rejoice to remember as a personal friend and ruling elder in the Presbyterian Church) made a visit early in 1928 to the Polytechnic to see what we were doing.

It was a great pleasure for me to show him around the grounds. My middle name through the years was "To show the Polytechnic to visitors." We drove around through Lovers' Lane and on to the Dairy where the finest herd of Jerseys supplied us with milk. (I bought and paid for the foundation stock for this Jersey herd with our own money. Evalina was a daughter of Flying Fox, the highest priced, $25,000, bull of the Isle of Jersey. The bull for the herd was bought from the U.S.A. Experimental Station in Mayagüez. I donated the herd to the college before leaving in 1937.) He saw the overflow water from the Water Works flowing through and washing the dairy refuse on down to fertilize and irrigate the farm and gardens. We walked through the hog pens made of concrete and just as clean as the dairy. He admired the healthy, clean hogs being fattened by the scraps from the kitchen and the mother hogs sustained by royal palm seed, inspected also the white leghorn chickens in modern houses and yards for our egg supply, came back up to Phraner Hall and saw the bedrooms furnished with mahogany furniture made by the students. We entered his car again and drove on to the carpenter shop where don Antonio Padilla, with Popo as assistant, directed some $30,000 worth of woodworking machines, guided by student skill, turning out doors, windows, chairs and all the furniture for the school. We entered Marquis Science Hall and were glad to sit down and feel the intense interest of teachers and students in the classrooms.

Then we went to see the boys feeding rock into the rock-crusher, mixing sand, cement and crushed rock into concrete and pouring same into forms in the construction of a faculty residence donated by don Arturo Lluberas of Yauco. On an adjoining site other boys were digging the foundation ditches and laying the reinforcing rods of Mary Roberts Cottage. The two hundred and more boys had to be kept at profitable employment, profitable for them and for their school. All the work was done by students in order to help them pay for their education. The manual labor was under the able supervision of my brother, Mr. Clarence, who saw that the students carried out the detailed plans of our architect Stoughton. I did overrule the specifications of the New York engineers by placing into buildings heavier rods and about 50% more rods than the specified requirements as earthquake insurance. Don Victor Capriles, with aid of students, was in charge of all the plumbing and electric installations. The morning shift of girls was singing as they sewed and did needlework, washed and ironed the boys' clothes and cooked the dinner for all students.

It was now nearing the noon hour and all labor was over and the Commissioner was really tired as we drove up to Loma Vista and made ready for dining with the students which was always a part of the tour. The dining room was a large iron-roofed shed with palm branches as walls. The first students came in groups, warmly discussing the high points of the classrooms or loudly laughing at a boy nicknamed "Mofongo," whom Mr. Clarence found sitting down, waving at the girls when he should have been working. The five-minute bell was ringing and the boys were running uphill to get there before the doors closed. It was a hilarious gathering as they loudly laughed and talked on their way to their regular seats. The bell rang again and all was quiet while a chosen student led them in their thanks to God. The uproarious mirth broke out again through the meal's half hour. Sr. Huyke entered into the most jovial hour of Polytechnic life. It was a real Puerto Rican meal, served by beautiful waitresses to their appreciative fellow students. The dinner was mostly produced by the farms and gardens, prepared and cooked by the girls. Before he left the dining room, the senior class had signed him up as their Commencement speaker for 1927.[4] He left the dining room deeply impressed with the high quality of our students, and of the cultural value of meeting together around the tables to eat as a family group.

The approaching 1928 Commencement arrived. Commissioner Huyke's address thrilled us all as only a poet and orator can do. His evident pleasure in addressing the students and faculty was only exceeded in the rejoicing applause of students and faculty, as he spoke of our beautiful campus and commended the means employed in the Polytechnic for the development of well-rounded Christian character, the very thing that Puerto Rico needed most . . . the development of the head, the hand and the heart.

During the afternoon, I invited the Commissioner and the Chief Justice of the Supreme Court, don Emilio del Toro Cuebas, our trustee, for a walk up to Borinquen Hall. We admired the surrounding hills and valleys from the roof garden. Also the various buildings which now seemed a part of the ancient landscape. I proposed to Sr. Huyke that he extend the work we were doing for a few hundred young people to the thousands of his students in the rural public schools. We sat down in Borinquen Hall's roof garden and discussed such, for an hour or more. It was providential that our college trustee and dear friend, the Chief Justice, was with us. He entered heartily into the discussion. He presented the practical reason for extending the Polytechnic idea to the whole Island's educational system, employing his persuasive arguments so clearly expressed with such dialectic energy of his whole soul during the hour of consideration. Finally, Sr. Huyke arrived at the same conclusion and said he would try to carry out our suggestion.

The next school year, 1928–1929, Commissioner Huyke brought together several one-unit rural schools into a single school which he called *"second unit."* This second unit [5] added to the regular studies given in first units the industrial training so much needed for rural home-life of the students. The course of study was extended through the tenth grade. Young people learned the art of living well in their country homes. The approval of the Legislature was extended to another year when he added two more second unit schools. Then Teddy Roosevelt, Jr., came to Puerto Rico as Governor, urged the multiplication of the "second unit" idea, which produced some thirty more "second units." Honorable James R.

Beverley (later chairman of Polytechnic trustees) succeeded Teddy as Governor and also approved the extension of these second units. In 1940 Dr. José M. Gallardo (a graduate of Polytechnic and of Park College, Missouri) was Commissioner of Education. He informed me that there were some one hundred second units scattered all over the Island. Instruction in the classroom had been extended to the tenth grade and included such additional training as "How to grow vegetables, to prepare same for their noon day meal, to care for rabbits and hogs for their meat supply, to raise improved classes of commercial chickens for meat and eggs, and to own their own goats for milk in the home." They were also taught how to repair their shoes, to cut and sew their dresses and to make furniture for their home. In fact, how to do the very things necessary for a rural home. We have seen our industrial ideal developed and duplicated a hundred-fold in the betterment of the rural homes through the second units.

Polytechnic Institute rejoices in the extension of our idea beyond anything we could possibly have ever accomplished. In the name of our trustees, of whom Chief Justice Emilio del Toro Cuebas is an outstanding member and the principal one to introduce the practicability of the idea in acceptable form to Commissioner Huyke, I wish here and now to thank the Honorable ex-Commissioner of Education, don Juan B. Huyke, for his great service in introducing this industrial education into the public school system, and the Honorable Chief Justice don Emilio del Toro for the lion's share in persuading Commissioner Huyke. *Mil gracias, amigos míos.* Polytechnic cast its bread upon the waters and reaps a hundred-fold.

One other thing to remember that when I had not a penny to pay my passage to New York, Mr. R. A. Nadal, agent of the New York and Porto Rico Line, recommended and Mr. D. L. Mooney, president of the line, granted me free passage to and from New York as long as I was in the Polytechnic.

Still one more favor, President Villard of the American Railroad sent me a pass yearly over his road during my sojourn as president of Polytechnic.

Mr. A. H. Bull, Sr., owner of the Bull Insular Line, gave us free carriage on his vessels to Puerto Rico for all building materials.

Our gratitude goes to all the periodicals of the Island for their publicity given to the Polytechnic. The *Puerto Rico Ilustrado*[6] ran a series of pictures from time to time showing the many steps of progress during all the years. *El Mundo*[7] was always free in its support, so was the *Porto Rico Progress* and the *Puerto Rico Evangélico.* This publicity was a great help in our work. We thank you, one and all.

It took a lot of good people, all of whom I cannot mention here, to produce the Polytechnic Institute of Puerto Rico. For their cooperation and fellowship, I thank you. Hats off to Puerto Rico! And to Puerto Ricans!

# PART V

# Appendices

# Appendix A

## Tributes

EDITOR'S NOTE: *The following pages contain tributes to the Polytechnic or to Dr. Harris that he himself seems to have valued especially.*

THE BOARD OF HOME MISSIONS OF THE
PRESBYTERIAN CHURCH IN THE U.S.A.
156 FIFTH AVENUE, NEW YORK

OFFICE OF SECRETARY

April 19, 1915

The Polytechnic Institute in Porto Rico is a brave and increasingly successful attempt to meet the gravest need of the Island, whether that need is estimated in terms of the spiritual or general social approach. The complete salvation of this people must come under God through an intelligent, consecrated and well-balanced leadership raised up from among the people themselves. Porto Ricans need the spirit and the skill for work. Young people at the Polytechnic are gaining these. The commonest expression one hears among thoughtful Porto Ricans in referring to the Institute is *"The San Germán School is giving Porto Rico just what it needs."* This is Christian character, the capacity for hard work and the sense of responsibility for the common good.

*J. E. McAfee*

*PORTO RICO PROGRESS*

(October 28, 1922)

### The Optimist of San Germán

Faith and hard work, vision and determination have brought the Polytechnic Institute at San Germán into its eleventh year with more students than ever before and a greater outlook for the future if we may accept the word of Dr. J. W. Harris, president and chief motive force of the institution. And his word is considered pretty good. The new science building, erected chiefly by the students themselves, and which will be furnished and dedicated in February, probably has been a distinct achievement of the current year, which really marks an important period in the school's history.

Why the Polytechnic has succeeded can be readily understood if one cares to read the last annual report of Dr. Harris to the Board of Trustees. Optimism is the dominant note, but there is pathos and humor, courage and foresight and even romance and a touch of the dramatic are not lacking. Dr. Harris didn't miss his calling but his opening paragraphs give every indication that he would have made his mark as a writer of advertisements that approach literature. This is the way he starts:—

"This, the tenth year, has been the most remarkable year and the best of the ten. It has been remarkable in the number of applications for admission constantly coming into the office. There has been an average of about three applications daily during the school year since September, fully 500 more than we could admit. It has been a gratifying year to know that so few of those admitted have left. It is an epoch in that for the first time we offered the first year of college work, and of the 13 graduates from the fourth year high school last June, ten returned to enter the Freshman college class.

"For the first time in our history local receipts for tuition and board passed into the teens, . . . and for this year were estimated at $13,000 but reached the handsome sum of $14,808 or seven-sixteenths of our total expenses. . . . It was a thrilling year. For a second time a storm unroofed several of our houses. It did it so cleverly this time that several girls did not know the roof had gone till they were pulled out from under their beds where they had fallen asleep from weariness.

"It has been a year of surprising realizations. One of the happiest surprises of the year to the teachers and students is to watch daily the walls of the beautiful new Science Hall growing into reality. This building is bringing renewed hope and assurance to all Porto Rico. There is no other building in the island that can compare with it in imposing and architectural appearance. . . . The strength of a giant, the beauty of youth and the simplicity of true greatness have been worked into the design of this our first large building by Mr. Stoughton, our architect, till one feels the impressiveness of refined character expressed in concrete."

There were 347 students enrolled last year and the average per capita cost for board during the year was $4.96 monthly, the report states, and elsewhere says "Our graduates have been awarded the highest marks in the Summer Normals of the island for the past five years."

Dr. Harris has come to dread the summer months, he says. "It is hard to select the few from among so many worthy young people, nearly all of whom are equally qualified for admission. . . . It gives a man the cold sweats to have to say 'no' to an applicant especially when he knows the student has no other place to go. Of the 438,743 children of Porto Rico, 249,784 can not find a seat in the public schools. The neighboring islands have no schools worthy of the name. Santo Domingo and the Virgin Islands are looking to Porto Rico for a place to educate their children."

Students arrive at Polytechnic in "Packards and Fords, on the train or in ox cart, horseback and on foot." How hard it must be to say "no" and turn students away is indicated by this story which Dr. Harris tells:—

"I recall a father riding a thin pony with his long shanked boy walking at his side. The father had been recently hurt in a mine. The last student possible to admit without some charge had been admitted. The father with the boy started to leave but stopped under the shade of a tree nearby the office. I saw tears rolling rown the father's cheeks, tears, not of intercession but of disappointment, of hopelessness for his boy's future. They both left. Later in the day he returned saying, 'My chest is crushed in. I am no good any more. My life is a failure. I want my boy to do better. I can leave him nothing. I want to give him an education. I have sold my pony and will pay five dollars monthly till the money is gone. Won't you take him?' What else could a fellow do?"

The field from which the San Germán school may draw students is not limited, and Dr. Harris sees the need.

"Take Porto Rico as a centre," he says. "Draw a circle of 1000 miles radius. It will touch or include 16 different nations with a population of 21 millions, sitting in the shade of walls built one hundred years before the pilgrims landed in America. To all these a Christian institution of learning like the Polytechnic Institute should be not only a place to educate their children but also a model of the highest type and the most modern in equipment after which all these countries may pattern, and an honor to the Christian people of North America."

It will take twenty years and two million dollars to make the Polytechnic what Dr. Harris dreams it will be. And every year he is making part of his dream come true.

## PORTO RICO PROGRESS

(*undated*) (ca. 1920/21, ed.)

### Some Day He'll Be Famous

Some day Will Harris of San Germán will be famous. But he will probably continue to wear his Texas Stetson and be just as modest as he is now.

Maybe if he were spoken of as Dr. J. W. Harris, president of the Polytechnic Institute of Porto Rico, he would be more easily identified. Already he might lay claim to fame, if he were that sort. For he has conceived a big idea and has gone far enough with it to prove that it is succeeding and will have still greater success.

No one now can foresee the future of the Polytechnic. But that it is to be a big factor in the educational life of the island is certain. Three hundred or so students there now know it is the right place to be even when they are hoeing in the garden or mixing concrete for Science Hall. For Dr. Harris has demonstrated to his own satisfaction and that of parents who send their sons and daughters there that work and study, properly mixed, make for higher scholarship. And study of the Bible, the greatest textbook ever written, is part of the daily program.

Co-education, Bible study, manual labor, a queer trio, perhaps, for a Polytechnic Institute. But it is working. It's growing every year and some day Porto Rico will find proper pride in this institution which it has so largely made possible.

## PORTO RICO PROGRESS

May 19, 1923

### One Happy Man

There is at least one happy man in Porto Rico. Rain or shine, year in and year out, regardless of politics, Don Antonio, Don Santiago or Don Roberto et al. he sticks to his task and is slowly but surely proving the truth of the saying that the only difference between the difficult and the impossible is that the impossible takes a little more time.

Will Harris—officially J. W. Harris, LL.D., President of the Polytechnic Institute, San Germán, Porto Rico—for twelve years or so has been doing the impossible. In that time an idea he discovered in his head developed and materialized to the extent that a large part of it can be seen crowning the classic hills near San Germán and much the rest of it can be seen carefully laid out on paper in such a form that anybody can understand it.

But the reason of his present happiness is two-fold: first a happy disposition and, second, something has happened that will keep it that way. He has been promised $250,000 by the Carnegie Corporation for the Polytechnic, provided he raises a like sum within three years. He'll do it, and he is happy; he's happy and he'll do it.

The only reason why there are not more students at the Polytechnic is because they can't be housed, fed and taught. Its student body has grown faster than its equipment. Students are turned away every year. It is a popular place despite the fact that each has to do a certain number of hours of manual labor each day, and despite the fact that the Bible is used as a classroom textbook. And in scholarship Polytechnic students outrank those of the public schools almost every time they are placed on a competitive basis.

So there are reasons Will Harris is happy. Porto Rico ought to be happy with him. Some day not far off the Polytechnic Institute will be one of the greatest show places of the Island, one of our greatest advertising assets. It's a sizable asset now and still growing.

## Scenes and Impressions in Puerto Rico [1]

by Rev. J. O. Atkinson, D.D. [2]
Mission Board Secretary of of the United Brethren Church

But the biggest thing I have seen, heard of, or read about in Porto Rico is J. W. Harris, and his Polytechnic Institute. Now this man Harris is an institution himself, and would make anything go. That sugar plant, with all its multiplied millions that we visited today, is nothing compared with Harris. It is worth a dozen trips all the way across the Atlantic and back, even if one has to swim, to see Harris and talk with him about what he is doing. To meet him in working clothes you would take him for an engineer or a farm hand. To talk with him about education you would take him to be a half dozen university presidents all made into one. To see him in the schoolroom you know he is a great teacher. To sit with him in his palatial home you discover he is a prince. And everywhere you see him you know him to be a man of God with great ideas for Kingdom service, and the heart and mind to put those ideas into practice.

Look here! People in Porto Rico vowed that a co-educational school would be a breeder of vice and immorality. Harris has proven that the opposite is true. People in Porto Rico declared that the rich would not work with the poor, and those who had money would not care to learn to work at anything. Harris has proven the opposite. He has a school of 277 pupils—young men and women. Some are rich and some are poor. But all work a certain number of hours each day. They study books in the schoolroom, but out yonder in the fields they are learning improved methods of farming. Harris is teaching these Porto Rican boys what a real hog is, and how it may be raised; what a dairy is and a garden, and chickens, and what a real cook kitchen and dining room look like. Why, this man is putting up one school building that is costing $75,000. It has in it 120 tons of steel, all sent here from the States. The plan of his farm, dairy, workshops, and school buildings calls for an expenditure of $2,000,000. Porto Ricans of San Germán are now raising $100,000 to put into his plant. He and his school will be worth ten times that to them in a few years. The plan was so stunning, outlandish, enormous, that no mission board would back him at first. Then Harris lined up with the God of Heaven and put his great heart and all that he was into the enterprise. He and God have won out. Now some of the wealthiest men and women in the States are behind his enterprise and put thousands into it. I put President J. W. Harris of the Polytechnic Institute of Porto Rico down as one of the truly great and wonderful men about whom one often reads, but seldom meets. He says his present urgent needs are for four cottages for teachers to live in, a girls' dormitory, a boys' dormitory, a dining room and bakery, waterworks, and a few such incidentals to cost a total of $288,500. And here is predicting that Dr. Harris will soon have these wants all supplied—and then he will be wanting twice that much more and will be getting it. All the men and women of faith and prayer are not recorded in the eleventh chapter of Hebrews, long as that chapter is, nor did all die with the patriarchs. Some are still living. And this man Harris is one of them. There is simply no telling what one man can accomplish in this world when that man flings himself with all he is and has upon the resources of God.

I am afraid I never thanked Dr. Atkinson for the above impressions. Aside from what he says about me personally I quote from *The Herald of Gospel Liberty* that which Mr. Marion Drury sent me, because: first he was the first secretary and Church official, other than the Presbyterian Church, to recognize what the faculty and students were doing in Polytechnic; and second because he relates the real power of God in the development of Poly. The United Brethren missionaries in Puerto Rico were the finest set of men as a whole ever to serve in early days of this century in Porto Rico. I certainly appreciated this man's boost. I shall also never forget that of Mr. E. P. Mitchell, of George D. Selden, president of the Erie City Iron Works, in his strong letter to the trustees in behalf of Poly.

I must not fail to express my warmest appreciation and gratitude to Mrs. Carnegie for her donations and especially for the letter she wrote and sent by private messenger in behalf of Polytechnic to Mr. Rockefeller. Mr. Rockefeller's reply in part was:

26 BROADWAY
NEW YORK

February 5, 1925

My dear Mrs. Carnegie:
    Since receipt of your note several weeks ago, expressing your great interest in the Polytechnic Institute of Porto Rico and mentioning the financial support which you and your daughter have been glad to give the institution, I have reviewed the request for aid which had been previously received. Because of the admiration and affection in which I held your dear husband, in addition to the high regard which I have always had for you, it would be a

peculiar pleasure were it possible for me to cooperate with you in this matter, which interests you so deeply.

From all that I have been able to learn, this school is doing an admirable piece of work. I have no reason to question for a moment its value or its usefulness. The reason why I am compelled to decline this request is that I have not entered the educational field, as a field. That field the General Education Board has cultivated, but unfortunately, the Board's counsel does not feel that its charter would permit it to make a gift to Porto Rico. If I were to make this gift I would be greatly embarrassed in view of declinations which I am constantly sending to educational institutions, both in this country and in other countries. To give to one and not to others, when I am financially able to do both, would be inconsistent and inexplicable, and would put me in a most embarrassing position.

No one knows better than yourself how necessary it is to follow certain principles and policies in giving if one would do the most good with the funds at one's disposal. This is often hampering and not infrequently causes very genuine regret, but unfortunately no other course seems possible.

It is therefore with very genuine disappointment that I am obliged to reply in the negative to your note. I feel sure I can rely upon your sympathetic understanding of the conditions which I have sought to describe.

Very sincerely,
/s/ *John D. Rockefeller, Jr.*

Mrs. Andrew Carnegie
2 East 91st Street
New York City


## *THE PARK STYLUS*[3]

February 11, 1927

## *Dr. J. W. Harris Is Educator in Porto Rico*

J. W. Harris, a native of Texas, came to Park College in the early '90's and entered the Academy; he finished the Preparatory course in 1898; in the following September he began his college work and received the degree of Bachelor of Arts from Park College in 1902. In the same year he entered Princeton Theological Seminary and completed his theological course in 1905. Porto Rico was calling for Christian leaders at this time and the Home Mission Board of the Presbyterian Church sent Mr. Harris to that field. There he has dreamed dreams and worked them out into concrete realities. In 1920 Park College conferred upon Mr. Harris the honorary degree LL.D. in recognition of his work in the field of education.

As a student in Park College, Mr. Harris was an important part of the industrial system of the college—being the baker. It was his task to bake sufficient bread for the entire student body. Some of the strong characteristics of Dr. Harris are industry, integrity and reliability. Any duty assigned either in the classroom or in the work department, church or social life was sure to be performed; nor did the one assigning him the work need to concern himself further about it.

In 1912 the Polytechnic Institute of San Germán was founded by Dr. Harris. In the history of the Latin-American countries no educational work similar in scope or purpose has ever been organized. The growth of the Polytechnic Institute has been phenomenal. The seal and motto of his Alma Mater *Fides et Labor* was not merely something to be admired but was a part of his very being and the granite foundation of his character. What faith and labor can do is being demonstrated by Dr. Harris in Porto Rico.

In June 1927 the Polytechnic Institute will graduate a class of twenty-five, granting the degree Bachelor of Arts. From an enrollment of one student in 1912, the Institution has at present time an enrollment of over 400. The school uses the quarter system, remaining in session for the entire year of four quarters. The campus consists of 200 acres with ten permanent buildings and a large number of modern homes for both teachers and students. The industrial plan is well organized, each student working twelve hours a week. The larger part of the construction of the buildings is done by student labor. The plans of Dr. Harris look forward to a plant estimated at a cost of $5,000,000. On his teaching staff Dr. Harris employs at the present time eight graduates of Park College.[4] It is not easy to estimate the value of the work of this unusual institution.

Dr. J. Will Harris was married in 1905 to Miss Eunice White, also a graduate of Park College in the class of 1902. Much of the success that has come to Dr. Harris is due to the inspiration and help of Mrs. Harris, who is Dean of Women in the Polytechnic Institute. They have five children.

## Some Phases of Missionary Work in Puerto Rico

Broadcast over WABC, New York, from the WEST END Presbyterian Church, by Myron D. Scudder, March 2, 1930, whose family has been connected with missionary work in India for 150 years.

One could think on the remarkable things done in education since the American Occupation, but that is a topic by itself, for though situations relate to Puerto Rico they may be taken as typical of missionary work in China, Japan, India, Africa, Cuba, Santo Domingo and South America—indeed wherever sacrificing and courageous men and women are able to go.

But don't think of missionary work as rounding up a few down-and-outs and preaching to them. An entirely different conception obtains when one comes face to face with facts and learns that in the wake of Sunday Schools, churches there follow schools, colleges, manual training, occupational instruction, improvement in sanitation and hygiene, and welfare organizations with their programs of casework, social centers and recreation. One or more of these, sometimes all, are instruments of evangelical Christianity and are effective in missionary work in proportion as the evangelical is stressed. In mission fields one sees, not a "declining church" which we hear so much about nowadays, but a church militant which is fighting mightily and successfully for better homes, better parents, better children, better neighbors, better industry—better everything. It is evident, therefore, that to contribute to the support of missions is not a mere matter of indulging a religious emotion; it is a definite way of promoting a welfare movement not only of international goodwill but of making every part of the world a better place in which to live and to make a living. A man who says, "I don't give to missions for I don't believe in missions," does not know what mission work is like or what it is accomplishing. If he is really moved by a wish to share his means for the good of others his giving is likely to be done with an eye to world benefit and he will be answering his own prayer, "Thy kingdom come."

An outstanding figure in Puerto Rico is Dr. J. Will Harris, who is supported by West End, founder of the Polytechnic Institute at San Germán. While a guest in the home of Attorney General Beverley, the latter said to me: "Dr. Harris has done more for Puerto Rico than any other man living." It was only a casual remark, but all the more significant because unpremeditated and offhand. Over and over again, sometimes from unexpected sources, came similar testimony.

Raised on a Texas ranch, Dr. Harris was graduated from Park College, then from Princeton Seminary, and for years has been a missionary representing West End Presbyterian Church of New York City. Those who only have seen him in his clerical gown in a pulpit don't know the real man. He must be seen on his great horse, with sombrero hat, top boots, lariat at saddle horn, all brought from the family ranch in Texas, directing the work of the Institute in a masterly way. Can he still use the lariat? Let the boy and girl who break the rule of the Institute that young couples may not walk out together after dark tell how they heard the clatter of Ranger's hoofs and the swish of the rope as it encircled them and towed them back to headquarters.

Founded in 1912 with but one student, the Institute has grown to a degree-conferring college with 400 students. The original campus has broadened to 200 acres and ranges over seven hills penetrated by deep glades rich with vegetation. Winding roads lead through all kinds of tropical beauty, and new roads are always under construction by student labor. Fifty acres are under cultivation—again by student labor. Spread over the rest of the estate are fine buildings, including a memorial cottage to Mrs. Keigwin (Dr. Keigwin, by the way, is president of the Board of Trustees), athletic field, yards for animals and poultry, ranges for grazing, fields for tree culture where 15,000 mahogany saplings have been set but recently to become a noble and exceedingly valuable grove fifty years hence, and the forest and jungle primeval. The Texas cowboy transplanted as a missionary to this Carribean Island builded better than he knew.

The daily round of activities begins early in the Institute. Besides classroom studies, religious education, recreation and three hearty meals there is a program of one to three hours of manual labor daily for boys and home economics for the girls. To insure a long enough day for such a comprehensive schedule for 400 students, the great bell on Berwind Dining Room rings at 5:30 in the morning. This bell was made for a steam locomotive engine and given us by President John H. Converse (a Presbyterian elder) of the Baldwin Locomotive Works in Philadelphia. Soon comes, at second ringing, breakfast, prayers, tidying up the rooms, followed by classes, assignment of work, study periods, recreation hours, everyone busy till bedtime at 10 P.M. Work, study, play whether in high school or college; some are preparing to preach, some homemaking, others for agriculture, mechanics, engineering or skilled labor, all this is a part of the new idea of missionary work. This program, supported by my personal observation and careful inquiry, leads me to a firm conviction that this is religiously inspired, educationally progressive and scientifically managed, an achievement of heroic proportions which, if adequately supported, has a future beyond the dreams of even an optimistic imagination.

The best rural schools are, in Puerto Rico, modelled after the Polytechnic Institute, with up-to-date buildings, playgrounds, gardens and provision for animal husbandry. Homemaking and manual training are outstanding features. In one large room children are being taught shoemaking, and in the barber shop they learn how to cut hair. A trained social worker is an important member of the faculty of these second units,[5] and she has an office to herself well equipt with files in which she keeps records of her visits in the homes, and where she interviews children and their parents. Spanish will always be the vernacular in Puerto Rico, but every one will be able to speak English also.

On the way to the steamer we stopped to make a memorable call on Hon. Emilio del Toro, Chief Justice of the Supreme Court, a man of unbounded prestige and affiliated with almost every good work on the Island. He is a trustee of the Polytechnic. A remark he made in our brief call is significant not only of the man himself but also of what is taking place in the Island. "Our job," he said, "is to develop the soul of the Island as well as the bodies of its people and natural resources."

The ship sailed at 4 P.M. The shores grew dim as I stood at the stern, the mountain peaks began to drop out of sight. As my gaze wandered to the southwest I saw in mind's eye the rugged features of Dr. Harris; I heard the great bell on Borinquen Heights call the students to prayer; I was once more in Mayagüez talking with Miss Clara Hazen of the Marina Neighborhood House; I saw Archilla and Santiago [6] tramping over the mountains telling the old, old story that is transforming the world; I thought of the goodbye of Domingo, the patriarch of Chamorro, as he pressed his hand over his heart and pointed up to God; I rode once again over the mountain trails. I heard once again the echo of the last words of Chief Justice Emilio del Toro: "Our job is to develop the soul of our Island as well as the bodies of its people and its natural resources."

Waving the last farewell to the Isle of Enchantment there rose in my heart the prayer: "God bless that little land; and may Thy kingdom come and Thy will be done in this and all other mission fields as it is done in Thy heaven of law, order, peace and love."

A True Friend of Puerto Rico
DR. JOHN WILLIAM HARRIS
Editorial

Our cover for this issue of the *Puerto Rico Evangélico* carries the picture of that good friend of the Puerto Ricans, Dr. John William Harris, founder of the Polytechnic Institute of Puerto Rico.

The arrival on the Island of this noble friend to take part in the anniversary celebration of the Institution held on Saturday, the 2nd of this month, has brought to mind innumerable recollections of those days, now past, connected with the glorious history of the Polytechnic.

The celebration to which we refer above was an overflow of enthusiasm, admiration and reverence for the Harris couple, and an avalanche of gratitude for the work these two outstanding educators-missionaries have dedicated to the minds and hearts of hundreds of Puerto Rican youths.

One had to see with his own eyes the different acts carried out during the day to realize how this anniversary, concentrated entirely on one person, or rather on two people, is the most beautiful and significant birthday the Institute has observed in all its years of existence.

The pen is incapable of describing, line by line, all the details and various shadings of this happy festival, for which reason we shall not attempt that but shall address ourselves to certain other ideas we believe quite pertinent at this time.

Dr. Harris should feel very proud of the work he left firmly established on the Hills of Sta. Marta and that speaks so eloquently of the beautiful idealism that he cherishes in his soul. With little of material equipment but an abundance of enthusiasm, vision and faith, he did that which no one else in Puerto Rico has done up to now. His dreams were infused with love and sacrifice, as in no other way can tasks like this be performed that are often rare miracles and are possible only through the spell-binding power of sublime faith.

The distance from an old farmhouse and a few students to a dozen modern, well-equipped buildings and two hundred or more students is no small accomplishment to be viewed with indifference. The material value of the effort to be seen in the lands and buildings can possibly be reduced to more or less definite appraisal, but the spiritual value of the harvest of souls rises beyond all possible estimate.

The artist that places on canvas or the walls of a palace the dreams that come to life under his skilled and responsive hand, or he who from a shapeless mass of clay or marble produces the immortal lines of perfection and beauty is worthy of being proclaimed a genius, as, also, a visionary who can give form to an idea, place within understandable limits what is essentially abstract. But the apostle, the artist of souls, who succeeds with unswerving zeal in entering the hearts of men and women and shaping them by the warmth of his enthusiasm and beliefs, so as to awake in them a new vision of their destiny and an ennobling and uplifting vision—that person is a creator in the real sense of the word and, as such, deserves a place at the very heights of Olympus. The work in clay, wood,

# Puerto Rico Evangélico

## QUINCENARIO DE RELIGION, EDUCACION Y SOCIOLOGIA

"He sido puesto para la defensa del Evangelio." Filipenses 1:17

| Año XXVIII | Ponce, P. R., Marzo 10 de 1940 | Número 17 |

Un Verdadero Amigo de Puerto Rico.

# DR. JOHN WILLIAM HARRIS

**EDITORIAL**

ENGALANAMOS la portada de este número de "Puerto Rico Evangélico" con el retrato del gran amigo de los puertorriqueños, Dr. John William Harris, fundador del Instituto Politécnico de Puerto Rico.

La llegada a la Isla de este noble amigo para participar del aniversario de la institución, el cual se llevó a cabo el sábado 2 de los corrientes, ha traído a la superficie innumerables recuerdos que se relacionan con los días idos que hoy constituyen gloriosa historia politecniana.

La celebración a que hacemos referencia fué un desbordamiento de entusiasmo, admiración y reverencia por los esposos Harris, y un derramamiento de gratitud por la obra que estos destacados educadores-misioneros han hecho en la mente y corazón de centenares de jóvenes puertorriqueños.

Había que ver con ojos de carne los distintos actos en que fué repartido el día para uno darse cuenta de que este aniversario, por la particularidad de enfocarse todo sobre una persona, más bien, dos personas cumbres, es el cumpleaños más hermoso y significativo que el Instituto ha celebrado en los años que tiene de vida.

La pluma es incapaz de describir, línea por línea, todos los detalles y matices de la alegre fiesta, por lo que renunciamos a la empresa para apuntar en unas cuantas consideraciones que creemos atinadas en la hora actual.

El Dr. Harris debe sentirse orgulloso de la obra que ha dejado firmemente establecida en las Lomas de Santa Marta, y que habla con elocuencia del hermoso idealismo que albergó su espíritu. Con unos pocos materiales pero con abundancia de entusiasmo, visión y fe, hizo lo que nadie en Puerto Rico ha hecho hasta la fecha. Sus sueños fueron amasados con amor y sacrificio, que no de otra manera se pueden llevar a efecto tareas que parecen inverosímiles, y que con frecuencia son milagros raros que sólo se realizan al conjuro todopoderoso de la fe.

El trecho que hay que recorrer desde un rancho viejo y unos cuantos estudiantes hasta una docena de edificios modernos, bien equipados, y un estudiantado de doscientos o más jóvenes, no es poca cosa para mirarla con indiferencia. El valor material del esfuerzo que se visualiza en tierras y edificos posiblemente puede reducirse a números más o menos determinados, pero el valor espiritual de la siembra de almas escapa a toda apreciación posible.

El artista que trasmite al lienzo o a las paredes de un palacio los sueños que cobran vida en su mano adiestrada y dócil, o el que arranca del montón informe del barro o del mármol las líneas inmortales de la perfección y de la belleza, es digno de que se le aclame como un genio, como un iluminado, que puede dar forma a la idea, límites materiales a lo que es esencia impalpable. Pero el apóstol—artista de almas—que logra, con una determinación inquebrantable, adentrarse en las vidas de los hombres y de las mujeres para modelarlos al calor de sus entusiasmos e ideología, de manera que se engendre en ellos una nueva visión de su destino—visión que ennoblece y levanta—, ése es un creador en todo el sentido de la palabra y, como tal, merece un sitio en las altas habitaciones del Olimpo. La obra hecha en

stone or metal collapses, corrodes, is mutilated and is a work for a time only; the work carried out silently in the spirit in the sacred realm of the intelligence and the conscience, is a work of eternity. Neither the years nor centuries can measure or weigh it, because he who has placed a man in the clearly defined path of his destiny has escaped from the limits of time and space to cooperate with God in the transcendental region of eternal values.

It is from this point of view that the work of Dr. and Mrs. Harris in the Polytechnic Institute shines out like the radiance of the sun. A good businessman with the preparation of an expert and the vision of human glory can build up an institute of a kind financially and make it prosper in numbers, but requires the makings of an apostle, of a sacrificial life, to raise up in the hearts of men and women that greatest of all monuments: an industrious, honorable life, inspired by the highest of ideals. And this is the work the Harrises have performed in Puerto Rico.

Soon Dr. and Mrs. Harris will leave for the north to return to their peaceful home in Texas, but their heart, for it is one alone between the two of them, will remain in Puerto Rico, made of the lands, buildings, equipment, facilities that, on an infinitely greater scale, have been changed into lives, noble actions, to a spiritual essence.

May God give Dr. Harris and his distinguished wife a happy return to their native land, followed by many more years of quiet, happy life, always surrounded by fruitful remembrances of the immortal labor carried out for Puerto Rican youth.

el barro, madera, piedra o metal, se derrumba, se corroe, se mutila, y es obra para un tiempo; la obra que se realiza en el silencio de los espíritus, en el sagrado recinto de la inteligencia y de la conciencia, es trabajo para la eternidad. Ni los años, ni los siglos, podrán medirla ni pesarla, porque el que ha puesto a un hombre en la clara senda de su destino, se ha escapado de los límites del tiempo y del espacio para colaborar con Dios en la trascendente empresa de los valores eternos.

Es, desde este punto de vista, que la obra de los Harris en el Instituto Politécnico de Puerto Rico brilla con destellos de sol. Un buen comerciante, con la preparación del perito y la visión de la gloria humana, puede levantar financieramente una institución cualquiera y hacerla prosperar en cifras, pero se necesita madera de apóstol y de crucificado para levantar en los corazones de los hombres y de las mujeres el más grandioso de los monumentos: el de la vida laboriosa, honrada, inspirada por los más altos ideales. Y las dos obras las han realizado los Harris en Puerto Rico.

Los esposos Harris se marcharán pronto al Norte, de regreso a su apacible hogar en Texas, pero su corazón— el de los dos es uno solo—lo dejan en Puerto Rico multiplicado, hecho tierras, edificios, equipo, comodidades, pero, en escala infinitamente mayor, convertido en vidas, en nobles acciones, en esencia de espíritu.

Dios conceda al Dr. Harris y a su distinguida esposa un retorno muy feliz a su tierra natal, y luego, muchos años más de vida tranquila, feliz, continuamente bañada en los fecundos recuerdos de su obra inmortal realizada en la juventud puertorriqueña.

## *Presenting Dr. J. Will Harris for the Honorary Degree of Doctor of Divinity, Polytechnic Institute of Puerto Rico, May 8, 1948*

I shall read you first what *Who's Who in America* says of Will Harris and then what those say who know him best.

"HARRIS, JOHN WILLIAM, educator; b. Dripping Springs, Tex., Jan. 12, 1876; s. William David and Annie Evelyn (Buckow) H.; B. A., Park Coll., Parkville, Mo., 1902, LL.D., 1920; grad. Princeton Theol. Sem. 1905; LL.D., U. of Puerto Rico, 1940; m. Eunice Evelyn White, May 17, 1905; children—Helen Evelyn, William Donald, Margaret Alice, Robert White (dec.), Charles Cleland. Ordained Presbyn. ministry, 1905; went to Puerto Rico as missionary, 1906; founder, 1912, and pres. Poly. Inst. of Puerto Rico, pioneer co-educ. college of liberal arts in Latin America to hold membership in Middle States Assn. of Colleges and Secondary Schs., Assn. Am. Colleges, and Nat. Commn. on Christian Higher Edn., retired as pres. on Founder's Day, March 2, 1937, trustee of the institute since 1912. County committee-man Agrl. Adjustment Administrn. Pres. Nat. Farm Loan Assn. of Pearsall, Tex., 1940-44; dir. Winter Garden Nat. Farm Loan Assn. since 1944; made Survey of Southwest Tex. for Austin Presbytery, 1945. Hon. life mem. Lions Club, San Germán, Puerto Rico. Mason. Home: El Guajolote Ranch, Dilley, Tex."

To this bare outline in *Who's Who in America,* the people who know Will Harris intimately would add:

A man who saw visions and dreamed dreams and set out to make them come true; who built a great college on nothing but faith and hard work; an unremitting toiler in the vineyard of the Lord; the man who has done more for the spirit and lasting good of Puerto Rico than any other person who has sojourned among us; the man who with the help of his devoted and beloved wife has built the most lasting edifice it is given to man to build, a shrine in the hearts and consciences of men and women.

> " . . . and the elements
> So mix'd in him, that Nature might stand up,
> And say to all the World, '*This was a man.*' "

It is most fitting that here on these old steps where Will Harris over 35 years ago made the modest start of this great institution, the Institute now honors him with the degree of Doctor of Divinity and he honors the Polytechnic Institute by accepting it.

James R. Beverley
President, Board of Trustees

## *Romance*

AL FUNDADOR DEL INSTITUTO POLITECNICO
MR. J. W. HARRIS.

A su regreso a Puerto Rico con motivo del
aniversario de la fundación de la gran institución docente radicada en San Germán *

Sobre esta verde colina
Que se nombra Santa Marta
Un gran centro educativo
Orgulloso se levanta
Y en el tenemos ahora
Al hombre que lo fundara
Quien hace ya algunos años
Desembarcó en nuestras playas
Trayendo por equipaje
Ilusiones y esperanzas
Que se convirtieron luego
En la realidad soñada. . . .
¡El Instituto! Su obra
En la que puso su alma. . . .
Mr. Harris vive en Tejas
Allá por tierras lejanas
Envuelto por ilusiones
Arropado en esperanzas
Para terminar la obra
Que comenzó en nuestra patria,
Obra de bien tan hermosa
Por ninguna superada. . . .
¡Jóvenes del Instituto!
A vosotros que os alcanza
Todo el bien que a manos llenas
El buen hombre derramara,
Ya que lo tenéis delante,
Acoged bien sus miradas
Para que la luz de ellas,
Brillante luz de esperanza,
Avive las ilusiones
Que sentís en vuestras almas
¡Y nunca olvidéis al hombre
Que piensa en cosas tan altas!

Marzo 2 de 1946                                        *Juan Angel Tió* [7]
San Germán, P. Rico

* To the founder of the Polytechnic Institute, Dr. J. W. Harris. On his return to Puerto
Rico on the occasion of the anniversary of the founding of the great educational institution
located in San Germán.

### Al Dr. John William Harris
#### Hijo adoptivo y predilecto de
#### San Germán, P. R.*

Dr. Harris: tu tierra sangermeña
De la más grande de tus obras dueña,
Te ha recibido llena de alegría;
 Pues aunque estés de San Germán ausente,
Esta ciudad te tiene muy presente
 En cada pensamiento, cada día.

Parece que fué ayer que tú iniciaste
Esa obra feliz que terminaste
Poniendo en ella el corazón entero;
Parece que fué cuando saliste
Pueblo por pueblo, y tu misión cumpliste
Con empeño tan hondo y tan sincero,

Que a él le debe mi ciudad la gloria
(Que con tu nombre pasará a la Historia)
De tener un plantel en cuyo seno,
Se forjó tanta clara inteligencia
Que en el foro, y el arte, y en la ciencia
Han llevado un blasón que es algo bueno.

Allí la juventud, llena de ensueños
Pasa instantes felices y risueños
Rindiendo culto a la ideal Minerva;
Y al marchar por la senda de la vida
En un pliegue del alma agradecida
Su recuerdo dulcísimo conserva.

Y el estudiante pobre, el que ha nacido
En hogar que no fué favorecido
Con el beso feliz de la fortuna;
Que aunque tenga un talento prodigioso
Si no sucede un hecho milagroso
No tiene de triunfar opción alguna,

Halló, al llegar a ese plantel, las puertas
Gentil y bondadosamente abiertas
Para lograr su ambicionado anhelo,
Y en el colmo de toda su alegría
Brota en su alma rauda melodía
De gratitud, que se remonta al cielo.

¡Salve, John William Harris, que pusiste
—Cuando esa obra tan sublime hiciste—
Un párrafo de luz en nuestra Historia!
Tienes un monumento levantado
En el alma de un pueblo que te ha amado
Y siempre ha de tenerte en la memoria!

*Rafaela Camacho Ramírez* [8]

San Germán, P. R. 1946

* Favorite adopted son of San Germán, P. R.

# Appendix B

## The Claims of Juan Cancio Ortiz

LET US TURN ASIDE from my school in San Germán. I wish here to recount the historical data of El Instituto de Agricultura, Artes y Oficios de Lajas,[1] founded by don Juan Cancio Ortiz, and later confused with PIPR.

The factual account herein related is based on Catalog No. 1, printed by don Manuel Ramírez [2] on his Excelsior Press in San Germán of July 15, 1907, prior to the opening of the Instituto de Agricultura, Artes y Oficios on September 1, 1907, and on Catalog No. 2 for the school year of 1908–1909, printed by the Primavera Press, 28 Allen St.,[3] San Juan: and on first-hand information given me at the time by Paul E. Taylor, who lived on Luna St. in San Germán near our home.

Taylor was inspector of public schools under E. G. Dexter,[4] the Commissioner of Education of Puerto Rico. Taylor was one of the many men sent to Puerto Rico to help develop the schools after the American occupation. He was one of the directors of the Instituto de Agricultura, Artes y Oficios of Lajas appointed by the Lajas City Council on March 21, 1906, to help organize it.

Taylor was the guiding hand and Benito Cumpiano of Lajas public schools was liaison man in the setting up of this school.

Soon after the Occupation of Puerto Rico by the Americans, 20 young men were sent to the States by the Department of Education to be prepared for teaching in the public schools. One of that number was a brilliant lad whose family lived on one of the Vivoni Plantations near Palmarejo, where don Juan Cancio Ortiz lived. The boy's name was Arturo Grant. He was sent to Booker T. Washington's Tuskegee Institute in Alabama. He wrote a long letter to don Juan Cancio Ortiz about Tuskegee Institute. There also appeared in *El Tiempo,* a daily in San Juan, a story of the life of Booker T. Washington and his Tuskegee Institute. Dr. José Celso Barbosa [5] was the writer of the article and editor of *El Tiempo.* Don Cancio later told me that this letter from Arturo Grant and this article in *El Tiempo* impressed him so deeply that he was led to propose such a school be established in Lajas. Incidentally, José J. Osuna was one of the 20. He was sent to Carlisle Indian School in Pennsylvania.

Don Juan Cancio Ortiz was a farmer and merchant, a man of wealth, and president of the Lajas City Council. I quote from Catalog No. 2, page 7, under General Information:

On March 21, 1906, don Juan Cancio Ortiz, President of the City Council of Lajas, presented a very luminous project of an Agriculture, Arts and Trades school to be located in, or near, Lajas; in the realization of this school he asked that the City Council appoint a committee for the organization of this school, which committee later was named as the Board of Directors of the Instituto de Agricultura, Artes y Oficios of Lajas.

The City Council forthwith named the committee composed of the following:

> Governor of Puerto Rico, honorary president [6]
> Commissioner of Education, E. G. Dexter, honorary vice president
> Juan Cancio Ortiz was named president
> Fernando Calder was named vice-president *
> Paul E. Taylor, inspector of schools
> Quintín Ramírez, president of the School Board of Lajas
> Francisco Feliú, an agriculturist
> Benito Cumpiano, secretary and professor of Lajas schools

The catalog does not state it, but I understand that Juan Cancio Ortiz subscribed $1,000 for the proposed school. It stated in Catalog No. 2, page 7, that a total of $4,000 was raised, including the $1,000 given by the Guánica Central. With this $4,000 there was erected a two-story wooden house, 60 feet long by 30 feet wide, and an adjoining cistern for rain water with a capacity of 75,000 liters.[7] The second floor was used as a boys' dormitory. The first story was used for classrooms, dining room, kitchen and small office.

Don José ("Cheo") Ramírez and the Zapata family each [provided] two acres of land, a total of four acres. On one acre of this land the four buildings were erected.

An appeal was made for contributions to all municipal governments, to individuals and to the Legislature. Response was considered good; even women and girls moved by the appeal subscribed to the school paper *El Excelsior,* "para arrancar de las calles a niños desamparados," ** a forerunner of Boys' Town decades later.

The Legislature, on motion of Representatives Vincente Trelles Olivia and Santiago Vivaldi, voted a contribution of $3,000 yearly. Luis Sánchez Morales secured the approval of the Executive Council of the Legislature's $3,000 yearly contribution. City Councils paid the expenses of homeless and abandoned boys whom they sent to the Instituto in Lajas. Thus some thirty boys came as boarding students. The rural public school of [Bo.] Palmarejo was brought in as day students and others from homes nearby were enrolled. The Lajas School Board united the Palmarejo rural school with that of don Cancio's, making a total enrollment of 159 for the first year, under Taylor as superintendent.

---

* Actually chairman and vice-chairman.
** To bring in (literally to drag) abandoned boys from the streets.

With the additional $3,000 annual gift from the Legislature three more build-ings were erected, a total of four houses; the second building was used for classes which were under the supervision of Paul E. Taylor. Teachers were supplied by the Lajas School Board with approval of the Commissioner of Education.

Juan Cancio Ortiz attempted to supervise the boarders and to teach agriculture in 1907–1908. Fernando J. Rodil was later sent by the Commissioner of Education to be the principal from 1908–1910. Juan Cancio Ortiz had rapidly increasing responsibilities as owner of three stores, extensive sugar cane plantations and cattle ranch, which demanded all his time and thought. Taylor, probably the only man connected with the Board of Directors with a knowledge of Tuskegee Insti-tute, had returned to the states in 1908. Juan Cancio Ortiz did not know Tuskegee. He was a brilliant businessman, a fine Presbyterian elder and gentleman, but a man self-educated and could not organize what he had never seen nor attended—an industrial school, of all schools the most difficult to plan and direct.

The school building was furnished with desks, books, wall maps, etc. by the government. The courses of study they followed were the courses of the Depart-ment of Education for the first eight grades. The school had two typewriters and a proposed business course, purchased an anvil and a bellows but had no one who could teach their use.

On page 17 of Catalog No. 2, it is stated: "No habrá religión oficial. Cada alumno estará en libertad de asistir el culto que estimare conveniente de acuerdo con sus padres y sus propias creencias. En los ejercicios de apertura los profesores alternando desarrollarán un curso de moral." *

The Ortiz school permitted no religious instruction of students, and no re-ligious services were held on the grounds. Don Juan Cancio Ortiz was ordained by me as an elder in the Palmarejo Presbyterian Church and built a chapel nearby, but not on the campus of his school. To this chapel students were welcome but few boarders ever attended. A U.S. Army chaplain heard of the chapel and paid don Cancio the cost of it.

The ideal of don Juan Cancio Ortiz was Tuskegee Institute adapted to the needs of Puerto Rican boys, especially for those whose fathers had no interest in their betterment and had never recognized them as legal children; boys who could be trained how to support a family as worthy citizens of *La Patria*. This was the urge in the soul of Juan Cancio Ortiz and what he wished to see done in this school, but did not know how to do it. His directors modeled the school after the public schools under supposedly private direction. That is what Juan Cancio Ortiz saw developed in his school, a forerunner of Boys' Town of today. "The industrial training of boys to work would never succeed in Puerto Rico, if these

* There will be no official religion. Each pupil is at liberty to attend the services he thinks best according to his own beliefs and those of his parents. In the opening exercises the instructors will take turns in developing a course in morals.

boys reached the 8th grade," was the opinion Juan Cancio became convinced of as his school got into operation.

Student life of the boarding department left much to be desired. The straw that broke the camel's back was when one of the students was killed in a fight, along with other things that caused the Legislature in 1908 to advise the directors that the $3,000 would not be allowed after the scholastic year of 1909–1910. Automatically this prohibited gifts from City Councils. So, it was conducted with a view to closure in June 1910.

President Ortiz offered the property to the Presbyterian Home Mission Board as a site for the Theological Training School in Mayagüez. The Presbytery of Puerto Rico met in April 1910 in Palmarejo to consider this offer. It was there discovered that the buildings were good, but had been erected on land the title of which was held by two different owners, both of whom wished to have the buildings removed. The other three acres originally lent[9] to the Instituto had been repossessed and planted in sugar cane. Presbytery acted as follows:

In meeting of Presbytery in Lares, September 13–14, the Committee appointed to consider and get approval of the Presbyterian Board of Home Missions reported that the Board of Home Missions replied that while it looked upon Sr. Ortiz's offer with deepest interest and sympathy, nevertheless it was impossible to accept Mr. Ortiz's offer.[10]

Don Juan Cancio Ortiz then moved his family to Mayagüez, put his two boys, Ernesto and Alfredo, in the Theological Training School of Mayagüez and his charming daughter, Ernestina, in the Colegio Americano under the Home Mission Board of the Presbyterian Church and saw his hopes vanish and his Directors' Board dissolved in June 1910.

Harris opened his school in San Germán, without a name, in [February] 1907,[11] in a very small house of a poor family with a handful of little tots who could not find a seat in the San Germán Public Schools, with Miss Guillermina Nazario of [Bo.] La Pica as teacher. Benches made of boards served in the absence of anything better. There were no books, only a small homemade blackboard, on which Guillermina wrote words and the children learned to read and to write and to cipher on cheap paper tablets with pencils. They memorized Bible texts, studied the Sunday School lessons for the following Sunday in the Church . . . learned to sing the hymns and "America," also learned to pray for their parents, brothers and sisters, neighbors and the children of heathen lands who had not heard of Christ. It soon outgrew the small room.

I bought a lot from don Pancho Rivera by the side of don Juan Ortiz Perichi's house on Luna Street. He did not want the school so near, so traded me a much better location at the top of the hill near where Luna Street turns left and Javilla Street begins to the right within a couple of blocks of Porta Coeli. There I built on the north side of Javilla Street a concrete one room school, reinforced with barbed wires, which was used on Sundays for Sunday School and Church services. Miss Eva Espada was added to the teaching staff and the school gradually grew in numbers of enrollment and finally to the sixth grade as the lower grades found admission to the public schools and were discontinued. Doña Pepita Nazario, wife of Rev. José A. Martínez, was our Bible reader who visited the children's mothers in their homes regularly for prayer and Bible instruction.

We started out with no financial backing, depending on the Lord's leading and on small weekly fees of 5, 10 and 15 cents, or nothing from those who could not pay. The fees increased with the years. The Presbyterian Woman's Board heard of us through our dear friend, Mrs. Adah Brokaw McAfee, wife of J. E. McAfee, Secretary of the Home Mission Board in New York, and sent us monthly the $25 salary[12] of Guillermina Nazario. I advanced the money for the concrete building which was repaid to me by the Woman's Missionary Board in the way of rent by the month.

This concrete building could not hold comfortably over 100 and it was necessary to run a double header—one section in the A.M. and another section in the P.M.—hard on the dedicated teachers but never a complaint for they taught to serve and to advance the children, not merely for their monthly $25 check.

I then bought an acre of land adjoining the property of the Presbyterian Church in San Germán from José M. Acosta, on which I proposed to begin to provide for imminent demands for higher education. San Germán offered the [old Spanish] barracks[13] for my proposed expansion into more advanced schooling.

When that failed Juan Cancio Ortiz offered me his IAAO de Lajas which had bloomed and died. That too failed. Then came the 100 acres from Francisco Lagarde on the Santa Marta Hills, which had been reserved for four centuries by the Lord for the coming of what is now[14] wrongly named the Polytechnic Institute of Puerto Rico. The objective from the first was to secure students from the best though poor families, to advance new standards within the needs and demands of the development of youth in Puerto Rico for a way of life to be lived for man and God and *centering around the Christian home as the greatest institution in the world.*† I always had both sexes enrolled.

Don Juan Cancio Ortiz, with all sincerity and frankness, said at the time he gave me the paper of transfer of buildings from IAAO de Lajas to me for my school in San Germán, that he would never give any financial aid in my school's development. He never did give a dime to the Polytechnic up to the time I left, March 2, 1937.

# Appendix C

*Twenty-eighth Anniversary Address*
*by Dr. John William Harris, March 2, 1940*

Honorable President of the Board of Trustees, Gov. Beverley, and fellow
    trustees;
President Morris, Faculty and Student Body;
President of the Alumni Association, Dr. Rodriguez, and Alumni and Friends:

It is an unexpected joy for Mrs. Harris and me to be here today, on the Twenty-
eighth Anniversary of our college. We have been so royally received by you all.
The reception of the city of San Germán and all the students of the public schools
of San Germán, led by its band and escorted by the Boy Scouts and some 5,000
friends of San Germán on the day of our arrival, was most kind and touching.
Had we known how much the people of our adopted town cared for our college
and for us, we might never have left the Polytechnic. We knew we loved the
people of our town and Island but did not know they really cared much for us
till we returned the other day and saw the great crowd at the station and learned
since of their increased support of and interest in our college. The warm, filial
love of the alumni under the leadership of their president, Dr. José M. Rodríguez
Quiñones, expressed first by their making it possible for us to be with you on this
occasion and secondly by your many kind attentions and thought of our comfort
since we arrived here as your guests have made us most happy. The welcome
you have given us into your beautiful and well-kept homes, from one end of the
Island to the other, convinces us that co-education in this college has been a success, for most of the homes are fathered and mothered by graduates of Polytechnic Institute. Our dreams for you, our spiritual children, in finding you happy
and working hard in your service for God and man in Puerto Rico, have been
realized. The paternal and increasing love of overflowing hearts go out to you
all: alumni, faculty, students, to the town of San Germán and to the people of
Puerto Rico. We thank you.

This school was conceived in prayer and communion with God. The Lord com-
missioned me to the presidency of this school before there was a school. I never
forgot that commission. It ennobled me to stand up under trials and to endure
hardships. The thought of that commission to serve here as founder of this school
made me overcome the pent-up feelings of resentment, when misrepresentations

came my way. It was a great joy to work with God and you here in planning and building up this school.

I began as president of the school having never been appointed nor elected as such by the trustees, for there were no trustees when I first signed my name as president. I left the college March 2, 1937, without resigning and of my own free choice, convinced that such was at that time God's will for me to do. To begin as president without an election, to serve 25 years and then to end without dismissal or resignation, is a distinction probably no succeeding president can ever claim.

I organized two boards of trustees during the twenty-five years of service. Both boards, especially the last, or present board, gave me much appreciated help and enthusiastic support. The board of 1920 left me free to work out policies, standards, requirements, curricula, to fix salaries, "to hire and to fire," and to raise the money to develop the school. One of the main reasons for my leaving in 1937 was a desire to have the trustees take a more personal and active part in the support and direction of the school. It had always been a one man's work. Such a condition could not continue without jeopardizing the future permanent life of the school. I made it clear to every trustee whom I secured on the board organized in 1920 that he would not be held responsible for raising money to support the school. (This was my first great mistake in dealing with the trustees.) Their work was to endorse me in raising money and to guarantee to donors that such money would be fully accounted for and rightly used.

The loyal and hearty endorsement by the trustees (many of whom are now in Heaven) greatly helped me in securing money to carry on. They gave personally of their own money and that liberally. The largest single gift came from Mrs. Caroline S. Phraner, of $60,000 for Phraner Hall, in memory of her late husband and treasurer of our college, Mr. F. S. Phraner. I certainly appreciate to this day their loyal help and benefactions to the Institute. Grateful mention is also made of the generous aid of the Carnegie Corporation from time to time, beginning with $250,000 in 1923. I hope you who are now alumni and you who live here and the others who will live here will always show your gratitude to these many donors, both in the U.S.A. and in Puerto Rico, by your wise use and care of the grounds, of the buildings and of the endowment they provided for your welfare and advancement in the service of mankind. To them, one and all, I find it impossible to express in my own words, my gratitude. I therefore quote the last lines of a poem written by Mrs. Harris, many years ago:

> The echoes of feelings unspoken,
> The strongest of all to lose,
> Gave one purpose to the many,
> To be meet for the Master's use.

Let us not forget that this college is a private institution, erected and endowed by donations of Christian men and women. Let us always remember that the purpose of this college from the first, and later stated in the articles of incorporation of 1920, is a Christian institution. The continuance of the Polytechnic cannot be justified by monumental buildings and picturesque landscape. The excellent curriculum of academic courses in the arts and sciences and a large enrollment of eager, bright students, can not justify its continuance. The training of the students in industrial arts was once the pioneer work of this school. Such training is now being given in a more efficient way in 96 Second Units on the Island. PIPR must continue its preparation of leaders for the Second Units.

The distinguishing mark of the Polytechnic is found in the *religious standards* and *life* † of those who, as trustees, teachers and students, worked and are now working together in building up this college.

They purposefully built this curriculum for the discipline and guidance of the head to think logically, of the hand to respond skillfully and of the heart to inspire and to sustain the just equilibrium of the head and hand in service to God and man.

The purpose of all that is done here and all that is standard here is to build Christ-like character in those who study here. The basic duty of man to man is found in Christ's command—"As ye would that men should do to you, do you also to them likewise;" and of man's duty to God, in Christ's command to Saint Peter: "Follow thou me." The open Bible is to be used as a textbook for all students. Its precepts to be inculcated by instruction and by example of those who teach here.

As we have visited our graduates in their homes and in their work, during the last few weeks, we have found that these Christian principles are the distinguishing marks in the personalities of our alumni. This institution therefore is a college whose distinguishing mark is an exponent of true religion.

"The charm of true religion," says my old college professor of Greek, J. E. McAfee, "is that it supplies dynamic for high achievement and spiritual triumph. The charm of youth is its capacity for such achievement and triumph. *True* education weds the two in holy wedlock."

This, then, is what differentiates the Polytechnic from other schools—its emphasis upon true religion in Christ Jesus. The continued improvement in methods and means for the application of true religion in the Polytechnic, to the lives of each succeeding generation, will always require renewed and prayerful consideration by those directing this college. In order to keep the emphasis on the dynamic in religion rather than on the form and rituals of religious services, the faculty as a whole will have to live as though Christ died yesterday, rose today and were coming tomorrow, forever wide awake and watchful.

Let us always remember that there is no such cleavage as: This is sacred and that is secular—for life is one. All of life and of life's contacts, including the material as well as spiritual world, are sacred and are to be used for the glory of God and for the good of man.

Here stands Popo by my side as he stood there on those Steps 28 years ago today. Let him, for the time, be the representative of the more than 3,000 students who have been enrolled in this institution since March 2, 1912. Let us here today assembled dedicate ourselves and let all this great number of old students and graduates rededicate themselves anew to the accomplishment of this work. Let us here resolve that daily we will work and pray for and serve the Polytechnic Institute, in this our Father's world, till the day arrives that the fatherhood of God and the brotherhood of man in Christ Jesus unites all governments and all creeds into the one and only true government, the Kingdom of God on earth.

You, trustees, faculty, alumni, students, and friends of this college must give of your money, of your time, and of your purified and matured thoughts in service for the perpetuation of the original purpose of this college as a Christian institution. Others in the past supported this college. Let us sustain our Alma Mater as a college where all, rich and poor alike, may find expressed here (in the clean, pure examples of Christian teachers, and in the contagious aspirations of students for higher and nobler living) a new way of life adapted to the Puerto Rican needs of a growing, Christian civilization.

Let us here and now dedicate ourselves to making:

> The mind of the Master of Galillee
> The master of the mind of all men.

# Appendix D

## Casa María . . . Its Function

The SANTA MARTA trail leads up from Costello to Heylman Hill on top of which is CASA MARIA overlooking the Seven Hills of Polytechnic. Four hundred years ago Indians carried on their shoulders rock from a nearby quarry just above the dairy barn down Santa Marta trail for the construction of Porta Coeli as a convent for training natives for the Christian way of life. Now comes a precious soul in human garb with vision and resources accompanied by her husband . . . Mary Tooker Heylman and Captain Harry Heylman. When they bought the surrounding land they were planning a home for President and Mrs. Harris's retirement. In the meantime they would use it during the winter months in the tropics. Mary made the plans for landscaping. Harry supervised the digging of holes through rocks which he filled with rich ground hauled from the cow barn in which to plant trees.

Dr. and Mrs. Nathaniel N. Britten, of the New York Botanical Gardens, selected and provided the trees and shrubs for what grew into the Britten Arboretum. Paths led around through the gardens over bridges they named Beverley Bridge, Judge del Toro Bridge, etc. Cacti brought from over the world were planted near by, and white pigeons by the score sailed around. A really beautiful place. Dr. Britten was President and Founder of the New York Botanical Gardens.

In Casa María I lost face with Harry and Mary. When Casa María was about completed they told me it was for us upon our retirement. I was thoughtless and cruel in saying: "When I retire I want to go to Texas and build another college like this." Fire flew out of Harry's eyes as his face flushed with anger that exploded in vituperation upon me for such a decision. He said that they would never have built it for anything else but for our retirement. They continued to love Eunice but not me.

Heylman Hill with continued improvement of the Britten Arboretum for field excursions of the botanical classes of students is a real goal of far greater value than a mere home for a retired president. The professor of botany should live in Casa María and direct the care of the arboretum with labor done by students who are working their way through college and not by hired men. That is the function of Casa María. The added value of Heylman Hill is a place where student conferences may be held for orientation in the Christian way of life. . . .

a solitary place for prayer groups and meditation in life commitments for all-out dedication of life to man and God. No college would ever think of it as the home of a retired president or of a president. If the president didn't maintain and improve it, who would. No president has time so to do. Make it according to original purpose an arboretum. And let the professor of botany live there and in addition to classroom work supervise in general the upkeep of the Britten Arboretum.

# Appendix E

## The Wedding of Nieves and Cola

"How are you, don Paco?"

"Nothing uncommon; and you?"

"Oh, I am always well, thank the Lord."

It was the salutation of a young man who came to pay his respects to the family of don Paco. Turning over a box, the youth sat down in the one room of royal palms which served as flooring for the parlor, sitting-room or general bedroom as the needs demanded.

The youth, Nieves by name, is tall, straight as an arrow, with a well-shaped head and determined, clear-cut features.

It is his third general visit to the family. For custom demands that he visit the entire family three times, after which he makes known on which of the daughters he wishes to call. Cola is the one chosen. He visits her several times. The mother or an older sister always sits in the room with them, or walks with them to the spring for a gourd of water.

Nieves sends his oldest brother to ask for the hand of Cola. Paco, the father, consents. The wedding garments require some time in the making. All laces are handmade, as is also the bridal gown. The gorgeously plumed hat is hired for the occasion. It has adorned the heads of all the brides of the district for years and years. Once more it is called for. The groom is in his only dark suit. All the night is passed in getting ready for the wedding. In the morning after early mass they present themselves before the priest at the parochial house. The betrothal had been announced two weeks previous.

"Father," says the groom, "I want you to marry us."

"Certainly, with the greatest pleasure, Nieves, and what is your bride's name? Cola? Yes, now I have it. I shall be at the altar of the church in a moment."

The bride, led by her oldest brother, together with the bridal party, retire to the church, while the groom remains with the priest.

"For a special mass it will cost so much; and for the Blessing of the most Holy Church and the Mother of our Lord so much more—in all the sum is reasonable."

Nieves figures the amount and finds that it will take two months' earnings from his little farm to pay the fees of the church.

"Can you not take part of the money now, Father Augustine, and let me pay the remainder later?"

"No, Nieves, I cannot do that. I must have it all now."

The families of the bride and groom have spent everything for the wedding feast of wines, etc., and have no money left. With slow tread and heavy hearts they all turn homeward. The lonely palms stand out on the hilltops, swaying in submission to a fixed law, as this bridal party wend their way over the stony path, disappointed yet submissive to the rigid laws of Rome.

Nieves goes to work on his farm with double strength to raise the amount required. A hurricane sweeps over and destroys everything, even his own little palm-bark house. He hires out at twenty-five cents per day; but he must support his father and mother and aged grandmother.

The first month comes and goes, then the second, third, and at last, a year has passed. Nieves has less money and is in harder circumstances than ever before.

All the time he and Cola have planned for the wedding day. Desperate with waiting, he goes to the priest and asks to be married on a promissory note!

"No, Nieves, Father Augustine cannot do that. You must bring the money."

"Here is your coffee, Father," spoke a boy of eight who was the second illegitimate son of Father Augustine, the priest, so zealous for the welfare of the church (in money matters!).

Again Nieves leaves the church, but this time considering certain facts with which he is familiar, and which the sight of the boy and coffee fixes in his mind more vividly than ever. He goes to Cola.

"Cola," he says, "I have worked hard a year and more and have not the amount required by our church. Come and live with me and both of us perhaps can make enough to pay for the ceremony later."

She goes with him. They reconstruct the house blown down by the storm. Their bananas have grown up again large enough to bear. They live on bananas, corn, beans and coffee. Their parents die. The little farm is sold and divided among the dozen and more heirs. Each takes his fifteen or twenty dollars.

Nieves moves to a distant Barrio Caín Alto, beyond San Germán, and settles down to work. He buys a small farm on time and is doing well. Spanish rule comes to an end, and the Stars and Stripes float over the Island. Civil marriage is offered gratis to all who are living as do Nieves and Cola. But they are told by the priests that civil marriage is concubinage and a great part of them refuse to accept it. Not so in the case of Nieves and Cola. They had grown so accustomed to the unmarried state that they do not wish to be married. Years go by. Seven children come to their home. Four born under the Spanish flag and three under the Stars and Stripes.

And now twenty years have passed since that wedding hat was rented. In the meantime the Evangelical faith has been sown broadcast. Nieves' family is reached. He hears the Gospel and likes it; he attends every service of the Evangelical church for two years. His older children accept Christ and are baptized. He wants to follow, but must be married. "The old obstacle coming up again," he thinks. But how changed! Fifteen to twenty-five dollars, now fifty cents. Then a priest to be served, now a minister to serve.

He wished to join the church. His wife refused to be married . . . the reason she stated was that he had no right to whip her if she remained unmarried to him! The groom was Nieves Lugo, a cousin to Juan Cancio Ortiz.

At last Cola consents to be married. The children prepare the wedding feast of their parents. The wedding gown is bought. The fatted pig is killed. The coffee is roasted and pounded. The oldest son is sent to lead the invited guests from the town church up the mountain road to their home. Gladness rings out through the valleys and the palm branches seem to wave with joy as the wedding party moves on, up the serpentlike path, to the top of the mountain.

After the usual salutations the party is seated on benches and chairs, or take turns swinging in the hammocks. The mother, the bride of the day, withdraws to adorn herself for the occasion. We inspect the house. It was built about 1760. The walls and beams are native wood, a kind of walnut; the floor is part satinwood; the roof, tile.

The usual words are said, and now come the congratulations. First, the children solemnly shake hands with their father and then kiss their mother. All in all, it might appear funny to an onlooker were it not for the tears in the bride's eyes and her whispered words to her children as she embraced them:

"Now you are my *own* children—my *own* children."

And so they were married. Not because the law commanded it, not because the rules of the church made it imperative, but because the New Life they were living, the New Word they were studying and the God they learned to obey in a new way, taught them what they ought to do.

In the early evening, after the guests have gone, don Nieves calls his children to him as he sits in the doorway, and tells them that family worship is now a part of every day's program. He reads a chapter from the Bible, and they kneel in prayer, the oldest son leading, thanking God for His goodness and asking greater faith. And then they sing:

> "Once I was blind, but now I see,—
> The light of the world is Jesus."

# NOTES

## Chapter 1

1. Later Gen. Miles (1839-1925) led one of the American invasions of Puerto Rico, entering through the port of Guánica, July 25, 1898.
2. Dr. J. A. McAfee was co-founder of Park College with Col. G. P. Park, according to a letter from Park College historian Frances Fishburn and *Park College 1875-1895,* published to celebrate the 20th anniversary of the college.

## Chapter 2

1. Interestingly enough, Dr. Harris was college baker during part of his years at Park College.
2. Dr. Lowell M. McAfree, son of the co-founder.
3. Instructors respectively of Latin, English and mathematics.
4. Instructor in the college preparatory school and later of history and composition in the college.
5. Jonathan Frederick Huckvale attended the preparatory school during 1894-97 but did not enter college on graduation from the school.
6. Dr. Cleland Boyd McAfee, professor of mental and moral philosophy.
7. Dr. Frank Sheldon, minister, author and public speaker. *In His Steps* was a best seller for many years.
8. Frank Koehler was in charge of gardens, orchards and farms at Park College, 1895-1902. He was also owner of a woodyard.
9. A 19th century Presbyterian evangelist, lecturer and publisher of a religious weekly.
10. Dr. Geerhardus Vos, professor of Biblical theology at Princeton Seminary.
11. This attitude toward grades created some tension between Dr. Harris and some of the Polytechnic faculty later, when the latter were interested in upgrading academic standards in order for the school to receive stateside accreditation.

## Chapter 3

1. These quotations from the Gospel of St. John are arranged here according to Dr. Harris's instructions on the margin of the manuscript. Capitalization and underlining are his.
2. Exodus 33:20-23 "But you must not see my face," he said, "for man cannot see me, and live." However, the LORD said, "Here is a place by me; station yourself on the rock; and when my glory passes by, I will put you in a cleft of the rock and cover you with my hand until I pass by; then I will take away my hand so that you may see my back, while my face shall not be seen."
3. Superintendent and business manager and in charge of the Work Department and Industrial Enterprises at Park College.
4. Rev. Samuel F. McAfee, Park College professor of Biblical history.

5. Government-run boarding school for Indians and other minorities, Carlisle, Pennsylvania.
6. George F. Girard from Hiawatha, Kansas, attended the preparatory school, 1898-99 and entered Park College, 1899-1900, but did not finish.
7. Arthur M. Mattoon, professor of mathematics and astronomy.
8. In Princeton, N. J.
9. Rev. C. A. R. Janvier, former missionary to India, pastor of the Holland Memorial Presbyterian Church, Philadelphia.
10. Oklahoma.

## Chapter 4

1. This was the official spelling from 1898 to 1932, at which time the American government went back to the Spanish spelling. Dr. Harris uses both spellings indiscriminately, regardless of date. (Joint Resolution of Congress, May 17, 1932)
2. After the United States occupied Puerto Rico, representatives of major Protestant churches met and assigned areas to each church to avoid competition for converts. Until 1898 the Episcopal Church (Church of England) was the only non-Roman Catholic Church permitted in Puerto Rico. It did not participate in this territorial distribution.
3. Continental, i.e., non-Spanish stateside-born American citizen.
4. Graduated in the first high school class, 1916; went on to graduate from Park College. Later he served twice on the Polytechnic faculty, 1922-23, and 1926-27, and had a distinguished teaching career in various stateside universities. He was Commissioner of Education in Puerto Rico, 1937-44. Upon retirement he matriculated in the Inter American University Law School and is now a practicing attorney. He received the first honorary degree granted by the Polytechnic, an LL.D., in 1937.
5. Mexican president, dictator and "strong man," 1877-80 and 1884-1911.
6. Lcdo.—licenciado, i.e., licensed after having passed a special qualifying examination to practice, e.g. law, pharmacy. Mr. Pedro Amado Rivera is a practicing lawyer.
7. Dr. Cástor Lino Rivera was really a medical doctor, not a dentist.
8. Holiday, especially the 10-day patron saint festival of a town.

## Chapter 5

1. Barrio: In Puerto Rico a legal urban or rural division of any municipality corresponding roughly to either township or ward in many states. The term is also used to denote a specific neighborhood or area, especially within a city or town for what is really a subdivision within the legal boundaries of a barrio. The term, whether applied to the legal division or a neighborhood, carries no connotation whatsoever about the economic or social status of the area or its residents. Names of barrios in the text will be identified by [Bo.]
2. The bioluminescence of the bay is caused by the unusually large population of luminescent dinoflagellates that inhabit it. This particular bay was scientifically discovered by Dr. Boyd B. Palmer, a teacher at the Polytechnic Institute and Inter American University from 1924 until retirement in 1964.
3. Mrs. Harris was pregnant with Helen when the Harris family arrived in July. Helen was born three months later.
4. In 1921, when the first college class enrolled but failed to complete the required

four years because Puerto Rican public schools were desperately in need of teachers, offering salaries they could not refuse. Teacher licenses were granted on completion of eighth, even sixth, grade for work in primary grades or rural schools.

5. In Salud Street. The building was torn down in 1972 by the Corporación Renovación Urbana y Vivienda.

6. A later story is that Ortiz Perichi did not want Harris's school alongside his home, so he traded the lot for one on Javilla Street, just off Luna Street.

7. A story, as told by Dr. Harris, about a couple for whom marriage fees were beyond reach so that the ceremony had to be postponed for some 20 years is found in Appendix E, page 183.

8. Evidently a gentlemen's agreement, as the deed of purchase is dated January 10, 1910. These plans date from 1909.

9. José M. Acosta; "Pepe" is a nickname for José.

10. Businessman and, at one time, mayor of Salinas, Kansas.

11. Owner of almost all land beyond the north limits of San Germán as far as Lajas.

12. Site of the present Presbyterian Church on Luna Street in San Germán. At that time all Presbyterian Church property in Puerto Rico was owned by the Board of Home Missions.

13. Date of transfer to the Board is April 21, 1910.

14. Offer made in 1909.

15. All were members of the San Germán City Council.

16. Large property owner who later gave land for La Concepción Hospital, San Germán.

17. A graduate of Polytechnic Institute from the academy in 1924, who went on to get his degree in law. He was at one time Presiding Judge of the Insular Court of Puerto Rico.

18. Probably the Cruces River that flows between Sabana Grande and San Germán before joining the Guanajibo River that goes through San Germán. Dr. Harris uses the name "Río Grande" for several rivers.

19. He employed Miss Nazario and opened the school in February 1907, not 1906.

20. Ensenada, barrio of Guánica and location of the hospital for Guánica Central.

21. Guanajibo River.

22. There were already a few automobiles in Puerto Rico, as mentioned earlier.

23. Usually a private or parochial preparatory school, equivalent to an American high school. However, it is also sometimes used to describe a college.

24. Prosperous businessman and large landowner of Lajas and Mayagüez. Inspired by what he had heard and read about Tuskegee Institute, he tried to start a similar school in Palmarejo, a barrio of Lajas, El Instituto de Agricultura, Artes y Oficios (IAAO). However, the school failed. For a description of this school and its problems, see Appendix B, page 172. Acting mayor of Mayagüez, 1918.

25. These were the four buildings of the failed IAAO de Lajas.

26. To San Juan, capital of Puerto Rico.

27. Doña Guesa Schroeder, an elderly lady, an immigrant from Holland.

28. From 1899, when a public school system was organized for the first time in Puerto Rico, until 1919, every town had its own school board, a system copied from Massachusetts. The first Commissioner of Education, Dr. Martin G. Brumbaugh, had previously been head of education in that State and tried to transfer it to Puerto Rico. Puerto Ricans had no experience with a public school system like that established in many States. For many reasons, especially in matters of finance and employment, local school boards were eliminated as unsatisfactory and all administration was placed under a centralized Department of Education. With more experience in school management, the current trend is to return some control to local districts.

29. See the account of the IAAO de Lajas in Appendix B, page 172.

30. Hills of St. Martha. Historians of Puerto Rico and the Catholic Church have been unable to locate the source of this story.
31. "Paco" is a nickname for Francisco.

## Chapter 6

1. Evidently a *bohío* or round hut built from palm fronds with a conical roof, like those used by the pre-Columbian Indians and by poor country people of the Island. Its use has disappeared in the last generation except mainly for recreational or tourist purposes.
2. Mr. McCahan made many contributions to the Polytechnic, including that for the first girls' dormitory.
3. The $500 for extending the option plus $275 rent, a very high rental for that time.
4. The only one still standing is Harris Hall, so named in 1940 in honor of "Mr. Clarence" Harris; it was originally built as a boys' dormitory with funds donated by Mrs. Arthur Curtis James Sr., and her son, Arthur Curtis James, Jr. Later it was remodeled for faculty apartments and is now used for Home Economics office and laboratories.
5. Colegio Puertorriqueño, incorporated in 1913.
6. President of the Executive Council of Porto Rico, 1902-04, appointed by President Theodore Roosevelt. Later, he set up his own law office in San Juan.
7. Governor, 1909-13.
8. Bishop Van Buren and the Reverends Wilson, Detweiller and Huffman were in charge of the work of their respective denominations in Puerto Rico.
9. From San Germán.
10. Deputy U.S. Marshal in Mayagüez.
11. Presbyterian Hospital, San Juan; he was head of medical services.
12. Well-known columnist and humorist of the day.
13. A loss of $166.66 yearly was a real blow for the institution at that time.

## Chapter 7

1. Leopoldo Ortiz Vega, one of the original twelve students.
2. Graduate of the first college class of Polytechnic Institute. Later completed medical school in the continental U.S.A. and practiced medicine until retirement in Arecibo where he still lives. He is a long-time member of the Board of Trustees of the University, of which he is now chairman, and has been president of the Polytechnic Alumni Association.
3. Probably *comején,* an ant-like termite.
4. This building was later reduced to one story and used as a faculty residence until torn down to make room for today's Religious Center.
5. Wife of a prominent New York financier.
6. Emancipation of slaves by Spain took place March 22, 1873.
7. British-born financier in New York.
8. Dr. Harris usually calls him Lcdo. Acosta, although his paternal name is López.
9. Refers to the deed to the original 100 acres bought from Francisco Lagarde, not to the 40 acres later acquired from the former slaves.
10. Well-known Presbyterian minister, president of Union Theological Seminary, trustee of the Polytechnic, member of the Board of Home Missions, author on Bible and religion.

11. Howard A. Sackville, husband of Dr. Harris's sister Minnie.
12. Northfield Academy for Girls, East Northfield, Massachusetts.
13. Charles A. Leker was at Polytechnic in 1916, again from 1927 to 1952, when he retired to return to Missouri. Served as dean 1928-35 and as chairman of the Psychology Department, 1935-52.
14. Mrs. Palmer was English teacher and chairman, English Department, 1923 to retirement in 1964. At that time she received the honorary degree of L.H.D.
15. Dr. Palmer was teacher and chairman, Biology Department, until retirement, 1924-64. He had organized the department in 1924. On retirement he received the honorary degree of Litt.D. and was made professor emeritus. He still lives in Atwater Cottage on the campus.
16. Dr. Vélez was teacher and chairman, Botany Department, from his graduation in 1930 to his death in 1970. He was a world renowned authority in tropical botany.
17. Retired from Inter American University in 1961, after 36 years of service as secretary to four presidents. She received a citation from the Alumni Association in 1949 and again in 1966, at which time the University also gave her a citation.
18. With Polytechnic 1920-37, beginning right after her graduation from the Polytechnic high school with second honors.
19. Written at the time of "Mr. Clarence" Harris's retirement and return with his wife doña Mary to their Texas farm.

## Chapter 8

1. Minister, journalist, author and editor.
2. Dr. Harris's quotation is from his own Historical Statement of March 31, 1923.
3. At the time Dr. Harris was writing the dining room held 500 students.
4. A religious periodical, founded in 1912 by Dr. Philo Drury of the United Brethren Church and published in Ponce at that time. It is now published in Río Piedras.

## Chapter 9

1. A beautiful solid mahogany table, made by students, later used for faculty and guests in Costello Hall dining room and now in Casa María.
2. Retired from University of Puerto Rico and living outside of San Juan. Received a citation for his services to the Polytechnic and Inter American University on Founder's Day, 1972.
3. Rev. Toro, retired pastor of the Arecibo Presbyterian Church, who received the honorary degree of D.D. from the Polytechnic in 1954.
4. Manager, Hacienda Tres Hermanos in Rincón; later managed his own farm and studied law by correspondence. Now retired in Mayagüez.
5. Formerly chairman of the Department of Pathology, Howard University, Washington, D.C. Now retired to California.
6. George Villard.
7. Parts of the building could not be fitted on the flatcars and had to be hauled on ox-carts, according to Dr. Nito Rodríguez Quiñones, whose father supplied the oxen and carts.
8. Later missionary to Brazil; authority on Latin America and advisor to the U.S. State Department.
9. Wild mammee, evergreen tree growing to 60 feet, native to the West Indies.
10. Actually the distance was about 150 miles on the roads of that time, or nearly 240 kilometers.

11. Alers graduated from Berea College, Kentucky, with a B.A. and B.S. degree; went on to study electrical engineering and now lives in Michigan.

12. Marina Neighborhood had, by 1955 when Dr. Harris was writing, a regular school, kindergarten through sixth grade, as well as the Sunday School.

13. D. E. Waid, chief architect of Metropolitan Life Insurance Company.

14. On Bleecker Street in Greenwich Village.

15. See footnote 11 for correct information on Antonio Alers.

16. Until the late 1920's all travel between Puerto Rico and the mainland was by ship. By 1928 there was some traffic to nearby places on small lines like the West Indies Aerial Express, but international traffic really began with NYRBA (New York, Río, Buenos Aires) that was purchased by Pan American in the early 1930's.

17. The year referred to is 1955, official time to New York on a DC-6 was six hours.

18. The cool side.

19. June 2, 1918.

20. Judge, U.S. District Court in Puerto Rico.

21. El Morro, oldest Spanish fortification in Puerto Rico, dating from 1539.

22. The exact date of this incident is uncertain, as records are no longer available. Internal evidence, however, indicates it occurred in 1919-20. Loma Vista became the Harris's home in 1919; Marquis Science Hall was built in 1920-21. The investigating committee stayed at Loma Vista and funds for Marquis Science Hall were in great part a result of this visit.

23. This connection was severed by mutual consent in 1956.

*Chapter 10*

1. Later Commissioner of Education, 1930-36.

2. Commissioner of Education, 1912-21.

3. Julio Montalvo had been a member of the San Germán City Council that tried to give the old Spanish barracks to Dr. Harris in 1909.

4. Governor, 1913-21.

5. Capt. Heylman and his wife, Mary Tooker Heylman, built Casa María for use of the school (see Appendix D, page 181) and made many other contributions.

6. James R. Beverley was another Texan who came to Puerto Rico as Assistant Attorney-General in 1925, appointed by President Calvin Coolidge. Later he was Attorney-General and acting Governor on a number of occasions. He served as Governor from January 15, 1932, to July 1, 1933, appointed by President Franklin D. Roosevelt. He was a member for many years of the Board of Trustees of Polytechnic Institute and Inter American University and chairman of the Board. He received the honorary degree of LL.D. from the Polytechnic in 1941. The Beverley Student Center is named after him.

7. Isaiah 58:13-14
    If you turn back your foot from the sabbath,
    Not doing your own business on my holy day;
    If you call the sabbath a delight,
    And the holy day of the LORD honorable;
    If you honor it by not following your accustomed ways,
    Nor doing your business, nor indulging in idle talk—
    Then shall you find your delight in the LORD;
    And I will make you ride in triumph over the heights of the earth,
    And will give you the heritage of Jacob your father to enjoy;
    For the mouth of the LORD has spoken.

## Chapter 11

1. Chief engineer for Guánica Central, a sugar factory.
2. Even though the Master Plan was not followed closely, boys' and girls' dormitories were built very close to the sites originally planned. The girls' dormitories are named Borinquen and Lamar, the latter after Miss Mary Alice Lamar for many years a member of the faculty and dean of women. She was awarded the honorary degree of D.H.L. in 1965. The boys' dormitories were named Phraner and del Toro. Phraner Hall is presently used to house faculty offices.
3. Dr. Harris does not always use these same names for campus areas.
4. William E. Leffingwell.
5. Heirs of Mr. James R. Beverley have not been able to locate this plan.
6. Wife of financier William Thaw.
7. See Appendix D, page 181.
8. This building, usually referred to as the "Cow Barn," was converted into apartments for faculty.

## Chapter 12

1. Concrete buildings erected before the Master Plan and not considered permanent were McCahan Girls' Dormitory (1914) and the two sections of boys' dormitories (1914-15), which were later remodeled (1940) and named "Harris Hall" for Mr. Clarence Harris.
2. Mrs. Franklin Delano Roosevelt. The visit occurred in 1935.
3. There is no record of President Franklin D. Roosevelt's having visited the Polytechnic Institute.
4. Evidently referring to the farewell at the end of the investigative visit in 1919 or 1920. See page 75.
5. A ship of the Puerto Rico Line providing passenger and freight services between New York and Puerto Rico, torpedoed during World War II.
6. Famous 19th and 20th century evangelist and founder of Moody Bible Institute, Chicago.
7. If Sr. Camuñas, Commissioner of Agriculture, visited in 1917, he could not have stayed at Loma Vista, which was built 1918-19.
8. Teatro Sol, at that time a small elegant theater that served for many kinds of special occasions as well as stage productions and early movies. It has since been remodeled into a movie theater.
9. Colegio de Agricultura y Artes Mecánicas, CAAM, popularly known as "El Colegio" or simply "Colegio," i.e., the Mayaguez campus of the University of Puerto Rico.
10. Other expressions of praise for Dr. Harris or the Polytechnic Institute that Dr. Harris evidently cherished are found in Appendix A, page 157.

## Chapter 13

1. Until 1920 the Polytechnic Institute had been incorporated only in Puerto Rico. The decision to incorporate in Washington, D.C., was important to the growth and permanence of the school.
2. This political event which, as the text reads, would seem to have occurred 10 years

prior to Dr. Harris's writing these memoirs in 1955, may, in fact, refer to the 1952 acceptance by the electorate of the Commonwealth status.

3. The Commonwealth of Puerto Rico (Estado Libre Asociado), established in 1952, does not provide for as complete independence as the text implies, although there is a far greater degree of autonomy than existed before.
4. Now the Chase Manhattan Bank.
5. Su atto. amigo y SS. SS. — Su atento amigo y seguro servidor: Your devoted friend and loyal servant.

## Chapter 14

1. These four letters have been selected for inclusion because they are typical of Dr. Harris' methods of interesting people in the Polytechnic and of giving them an idea of the conditions at the struggling school in the early stages.
2. Second Units were at first in fourth to sixth grades but later instruction was extended in these rural schools to cover tenth grade. With the 1944-45 reorganization of the Puerto Rican schools into the 6-3-3 system, Second Units were incorporated into the junior high level and now go only to ninth grade.
3. Theodore Roosevelt, Jr., 1929-32.
4. The college class entering in 1921 completed two years only. See Chronology, pages xv-xvi.
5. Never published and manuscript has not been located.
6. See editorial from *Porto Rico Progress*, May 19, 1923, for local reaction to the fund drive, Appendix A, page 157.
7. Luke 4:18. "The Spirit of the Lord is upon me, because he has appointed me to preach good news to the poor. He has sent me to proclaim release to the captives and recovering of sight to the blind, to set at liberty those who are oppressed, to proclaim the acceptable year of the Lord."
8. Across from where the Harris family had lived in San Germán, not across from Loma Vista.

## Chapter 15

1. The river referred to here is the Guanajibo River which flows through San Germán. Several rivers of Puerto Rico are called "Río Grande," e.g., "Río Grande de Loiza," "Río Grande de la Plata."

## Chapter 16

1. Following his famous non-stop airplane flight across the Atlantic Ocean in 1927, Col. Lindbergh toured the entire nation and most European and Latin American countries. Everywhere he was feted and was the recipient of honors and distinctions. The Legislature of Puerto Rico presented him with this Resolution, which with its quotation from Patrick Henry provoked strong reactions on the mainland and in Puerto Rico. Its consequences as a serious threat to the Polytechnic and the future of the school are evident in Mr. Workum's message and Dr. Harris's request for clarification as published in the *Porto Rico Progress*. Other local papers gave equal prominence to the Resolution and the reactions locally and stateside.

2. An English-language newspaper, no longer published, whose owner and publisher, Harwood Hull, often visited the Polytechnic and was a staunch supporter of Dr. Harris and the school.
3. Emilio del Toro Cuebas was Chief Justice of the Supreme Court of Puerto Rico and a trustee of the Polytechnic. One of the boys' dormitories is named for him. In 1947 he received an honorary LL.D. from the Polytechnic.
4. Governor, 1923-29.
5. Governing Board of the Alianza Party, of which both Antonio Barceló and José Tous Soto were leaders.
6. This comment was added by Dr. Harris in 1955, when he was writing this chapter, as the Commonwealth of Puerto Rico (Estado Libre Asociado) was not established until 1952.

## Chapter 17

1. 1932, actually dean of the College of Education, University of Puerto Rico.
2. A strike instigated by a faculty member in 1930, who aspired to the deanship held by Dr. Leker and hoped, in this way, to discredit Leker and thus get the position. It was timed to take place while Dr. and Mrs. Harris were in the States. It actually involved only a very few students.
3. Written in 1934 in support of Dr. Fansler's report and as a plea for implementing his recommendations.
4. Dr. E. W. Akers, father of Mrs. Rachel Akers Palmer, a frequent visitor to the Polytechnic.
5. Judge Pedro Rodríguez, Judge at Large but residing in San Juan. As a cousin of doña Ana, wife of Dr. "Nito" Rodríguez Quiñones, he was probably fairly well acquainted with the Polytechnic.

## Chapter 18

1. These rambling reminiscences seem to have been written as Dr. Harris happened to recall an incident or a person, as there is no chronological order. They illustrate the wide range of Dr. Harris' contacts in his struggle over the years to found, locate and and maintain the Polytechnic.
2. New York financier and philanthropist.
3. Popular minister, lecturer and author of essays, drama and novels.
4. A senator and twice Secretary of State, not vice-president, although a candidate for the presidency in 1884.
5. Dr. John Harvey Kellogg.
6. Governor, 1921-23.

## Chapter 19

1. This was probably written as a farewell and admonition to faculty and students as he was preparing to relinquish the presidency of his beloved Polytechnic Institute and to return to Texas to realize his early dream of establishing a similar institution there. No evidence has been found of his having actually succeeded in such an undertaking.

## *Chapter 20*

1. An affectionate final tribute to Puerto Rico and Puerto Ricans that seems to have been written as a last, long look back over the years. His death came within months of completion of this manuscript.
2. Theodore Roosevelt, Jr.
3. Commissioner 1921-30.
4. This was the commencement address to the 1928 class, the second college class to graduate from the Polytechnic.
5. Second Units as an offshoot of the Polytechnic are described in footnote 2, Chapter 14.
6. A magazine dating back to Spanish days, purchased by the newspaper *El Mundo* in 1910 and published as a separate magazine until 1951, when, shortly afterwards, it appeared as a Sunday supplement to *El Mundo,* until discontinued September 1975. It is to the separate magazine that Dr. Harris refers.
7. Spanish-language newspaper still publishing and with the largest circulation of local papers. Other newspapers not mentioned here that also published helpful articles, editorials or letters were *La Democracia* and *El Tiempo.*

## *Appendix A*

1. Probable date, 1924-25.
2. Actually with the Christian Church and later the Congregational-Christian Church, now the United Church of Christ.
3. Park College campus paper.
4. According to the 1926-27 Polytechnic catalogue quoted here there were only seven Park College graduates on the faculty:
   Harris
   Eunice White
   Clarence Harris
   Barney N. Morgan
   José M. Gallardo
   Boyd B. Palmer
   Mary Barlow
5. All Second Units were supposed to have a trained social worker assigned to the faculty. In 1930, when Dr. Scudder visited Puerto Rico, there were 28 Second Units, each with its social worker.
6. Angel Archilla Cabrera and José Santiago Cabrera, cousins, were leaders in the Presbyterian work during the first half of the century. Dr. Archilla was head of the Presbyterian work and a trustee of the Polytechnic, which conferred the honorary degree of D.D. on him in 1937. Rev. Santiago was in charge of rural evangelism and Sunday Schools.
7. Senator, poet and old friend of the Polytechnic.
8. Wife of Ramón López Vega, one of the original twelve students in 1912, nursemaid to the Harris's children for many years.

## *Appendix B*

1. Institute of Agriculture, Manual Arts and Trades of Lajas.
2. Owner of a print shop and publisher of the local newspaper. Unfortunately, no copy of this catalogue nor of the one printed in San Juan has been found.

3. Now Fortaleza Street.
4. Commissioner of Education, 1906-12.
5. Dr. José Celso Barbosa, prominent physician and politician. Appointed to the Executive Council by four different Presidents: McKinley, Theodore Roosevelt, Taft and Wilson, 1900-17. Founded the newspaper *El Tiempo*.
6. Governor Beckman Winthrop, 1904-07, and Regis H. Post, 1907-09, were the governors during the years in question.
7. Approximately 19,000 gallons.
8. Executive Secretary of Puerto Rico, a presidential appointment.
9. The original typescript has "ceded" corrected by an unknown hand to read "lent" with the obvious intent of indicating that title to the land had never been transferred to the name of Juan Cancio Ortiz.
10. Apparently still 1910, but source of this quotation is unknown.
11. Original typescript gave November in error.
12. Standard teacher's salary at that time.
13. Old Spanish barracks mentioned on page 36.
14. Typescript contained handwritten note indicating the date as 1952.

# INDEX OF SUBJECTS

# INDEX OF NAMES

# INDEX OF PLACES